Ivan the Terrible

PROFILES IN POWER

General Editor: Keith Robbins

Ivan the Terrible

Andrei Pavlov and Maureen Perrie

London • New York • Toronto • Sydney • Tokyo • Singapore
Hong Kong • Cape Town • Madrid • Paris • Amsterdam • Munich • Milan

Pearson Education Limited
Edinburgh Gate
Harlow, Essex CM20 2JE
England

and Associated Companies throughout the world

Visit us on the World Wide Web at:
www.pearsoned.co.uk

First edition published in Great Britain in 2003

© Pearson Education Limited 2003.

The right of Andrei Pavlov and Maureen Perrie to be
identified as Authors of this Work has been asserted by
them in accordance with the Copyright, Designs and
Patents Act 1988.

ISBN 978-0-582-09948-7

British Library Cataloguing in Publication Data
A CIP catalogue record for this book can be obtained from the British Library

Library of Congress Cataloging in Publication Data
A CIP catalog record for this book can be obtained from the Library of Congress

10 9 8
08 07

Set in 9.5/12pt Celeste by Graphicraft Limited, Hong Kong
Printed and bound in Malaysia, LSP

The Publishers' policy is to use paper manufactured from sustainable forests.

Contents

List of Illustrations

Figures

Maps

Preface

This book has been a long time in the making. I was originally commissioned to write it as the sole author: other commitments intervened, and a start on Ivan's 'Profile in Power' was repeatedly postponed. By the mid-1990s, both I and the publishers were beginning to wonder whether it would ever materialise. Soon afterwards, however, a solution suggested itself. I had known and admired Andrei Pavlov's work for many years before we met for the first time at a conference in Berlin in 1998. We began to correspond, and later that year he sent me a copy of a substantial chapter on the reign of Ivan the Terrible which he had recently contributed to a Russian textbook for university students. This greatly impressed me as a synthesis and popularisation of recent Russian historiography of the period, including of course his own authoritative publications, which are based on many years of research in the archives. I proposed to Andrei that he co-author the Ivan 'Profile', and was delighted when he agreed. The contract was renegotiated with the publisher, and I discussed the practical details with Andrei in the course of a research visit to Russia in 1999.

The division of labour between us was largely dictated by our respective interests in the period. Andrei wrote the initial versions of Chapters 4 to 9 in Russian; I translated and edited these, adding some material and references of my own, and drafted the rest of the text. Andrei read and approved my complete English typescript, and we share joint responsibility for the final product.

Transliteration from Russian follows the simplified form of the British Standard (BS 2979-1958). Non-Russian personal names and place-names always pose problems, which I have tried to resolve on a 'common-sense' basis, sometimes at the expense of rigid consistency. Tatar and Lithuanian names mostly appear in transliterated Russified forms. Dates are given according to the Old Style (Julian) calendar, which was nine days behind the Western (Gregorian) calendar in the sixteenth century.

Maureen Perrie

List of Abbreviations

ChOIDR
Chteniya v Obshchestve istorii i drevnostei rossiiskikh pri Moskovskom universitete.

Correspondence
The Correspondence between Prince A.M. Kurbsky and Tsar Ivan IV of Russia, ed. and trans. J.L.I. Fennell, Cambridge: Cambridge University Press, 1955.

Kurbsky's History
Prince A.M. Kurbsky's History of Ivan IV, ed. and trans. J.L.I. Fennell, Cambridge: Cambridge University Press, 1965.

PSRL
Polnoe sobranie russkikh letopisei.

Rude and Barbarous
Rude and Barbarous Kingdom. Russia in the Accounts of Sixteenth-Century English Voyagers, ed. L.E. Berry and R.O. Crummey, Madison, WI: University of Wisconsin Press, 1968.

TODRL
Trudy Otdela drevnerusskoi literatury Instituta russkoi literatury (Pushkinskii Dom) AN SSSR.

Zak. akty
Zakonodatel'nye akty Russkogo gosudarstva vtoroi poloviny XVI – pervoi poloviny XVII veka. Teksty, Leningrad, 1986.

Introduction

Ivan the Terrible is one of the most controversial rulers in Russian history. Like Peter the Great – with whom he had much in common – Ivan has acquired a cultural significance which transcends that of most other historical figures, however eminent. Peter symbolises all the dilemmas of Russia's relationship with the West: the need for economic modernisation in order to ensure political survival, at the cost of cultural deformation; and the employment of barbaric means in order to bring about supposedly civilising ends. Ivan is associated with the contradictions of state-building. He has been seen as the founder of an autocratic monarchy which subordinated all of society to itself, sacrificing the freedom of the individual in the interests of the strength, security and order of the realm. To a certain extent, these images are simplifications: but Ivan's policies, like Peter's, raise profound questions about ends and means. Artistic representations of both tsars have been used as vehicles for the exploration of political morality in general, and have also raised more specific issues of Russian cultural identity. In Ivan's case, his conventional epithet has embued him with an aura of violence which has only added to the fascination which he exerts over so many people. In Russian the term '*Groznyi*', which is normally translated into English as 'Terrible', has the more positive implications of 'dread' or 'formidable'.[1] Nevertheless, in much popular Russian literature about the tsar the stereotypes of 'crazed tyrant' and 'evil genius' have been mercilessly exploited for their dramatic and melodramatic potential.

Historians have long been divided in their assessments of Ivan's rule.[2] The greatest disputes have centred on the period of the *oprichnina* (1565–72), when the tsar mysteriously divided his realm into two parts and embarked on a reign of terror. We shall consider the debates about the *oprichnina* in the chapters below which deal with that institution. Here, however, we shall examine general approaches to Ivan's reign as a whole. The American historian Richard Hellie has drawn a useful distinction between those scholars who attempt to provide a 'rational' explanation of Ivan's policies and actions, and those who offer instead an account of the tsar's behaviour as irrational and pathological.[3] The interpretation which

1

we shall put forward in this volume falls into the 'rational' category; but in the interests of comprehensiveness it may be worth pausing briefly to examine the alternative, 'irrational' approach.

Virtually all historians would agree that Ivan's personality influenced his behaviour. Unfortunately, we have very little information about the tsar's personal biography. This has not, however, prevented some scholars from drawing ambitious conclusions from the few facts that we do possess. Ivan's father died when he was only three years old, and his mother five years later, supposedly leaving him psychologically damaged from childhood onwards. The death of the tsar's first wife, Anastasiya, in 1560, has led to speculation about his emotional reaction to this new bereavement; and his frequent re-marriages have provoked conjectures about his ability to sustain close personal relationships. Popular historians, and the creators of literary and artistic works about the tsar, have made much play of Ivan's presumed psychological characteristics. Serious scholars, too, have justifiably argued that the tsar's personality, like that of all major historical figures, should not be discounted in interpretations of his reign.

Some have, however, gone much further, and argued that Ivan suffered from serious mental illness. From the late nineteenth century, psychiatrists began to take an interest in Ivan's 'case'. Basing themselves on the accounts of his reign provided by historians such as N.M. Karamzin (1766–1826), they diagnosed him as suffering from paranoia, an ailment which manifests itself primarily through delusions of persecution.[4] The professional historians were less impressed. Admittedly, V.O. Klyuchevskii (1841–1911), citing evidence of Ivan's capriciousness, suspiciousness and self-pity, observed that such qualities provided interesting material for 'a psychologist, or rather a psychiatrist'; but S.F. Platonov (1860–1933), while conceding that the tsar may have displayed elements of 'persecution mania', dismissed any suggestion that Ivan suffered from a specific mental illness or that he was insane. S.B. Veselovskii (1876–1952) explicitly rejected the psychiatrists' diagnosis of 'persecution mania' and argued that Ivan's fear of plots and of attempts on his life was well founded, if somewhat exaggerated.[5]

While psychoanalytical and in general 'psychobiographical' approaches to historical figures were ideologically unacceptable in Russia in the Soviet period, certain eminent Western historians were attracted by them.[6] Richard Hellie, in his historiographical introduction to an English edition of Platonov's popular biography of Ivan, argued that the tsar was paranoid, and that the *oprichnina* was a 'madman's debauch'. Paranoia, Hellie asserted, is a disorder of middle age, and it frequently occurs after the death of a spouse: Ivan was 35 years old when he introduced the *oprichnina* in 1565, five years after the death of Anastasiya. 'The sadism, debauchery, and sexual abuse institutionalized in the years 1565–1572', he added, 'suggest erotomaniac expressions of paranoia.'[7] In a later article, published in a collection of papers presented at a conference held in Chicago in 1984 to 'celebrate' the 400th anniversary of the tsar's death, Hellie developed some of these ideas more fully. He reinterpreted the evidence provided in R.G. Skrynnikov's accounts of Ivan's reign in order to argue that the tsar displayed features of three main types of paranoia: delusions of persecution, erotomania and megalomania. By 1566, Hellie claimed, Ivan was 'totally insane'.[8] In another article in the same collection, Robert Crummey argued that the tsar's brutal punitive expedition against his supposedly treasonous subjects in Novgorod in 1570 can best be explained in terms of paranoia triggered by his unhappy childhood and reinforced by alcohol abuse in later life. The symptoms of Ivan's paranoia included not only his suspiciousness, but also his 'reputedly frantic heterosexual activity'.[9] More recently, the Russian historian Sergei Bogatyrev has speculated further about the tsar's sexual proclivities in relation to his conclusion that Ivan suffered not only from 'persecution mania' but also from a 'flight reflex' – a tendency to distance himself both spatially and psychologically from his familiar environment.[10] Archaeological evidence has also been cited in support of the 'pathological' interpretation of Ivan's behaviour. The tsar's remains were exhumed in 1963 and, on the basis of indications that he had suffered from a painful bone disease, Hellie and Crummey suggested that his illness may have exacerbated Ivan's paranoia.

Intriguing as these conjectures are, they remain hypothetical. Psychology and psychoanalysis are not exact sciences, and the retrospective application of nineteenth-century theories to a sixteenth-century figure, on the basis of somewhat problematic sources, is fraught with dangers. Some of the psychiatrists' approaches are quite bizarre: P.I. Kovalevskii attributed Ivan's psychological instability to the discrepancy in age between his parents, and D.M. Glagolev diagnosed mental illness on the basis of the depiction of the tsar in an icon.[11] Influenced by psychoanalytic theories, Hellie, Crummey and Bogatyrev all seem to accept that the diagnosis of paranoia is confirmed by evidence that the tsar may have engaged in homosexual activity.

'Irrational' explanations of Ivan's behaviour tend to be invoked only when 'rational' interpretations are found wanting. Hellie and Crummey appear to have opted for psychiatric and medicalised approaches to the tsar's reign because they considered alternative explanations to be

inadequate and unconvincing. Until the 1960s, the dominant interpretation in Russian historiography was that of S.F. Platonov, who had
presented the *oprichnina* as a policy designed to weaken the old princely
aristocracy by destroying its large hereditary landed estates and redistrib-
uting them on a conditional basis to the new class of small-scale military
servitors.[12] In 1963, however, a collection of S.B. Veselovskii's essays on
the *oprichnina* was posthumously published.[13] Veselovskii was damningly
critical of Platonov's use of the evidence concerning land transfers on
which he had based his main conclusions. Veselovskii, as a result, partly
rehabilitated the older 'pathological' view of V.O. Klyuchevskii, who had
seen the *oprichnina* as a fruitless attempt by the tsar to resolve his conflict with the boyar aristocracy. Other distinguished Russian historians
– notably A.A. Zimin and R.G. Skrynnikov – subsequently provided
'rational' explanations of the *oprichnina* which significantly modified
Platonov's interpretation. But Veselovskii's attack on Platonov had tended
to discredit such approaches, particularly in the eyes of Western historians, and opened the way to 'irrational', psychosexual explanations such
as those favoured by Hellie and Crummey. In the present study, using
new sources and methods, we re-examine the evidence relating to land
transfers and conclude that Veselovskii's criticisms of Platonov's interpretation were largely unfounded.[14]

It may be worth adding at this point that we shall take issue with
another important element of Richard Hellie's interpretation. Hellie
argues that the tsar was able to behave in such a bizarre manner only
because there were no institutional restraints on the Russian monarch of
the kind which were provided in the West by the Church, by urban
corporations and the nobility. We, however, shall present the *oprichnina*
as, at least in part, an attempt by the tsar to free himself from the
constraints on his power provided by the boyars and the embryonic
social estates. Unlike Hellie, we see the weakness of institutional
restraints on the Russian ruler as a consequence, rather than a cause, of
the *oprichnina*.

Regrettably, extra-academic considerations have at times influenced
approaches to Ivan's reign. 'Rational' explanations of the *oprichnina* were
discredited in the eyes of some by the uses to which they were put in the
Stalin period. Although Platonov had been arrested on a trumped-up
charge in 1930 and died in exile in 1933, his classic study of the Time of
Troubles was republished in 1937, and a simplified version of his interpretation of the *oprichnina* dominated popular and textbook histories for
the next two decades. Artistic representations of Ivan the Terrible in the
Stalin era reflected the official view of the *oprichnina* as a 'progressive'

phenomenon and of the tsar himself as a great and wise statesman engaged in a heroic struggle to eradicate treason. The intended parallel with Stalin was obvious, and such positive accounts of Ivan's reign were condemned, after the dictator's death in 1953, as allegorical apologias for Stalinism.[15] 'Platonovite' interpretations of the *oprichnina*, such as those contained in the wartime accounts of S.V. Bakhrushin, I.I. Smirnov and R.Yu. Vipper, were viewed as justifications of state terror; and later attempts to provide 'rational' explanations of Ivan's behaviour have been subject to similar accusations. Hopefully such criticisms will fade away in the course of time, as the Stalin era recedes into the past. 'Rational' approaches do not, in any case, lead only to positive assessments. Recent accounts by Russian historians provide predominantly negative evaluations of Ivan's achievements, but even those who broadly approve of the outcome do not justify the means that were employed in order to achieve it.[16]

Any attempt to provide a 'rational' explanation of Ivan's behaviour inevitably encounters the problem of establishing his aims and intentions. This problem arises in part from the absence of direct evidence of the tsar's motives – an absence which fuels the assumption of scholars such as Hellie and Crummey that his actions were in fact motiveless or irrational. The outcomes of Ivan's policies may of course serve as an indication of his aims. But, as we all know from our experience of everyday life, the consequences of actions may be unintended ones. Nevertheless, historians often have little option but to deduce intentions from outcomes, and this is the approach we shall adopt in this study. It is, after all, not unreasonable to assume that achievements which are consistent with the interests of an historical actor represent the results that he intended. The context in which the policies were initiated is also relevant, of course, as is the appropriateness of the means to the assumed ends. But we shall be more concerned in this book with determining the results of Ivan's policies than with speculation about his motives.

In the last resort, of course, the validity of historians' interpretations depends on their use of evidence. Sources for Ivan's reign are plentiful, but not unproblematic. A substantial number of official Russian documents has survived, notwithstanding the fact that many were destroyed during the Time of Troubles in the early seventeenth century, while others perished in a disastrous fire in 1626. There are numerous narrative accounts, although the official chronicle frustratingly breaks off at the beginning of the *oprichnina* period. Because of the incompleteness of the Russian sources, the reports written by Western visitors to Muscovy in the sixteenth century – including the first English voyagers, who established commercial and diplomatic links from 1553 onwards – provide particularly valuable evidence. The testimony of these foreign witnesses was, of course, often influenced by their prejudices and misunderstandings of Russian customs, and – like all sources – must not be accepted uncritically.

Some evidence concerning sixteenth-century Russia survives only in manuscripts of the seventeenth century or later, and the problem of attributing the correct dates to the original versions of such sources has given rise to many heated academic debates. One of these controversies has overshadowed study of Ivan's reign, in the West in particular, for the last few decades. For many years historians considered that the correspondence between Tsar Ivan and Prince Andrei Kurbskii, one of his generals who defected to Lithuania in 1564, was a source of primary importance for evaluating the tsar's character and his views on the nature of his royal power. In 1971, however, the Harvard historian Edward Keenan published a highly controversial monograph in which he argued that the correspondence was not authentic, but was instead composed in the seventeenth century. Keenan went on to claim that the 'History' of Ivan's reign attributed to Kurbskii was also not genuine.[17] Keenan's arguments triggered a lengthy international debate which is still not entirely concluded. The overwhelming weight of scholarly opinion, however, is against Keenan and in favour of the authenticity of the sources which he questioned.[18] In this book we assume that both the 'Correspondence' and the 'History' are genuine (although none of our major arguments would be seriously undermined if Keenan's hypotheses were somehow to be confirmed).

While new sources of the traditional kind continue to be discovered and published, in recent years historians in both Russia and the West have begun to make use of new types of evidence. They have examined pictorial images such as icons, murals and frescoes, and explored the symbolism of churches and cathedrals – previously the preserve of specialists on art and architecture.[19] Rituals and ceremonies, such as coronations and processions, have been analysed in order to elucidate the symbolism of power.[20] Some scholars have also explored the ritualised violence of the *oprichnina* terror in an attempt to reach a fuller understanding of its meaning.[21] The semiotic approach of B.A. Uspenskii and his colleagues is particularly valuable because it helps us to comprehend many otherwise puzzling aspects of Ivan's behaviour in terms of the cultural system of his age, thereby avoiding the problems inherent in psychological interpretations which assume that the human personality is a constant entity which functions independently of its historical context.

Although it is organised on a primarily chronological basis, the present study does not aim to provide a biography of Tsar Ivan. Nor is it an account of 'Russia in the age of' Ivan IV: many important aspects of sixteenth-century Muscovite history are not covered here at all. Rather, in line with the aims of 'Profiles in Power', we shall focus on politics. We shall examine three main aspects of Ivan's power. The first major theme will be Russia's territorial expansion and the tsar's efforts, by means of diplomacy and warfare, to enhance the international prestige of his state. We shall discuss the significance of the Russian annexation of the Volga khanates of Kazan' and Astrakhan' in the 1550s, and examine the protracted Livonian War (1558–83), which ultimately failed to establish a Russian presence on the Baltic. A second issue concerns the development of the ruler's own power in relation to that of the boyars and other privileged landholders. In this connection the problem of the causes and consequences of the introduction of the *oprichnina* is, of course, a dominant concern. Finally, we shall pay attention throughout our study not only to the mythology of power, but also to its rituals and symbols: in a society with low levels of literacy these visual expressions of monarchical ideology assumed particular importance as a means of conveying to the population the grandeur of the tsar and the splendour of his realm.

Notes

1 See, for example, Marc Szeftel, 'The Epithet *Groznyj* in Historical Perspective', in A. Blane, ed., *The Religious World of Russian Culture*, The Hague: Mouton, 1975, pp.101–15.

2 English-language reviews of the historiography include: Leo Yaresh, 'Ivan the Terrible and the *Oprichnina*', in C.E. Black, ed., *Rewriting Russian History: Soviet Interpretations of Russia's Past*, New York: Praeger, 1956, pp.224–41; Anatole G. Mazour, 'Ivan IV and the *Oprichnina*', in his *The Writing of History in the Soviet Union*, Stanford, CA: Hoover Institution Press, 1971, pp.67–78; Robert O. Crummey, 'Ivan the Terrible', in S.H. Baron and N.W. Heer, eds., *Windows on the Russian Past: Essays on Soviet Historiography since Stalin*, Columbus, OH: AAASS, 1977, pp.57–74; Alexander Yanov, *The Origins of Autocracy: Ivan the Terrible in Russian History*, Berkeley, CA: University of California Press, 1981; and Maureen Perrie, *The Cult of Ivan the Terrible in Stalin's Russia*, Houndmills: Palgrave, 2001.

3 Richard Hellie, 'In Search of Ivan the Terrible', in S.F. Platonov, *Ivan the Terrible*, Gulf Breeze, FL: Academic International Press, 1974, pp.ix–xxxiv.

4 See Sergei Bogatyrev, 'Groznyi tsar' ili groznoe vremya? Psikhologicheskii obraz Ivana Groznogo v istoriografii', *Russian History/Histoire Russe*, vol.22, no.3, fall 1995, pp.285–308.

5 V.O. Klyuchevskii, *Sochineniya*, vol.2, Moscow, 1957, p.192; S.F. Platonov, *Sobranie sochinenii po russkoi istorii*, vol.2, St Petersburg, 1994, p.84; S.B. Veselovskii, *Issledovaniya po istorii oprichniny*, Moscow, 1963, pp.319–20.

6 For an early flirtation with psychological theories, see Bjarne Nørretranders, *The Shaping of Czardom under Ivan Groznyj*, London: Variorum Reprints, 1971 (first published Copenhagen, 1964), pp.130–37.

7 Hellie, 'In Search of Ivan the Terrible', pp.xix, xxiii, xxvii.

8 Richard Hellie, 'What Happened? How Did He Get Away With It? Ivan Groznyi's Paranoia and the Problem of Institutional Restraints', in Richard Hellie, ed., *Ivan the Terrible: a Quarcentenary Celebration of his Death* (*Russian History/Histoire Russe*, vol.14, 1987), pp.199, 209.

9 Robert O. Crummey, 'New Wine in Old Bottles?: Ivan IV and Novgorod', in Hellie, ed., *Ivan the Terrible*, pp.68–72; see also the chapter on Ivan's reign in Robert O. Crummey, *The Formation of Muscovy, 1304–1613*, London: Longman, 1987.

10 Sergei Bogatyrev, 'Povedenie Ivana Groznogo i moral'nye normy russkogo obshchestva XVI v.', in *Studia Slavica Finlandensia*, vol.11, Helsinki, 1994, pp.8–9.

11 Bogatyrev, 'Groznyi tsar'', pp.289–90.

12 Platonov, *Ivan the Terrible*; see also his *Ocherki po istorii smuty v Moskovskom gosudarstve XVI–XVII vv.*, Moscow, 1937, part 1.

13 Veselovskii, *Issledovaniya*. Veselovskii had been able to publish only one statement of his controversial views in his lifetime: 'Uchrezhdenie Oprichnogo dvora v 1565 g. i otmena ego v 1572 godu', *Voprosy istorii*, 1946, no.1, pp.86–104.

14 These conclusions are based on Andrei Pavlov's research: see, in particular, A.P. Pavlov, 'Opyt retrospektivnogo izucheniya pistsovykh knig', in *Vspomogatel'nye istoricheskie distsipliny*, vol.17, Leningrad, 1985, pp.100–20; A.P. Pavlov, 'Zemel'nye pereseleniya v gody oprichniny', *Istoriya SSSR*, 1990, no.5, pp.89–104; and A.P. Pavlov, *Gosudarev dvor i politicheskaya bor'ba pri Borise Godunove (1584–1605 gg.)*, St Petersburg, 1992, pp.149–217.

15 Perrie, *The Cult of Ivan the Terrible*.

16 An example of the former position is V. Kobrin, *Ivan Groznyi*, Moscow, 1989; for the latter, see Boris Florya, *Ivan Groznyi*, Moscow, 1999.

17 Edward L. Keenan, *The Kurbskii-Groznyi Apocrypha*, Cambridge, MA: Harvard University Press, 1971; Edward L. Keenan, 'Putting Kurbskii in his Place, or: Observations and Suggestions Concerning the Place of the *History of the Grand Prince of Muscovy* in the History of Muscovite Literary Culture', *Forschungen zur Osteuropäischen Geschichte*, vol.24, 1978, pp.131–61.

18 For a recent assessment of the debate, see: C.J. Halperin, 'Edward Keenan and the Kurbskii-Groznyi Correspondence in Hindsight', *Jahrbücher für Geschichte Osteuropas*, Band 46, 1998, pp.376–403; and Keenan's 'Response to Halperin', *ibid.*, pp.404–15.

19 See, for example, Priscilla Hunt, 'Ivan IV's Personal Mythology of Kingship', *Slavic Review*, vol.52, 1993, pp.769–809; Daniel Rowland, 'Biblical Military Imagery in the Political

Culture of Early Modern Russia: the Blessed Host of the Heavenly Tsar', in Michael S. Flier and Daniel Rowland, eds., *Medieval Russian Culture*, vol.2, Berkeley: University of California Press, 1994, pp.182–212; A.L. Yurganov, 'Oprichnina i strashnyi sud', *Otechestvennaya istoriya*, 1997, no.3, pp.52–75.

20 For example: David B. Miller, 'Creating Legitimacy: Ritual, Ideology, and Power in Sixteenth-Century Russia', *Russian History/Histoire Russe*, vol.21, 1994, pp.289–315; Nancy S. Kollmann, 'Pilgrimage, Procession and Symbolic Space in Sixteenth-Century Russian Politics', in Flier and Rowland, eds., *Medieval Russian Culture*, vol.2, pp.163–81; Richard S. Wortman, *Scenarios of Power. Myth and Ceremony in Russian Monarchy*, vol.1, Princeton, NJ: Princeton University Press, 1995, chapter 1.

21 A.M. Panchenko and B.A. Uspenskii, 'Ivan Groznyi i Petr Velikii: kontseptsii pervogo monarkha', *TODRL*, vol.37, 1983, pp.54–78; D.S. Likhachev, A.M. Panchenko and N.V. Ponyrko, *Smekh v drevnei Rusi*, Leningrad, 1984, pp.25–59; Hunt, 'Ivan IV's Personal Mythology of Kingship'; Yurganov, 'Oprichnina i strashnyi sud'.

Ivan's Inheritance

The Muscovite state which Grand Prince Vasilii III bequeathed to his infant son Ivan IV in 1533 was a comparatively recent formation, created by the annexation of neighbouring north-eastern Rus' principalities by the grand princes of Moscow. It was also only comparatively recently that Muscovy had established its independence from the Tatars who had exercised suzerainty over the Rus' lands since the thirteenth century.[1]

The dynasty of the grand princes of Moscow traced its origins back to the semi-legendary figure of Ryurik the Viking, who had in the ninth century been invited by the peoples of what is now north-western Russia to come and rule over them. In due course the Ryurikids (Ryurik's descendants) became the princes of the land known as Rus', which was inhabited predominantly by eastern Slavs. Their capital city was Kiev (in present-day Ukraine), and their state is thus frequently described as Kievan Rus'. In the tenth century it extended from Kiev in the south to Novgorod in the north; it subsequently expanded eastwards, to Nizhnii Novgorod on the River Volga, and to the foothills of the Ural Mountains.

In the thirteenth century the lands of Rus' were invaded from the east by the Mongols, a nomadic Asiatic people also known as the Tatars. Their military campaigns of 1237–40 were led by Batu, a grandson of Genghis (Chingis) Khan. In December 1240 the Mongols captured Kiev, before continuing westward into Poland and Hungary. Batu built his capital at Sarai, on the lower Volga, and the Rus' lands were incorporated into his realm, the Kipchak Khanate, which has become better known as the Golden Horde. With the construction of Sarai, the ruling élite of the khanate became settled and urbanised; and in the fourteenth century the Horde adopted Islam. The official language of the Horde was Turkish, reflecting the extensive assimilation of the original Mongol invaders to the indigenous Turkic peoples of the steppes.

By the time of the Mongol invasion, Kievan Rus' had acquired a complex political structure. The grand prince, the senior member of the

Ryurikid dynasty, was based in Kiev. From the time of Yaroslav 'the Wise' (d.1054) the other main towns were allocated to junior members of the dynasty on a hierarchical basis which (in theory, but not always in practice) determined the order of succession to the Kievan throne. From 1097 these towns were recognised as the capitals of separate principalities which were passed down within the same branch of the dynasty. In subsequent decades some of the principalities became increasingly independent of Kiev. One of these more independent principalities was Suzdalya, to the north-east of Kiev, which expanded and prospered in the twelfth century. Often known as Vladimir-Suzdal', its major towns were Rostov, Suzdal' and Vladimir, all of which served at various times as its capital. The town of Moscow, in the south-west of Suzdalya, is mentioned for the first time in 1147, in the reign of Prince Yurii Dolgorukii.

The Mongol invasion reinforced the growing division between the south-western and the north-eastern lands of Rus'. Kiev itself was severely weakened, and ceased to serve as a focal point for all the Rus' principalities. In the course of the fourteenth century the western and south-western lands – Polotsk, Turov, Volynia, Galicia, Smolensk, Chernigov, Pereyaslavl' and Kiev itself – came under the control of Poland and Lithuania, while the north-eastern principalities, including Suzdalya, remained part of the Golden Horde.

In spite of the political separation of the north-eastern principalities from the south-western lands, religion remained a unifying factor for the peoples of Rus'. Kievan Rus' had adopted Christianity in 988, with the conversion of Prince Vladimir I. Vladimir adopted his new religion in its Eastern Orthodox form, from Byzantium (Constantinople), and Rus' continued to have close relations with the Byzantine Empire throughout the Kievan period. Prince Vsevolod Yaroslavovich married a relative of the Byzantine Emperor Constantine IX Monomachus; their son, who became grand prince of Kiev in 1113, was known as Vladimir Monomakh. After the Mongol invasion, Kiev at first remained the ecclesiastical centre of the lands of Rus'; in 1299, however, Metropolitan Maksim, the head of the Church, moved from Kiev to Vladimir. In 1325 Metropolitan Peter took up residence in Moscow, which became the official seat of the metropolitan in 1354.

Although Mongol domination was for a long time described by Russian historians as the 'Tatar yoke', the overlordship which the khans of the Horde exercised over the Rus' lands mainly assumed the form of the exaction of tax or tribute. From the fourteenth century, the Rus' princes themselves acted as tax-collectors and administrators for their Tatar overlords. The Mongols asserted the right to appoint the princes, who had to travel to Sarai to receive the khan's *yarlyk* or letter of confirmation. In 1243 the khan granted Prince Yaroslav Vsevolodovich of Vladimir the titles of grand prince of Kiev and grand prince of Vladimir; thereafter, Vladimir replaced Kiev as the dominant principality of the Rus' lands. In general the Mongols respected the rules of dynastic succession to the grand princely throne which had operated in the Kievan period. In 1328, however, rivalry between the Tver' and Moscow branches of the dynasty for the position of grand prince was resolved by the khan in favour of the latter. Prince Ivan Daniilovich of Moscow became grand prince of Vladimir as a result of the khan's patronage, even though he had no legitimate claim to the throne according to the traditional principles of succession. Ivan I (nicknamed '*Kalita*' or 'Moneybags', because of his financial acumen) was therefore more dependent on the Mongols than his predecessors had been. Ivan Kalita and his heirs made frequent visits to the Horde; this custom familiarised the grand princes of Vladimir with Mongol methods of rule and administration, and may have inspired them to adopt similar practices in their own domains.[2]

The period of Mongol domination is often described as the era of 'fragmentation' of the Rus' lands. Not only did it witness the separation of the south-western principalities around Kiev from the north-eastern territories of the grand princes of Vladimir, but in the north-eastern lands themselves the principalities were increasingly subdivided. Vladimir-Suzdal' was split into Vladimir, Suzdal' and Rostov, which were in turn broken up; Beloozero and Yaroslavl', for example, were carved out of Rostov. These smaller principalities, which were inherited within a single branch of the dynasty, were known as appanages (*udely*) – a term which is sometimes used to characterise the period as a whole.

After Ivan Kalita became grand prince of Vladimir, however, the principality of Moscow began to expand through the annexation of neighbouring principalities. This process, commonly known as the 'gathering of the lands of Rus'', continued under his successors. Ivan III (1462–1505) annexed the great city of Novgorod, with its extensive northern hinterland, and added the principality of Tver' to his domains. His son, Vasilii III (1505–33), incorporated Pskov and Ryazan'. At the death of Vasilii III, Moscow not only ruled all of the north-eastern lands which had formed part of the Golden Horde, but as a result of wars with Lithuania it had acquired some of the territory of the Chernigov and Smolensk principalities of Kievan Rus', including the important fortress of Smolensk itself (see Map 1.1). With this westward expansion Muscovy acquired a population which included some of those east Slav peoples who were subsequently to become known as Belorussians and Ukrainians.

Map 1.1 Muscovy in 1533

By this time, Muscovy had emancipated itself from Mongol overlordship. In the middle of the fourteenth century the Golden Horde began to experience a number of internal crises which were to lead to its disintegration. Its main offshoots were the Crimean khanate, on the northern shore of the Black Sea, and the khanate of Kazan', on the mid-Volga. The remainder of the Golden Horde, which became known as the Great Horde, retained its base on the lower Volga, although its capital, Sarai, never recovered from its devastation by the Mongol warlord Timur (Tamerlane) at the end of the fourteenth century. The Rus' princes took advantage of the discord within the Horde in order to challenge their Mongol overlords. In September 1380 Grand Prince Dmitrii Ivanovich led a coalition of princes that defeated the Tatar warrior Mamai at Kulikovo, on the upper reaches of the River Don. Dmitrii, who gained the epithet 'Donskoi' from his victory, did not however succeed in overthrowing the suzerainty of the khan, who continued to dominate the lands of north-east Rus'. As the Golden Horde disintegrated, however, Moscow became more self-assertive. A confrontation on the River Ugra which took place in October 1480, between Grand Prince Ivan III and Akhmat Khan of the Great Horde, is often said to have marked the definitive end of the 'Tatar yoke'. In practice the grand prince was by this time an independent ruler, although he continued to pay tribute to the Mongols even after 1480. Following the destruction of the Great Horde by the Crimean Tatars in 1502, Ivan III sent the payments to the Crimean khan, but it was now little more than a token gesture.

By the reign of Vasilii III, the Great Horde had been succeeded on the lower Volga by the khanate of Astrakhan'; the steppes further east were dominated by the nomadic Nogai Horde; and to the north there lay the khanate of Siberia. These successors of the Golden Horde were fragmented and disunited, and they posed little threat to Muscovy. On the mid-Volga, the khanate of Kazan' was more formidable, but its relations with Russia were fairly stable. The greatest potential danger was presented by the Crimean khanate. Since 1475 Crimea had been a vassal of the Ottoman (Turkish) Empire, which had continued to expand, after its conquest of Constantinople in 1453, to the northern shores of the Black Sea. The Russians feared that in any conflict with the Crimean khan, the latter would receive the support of his master the Sultan.

At the time of the 'stand on the Ugra' in 1480, Ivan III had formed an alliance with the Crimean khan, Mengli-Girei, against the combined forces of Akhmat Khan of the Great Horde and King Casimir IV of Lithuania and Poland. The Muscovite association with Crimea expanded to include Kazan', when in 1487 Russian troops helped to place Mengli-Girei's stepson, Magmet-Amin', on the Kazanian throne. After the death of Ivan III, however, the alliance with Crimea was weakened. Mengli-Girei's successor, Magmet-Girei, sided with Poland-Lithuania in its wars against Russia, and in 1521 the Crimean Tatars attacked and besieged Moscow itself. The conflict between Moscow and Crimea was exacerbated by rivalry between them for influence over Kazan'. In 1523, after the murder of a Russian ambassador to Kazan', Vasilii III constructed a new fortress, named Vasil'grad (later Vasil'sursk) on the River Volga, just within the territory of the khanate, and in the following year he sent an army against Kazan' which overthrew the Crimean client Saip-Girei. Saip-Girei was replaced as khan by another Crimean prince, Safa-Girei, and the outcome represented a compromise which lasted until 1532, when Safa-Girei was deposed by the Kazanians and replaced by a Moscow candidate, Enalei.

In order to counter the growing threat from the Crimean Tatars, in particular, the grand princes began to strengthen their southern frontiers with chains of fortresses. With the annexation of Ryazan' in 1521, Vasilii III gained control of key strategic territory bordering the 'wild field' of steppelands that lay between his realm and the Tatar khanates to the south and east. In the late fifteenth century the River Oka had constituted the southern frontier of Muscovy; the fortification of the town of Tula, between 1509 and 1521, brought the defence line further south. On the steppe grasslands beyond the frontier there roamed bands of cossacks, mounted warriors who may have originated as offshoots of the Tatar hordes, but soon included many ethnic Slavs, fugitives from Poland and Lithuania as well as from Muscovy. They frequented the basins of the rivers which drained into the Black Sea and the Caspian – the Dnieper, the Don, the Volga and their tributaries – and supported themselves by fishing, piracy and brigandage. By the mid-sixteenth century some cossacks provided regular military service to Muscovy along its southern and eastern borders, while others remained free agents on the steppes.

At the same time as the grand princes of Muscovy were establishing their political independence from the Tatars, the Russian Church was becoming increasingly free of Byzantine influence. Until the fourteenth century, the Russian metropolitans were appointed by the patriarch (the head of the Eastern Orthodox Church) in Constantinople. After the death of Metropolitan Fotii in 1431, however, the patriarch delayed naming his successor. During the interregnum Bishop Iona of Ryazan' acted unofficially as head of the Church, and in 1436 he was officially nominated by Grand Prince Vasilii II as the new metropolitan. The patriarch, however, promptly appointed his own candidate, Isidor. At this time, the Byzantine Empire was under attack from the Ottoman Turks, who were threatening Constantinople itself. The emperor and the patriarch, hoping for military assistance from Catholic Europe, responded favourably to an approach from the pope concerning the re-establishment of Christian unity. Soon after taking up his new office, Metropolitan Isidor left Moscow to attend the Council of Florence, which was convened in 1437 to negotiate the re-unification of the Eastern Orthodox and Roman Catholic Churches. When Isidor eventually returned in 1441 to report that the Council had agreed to the union of the two Churches, he met with a hostile reception from the grand prince and the Russian bishops, who deposed him as metropolitan. In 1448 they named Iona of Ryazan' as his successor. When Constantinople fell to the Turks in 1453, the immediate reaction in Moscow was that God had punished the patriarch and the emperor for their heretical acceptance of union with Rome.

In appointing Iona as metropolitan without the approval of the patriarch, the Russian Church had effectively established its independence from Byzantium. The Church in Constantinople survived the capture of the city by the Turks, but it was now subject to the political authority of the Sultan. The fall of Constantinople meant that the decisions of the Council of Florence were largely a dead letter, and Moscow's breach with the patriarch was soon mended. But Ivan III's emancipation of his state from Tatar overlordship contrasted with the conquest of Constantinople by the Turks: Russia was now the only major Orthodox realm which was independent of non-Orthodox rulers. In 1472 Ivan III had married Zoe (Sofiya) Paleologue, a niece of the last Byzantine emperor, thus establishing a degree of dynastic continuity with Constantinople. It was in this context that the idea developed that Moscow was the spiritual heir to Byzantium. The best known version of this notion is the concept of 'Moscow the Third Rome', which we shall discuss in a later chapter. But it was preceded by similar theories. In 1492, for example, Metropolitan Zosima described Moscow as the 'new Constantinople'. And a literary work known as the 'Tale of the White Cowl', probably dating from the early sixteenth century, describes how the white cowl of the Novgorod archbishops, symbolising the purity of Orthodoxy, was passed from Rome to Constantinople and thence to Novgorod after the patriarch had a prophetic dream of the fall of Byzantium to the infidel Turks.

The creation of an independent metropolitanate in Moscow had implications for Russia's relations with Lithuania. Even after the metropolitan had moved from Kiev to Vladimir in 1299, he retained the title of 'Metropolitan of Kiev and all Rus''. When the south-west lands began to come under the influence of the predominantly Catholic states of Poland and Lithuania, their rulers on several occasions persuaded the patriarch to create a separate metropolitanate for their newly acquired Orthodox population. The two sectors were reunited under Metropolitan Kiprian in

1390, but in 1458 King Casimir IV of Poland and Lithuania succeeded in obtaining the re-establishment of a metropolitanate based in Kiev: the new metropolitan represented the united Church created by the Council of Florence. Thereafter it became an aim of the Moscow-based metropolitans to re-unify the Orthodox populations of Muscovy and Lithuania not just under the same ecclesiastical authority, but also under the same political ruler. As Ivan III and Vasilii III expanded their realm westward into the Chernigov and Smolensk lands, there seemed to be a real prospect that Muscovy could re-unite the principalities of Kievan Rus'. After his annexation of Novgorod in 1478, Ivan III regularly used the title 'sovereign of all Rus'', which echoed that of the metropolitan, and implied a territorial claim to the south-west lands which was of course contested by Casimir IV. Against this background, the Church began to produce a number of literary works which traced the lineage of the grand princes of Moscow back to Kiev and implicitly provided a legitimisation of their dynastic right to rule all the Rus' lands. The best known of these compositions is the 'Monomakh legend', concerning the transfer of royal regalia from Byzantium to Grand Prince Vladimir Monomakh of Kiev and thence to the grand princes of Moscow. This tale probably originated in the early sixteenth century; as we shall see, it was to constitute a prominent part of official ideology at the time of Ivan IV's coronation as tsar.

The Russian Church's assertion of its independence from Byzantium led to its adoption of a strongly anti-Tatar line. Until 1448 the Russian metropolitans had followed the Byzantine policy of accommodation with the Tatars. In 1261 the Church had established a bishopric at Sarai, the capital of the Golden Horde, and it regularly prayed for the khan. In return, the Church was granted various privileges and tax exemptions by the Tatars. This mutually advantageous relationship persisted even after the khans adopted Islam in the fourteenth century. The Byzantines' apparent betrayal of Orthodoxy at the Council of Florence, however, and the subsequent conquest of Constantinople by the Turks, gave the Russian Church greater ideological freedom. From the late fifteenth century, it began to formulate a vehemently anti-Tatar and anti-Muslim ideology which was to culminate in Metropolitan Makarii's rhetoric against the Kazanian Tatars in the middle of the sixteenth century.

The independence of the Russian metropolitanate from Byzantium meant that relations between Church and state were redefined. In spite of various disagreements and conflicts of interest on specific issues, the metropolitans and the grand princes had in general been mutually supportive of one another. Metropolitan Peter and his successor, Feognost, had backed the Muscovite princes' claim to the grand princely title; and when Moscow was chosen as the metropolitan's place of residence there began a programme of construction of churches and cathedrals which not only greatly beautified the city but also raised the status and prestige of its princes. In their turn, Ivan Kalita and his heirs supported the claims of the Moscow-based metropolitans to jurisdiction over Orthodox Christians in Poland and Lithuania. They also backed the Church's acquisition of extensive landholdings, and granted generous tax exemptions to monasteries.

In line with the emergence of the idea of Muscovy as the successor to Byzantium, from the late fifteenth century Church-state relations in Russia were increasingly theorised according to the model of the Byzantine Empire, where the secular and spiritual authorities supposedly acted in harmony. Muscovy acquired an understanding of the division of responsibility between grand prince and metropolitan which was similar to that between the emperor and the patriarch in Byzantium. The metropolitan was not to interfere in matters of state; conversely, the grand prince could not influence Church dogmas and doctrines. There was, however, a grey area of shared responsibility, which included the administrative and organisational aspects of Church life. The reign of Vasilii III was marked by sharp disputes among leading ecclesiastical figures on the precise line of demarcation between Church and state. Iosif (Joseph), the abbot of the Volokolamsk Monastery, headed a group (the 'Josephites') that placed greater emphasis on the power of the grand prince than did their opponents, who were led by the monks Vassian Patrikeev and Maksim Grek (Maxim the Greek). After 1522, when Metropolitan Varlaam was deposed and replaced by Daniil, the Josephites triumphed. Vassian and Maksim were found guilty of heresy, and the Church in practice became subordinate to the state. Even according to the predominant Josephite ideology, however, the Church had the duty to speak out against a ruler whom it regarded as a 'tormentor'; and the ruler in his turn had an obligation to promote and protect the Orthodox faith.

The theory of the secular power of the ruler which dominated in early sixteenth-century Russia originated in Byzantium. The authority of the grand prince, like that of the emperor, came from God, and was unlimited in its scope. Some foreign contemporaries believed that the Russian ruler's authority corresponded in practice to this image of autocratic (unrestricted) power. Sigismund von Herberstein, the ambassador to Muscovy from the Holy Roman Empire, wrote of Vasilii III: 'In the sway which he holds over his people, he surpasses all the monarchs of the whole world'.[3] In reality, the grand princes traditionally consulted their aristocratic advisers (the 'boyar duma'). There is considerable scholarly disagreement on the precise balance of power between the grand prince and his boyars. The American historian Nancy Kollmann has argued that the boyars shared power with the rulers, and that the supposedly exclusive power of the grand prince was merely a 'façade of autocracy'.[4] Other historians, however, attribute the dominant role to the sovereign.[5] A major theme of this book will be the division of power between the ruler and the boyars at various stages in the reign of Ivan IV.

How was the realm which Ivan inherited governed in practice? The unification of the Rus' lands around Moscow had led to a degree of administrative centralisation, as the previously fragmented principalities were integrated into a single state. The process of incorporation into Muscovy involved a particular culture-shock in Novgorod, where the city *veche*, an elected assembly, had traditionally chosen the prince. As their territory expanded, the grand princes of Moscow appointed servicemen known as *namestniki* to govern the provinces. These provincial governors represented the authority of the central government, and were regularly rotated in office. They received their remuneration through a system known as 'feeding' (*kormlenie*), whereby the local population provided them with supplies of food and paid them fees for their administrative and judicial services. The annexation of the formerly autonomous principalities led to the introduction of a uniform system of justice for all the lands which were under the jurisdiction of the grand prince. Ivan III's Law Code of 1497 introduced standardised judicial institutions and legal procedures that applied throughout Muscovy. In the capital itself, the main day-to-day activities of government were conducted by secretaries (*d'yaki*), officials who had originally operated as officers of the royal household, but who increasingly acquired broader state functions. At the beginning of the sixteenth century, however, the administration of the ruler's household was not yet clearly demarcated from the government of the state.

The dynasty itself became more centralised. The Moscow branch of the house of Ryurik – often known as the Daniilovichi – consolidated their position as grand princes of Vladimir. As the title passed down through the descendants of Ivan (Daniilovich) Kalita, the pattern of succession changed. The older system, bequeathed from Kievan times, involved collateral succession, in which the position of grand prince was inherited by his younger brothers before passing to the senior member of the next generation. With the ascension of the Daniilovichi, however, the succession became vertical, that is, it passed directly from father to eldest son. The new system, however, was confirmed only after a bloody civil war which followed the death of Grand Prince Vasilii I in 1425. The succession of Vasilii's son, Vasilii II, was challenged by his uncle, Prince Yurii Dmitrievich. The ensuing conflicts resulted in victory for Vasilii II, and he in turn was succeeded in 1462 by his eldest son, Ivan III. The vertical principle was not without its ambiguities, however. When Ivan III's eldest son, Ivan Ivanovich, predeceased him, it was unclear whether the new heir should be Ivan Ivanovich's son, Dmitrii, or Ivan III's eldest surviving son, Vasilii. The grand prince himself vacillated between them, and in the end it was Vasilii who succeeded his father in 1505.[6]

Although the younger brothers of the grand princes had lost their former preferential rights to the succession, they retained the prospect of inheriting the throne if the grand prince died without sons of his own. Nevertheless, their political importance diminished and the size of the semi-autonomous appanage principalities allotted to them was reduced. On the deaths of their brothers and cousins, the grand princes incorporated their lands into their own domains. They continued to be suspicious of their siblings. Ivan III, who had four younger brothers, apparently feared that they might challenge his own sons' claims to the throne: he arrested one of his brothers and restricted the marriages of the others, thereby reducing the number of prospective collateral heirs. When Vasilii III died in 1533, the only remaining appanage principalities were Dmitrov and Staritsa, ruled respectively by his two surviving younger brothers, Yurii and Andrei (see Figure 1.1).

While the appanage princes maintained their own courts and retainers, including military servitors, the formerly independent princes whose domains were annexed by Moscow lost their courts and their retinues, although in certain cases they retained extensive estates in their former principalities. Some of these princes moved to Lithuania, but the majority entered the service of the grand prince of Moscow. The Moscow court expanded as a result of an influx of displaced princes and their retainers. They included not only former rulers of the north-east Russian principalities and their descendants, but also some princes who had come to Moscow from Lithuania. Many of these were Orthodox Christians, opposed to the growing influence of the Catholic Church; some of them, living on the eastern border of Lithuania, transferred not only their retinues but also their lands to the grand prince of Moscow, thereby contributing to the territorial expansion of his realm. A similar category comprised Tatar princes, fugitives from their khanates, who entered the service of Moscow with their military retainers and were granted lands and privileges. An early 'service Tatar' of this kind was Kasim, a brother of the khan of Kazan'. Kasim supported Vasilii II in his dynastic war and

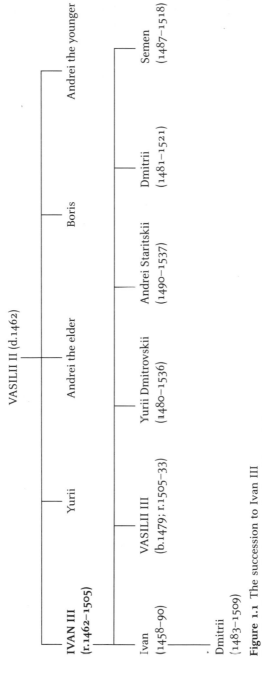

Figure 1.1 The succession to Ivan III

Note: Reigning grand princes are indicated in capitals

in return he was granted lands on the River Oka, south-east of Moscow, which became known as the Kasimov khanate.

This influx of princes and other servitors into the Moscow court not only expanded it numerically, but also made it much more heterogeneous. The court in the mid-fifteenth century still consisted primarily of members of a small group of élite families who were untitled (i.e. of non-princely origin) but had been in the service of the grand princes for several generations. These clans, sometimes known as the 'old Moscow boyar' families, had established a hereditary right to provide the principal counsellors of the grand princes and the chief commanders of their armies. Although they were not 'royal', they comprised a kind of aristocratic élite by virtue of the length of their pedigree. Because of their tradition of service at the grand princely court, however, they may more appropriately be described as a 'service aristocracy'. With the arrival of the princes, who began to compete with the older-established untitled clans for court positions, it is possible to speak of a composite 'princely-boyar' service aristocracy in Muscovy.

The princely and boyar families, however, constituted only the topmost stratum of a much larger category of servitors of the grand prince. At this stage, we encounter major problems of terminology. Russian historians often use the term '*dvoryanstvo*' to apply either to the servitor class as a whole, or to its non-aristocratic majority. In both applications, it is an anachronistic usage, since the word *dvoryanin* (literally, 'courtier') was used in sixteenth-century Russia only for a specific category of servitors (from '*dvor*', the royal court). For later periods, *dvoryanstvo* is often rendered into English as 'nobility' or 'gentry', although even then these terms imply somewhat misleading parallels with British social groups. For the sixteenth century, at least, terms such as 'service class' or 'military-service class' are more appropriate, although they have the opposite disadvantage of sounding rather clumsy and alien in English.

The problem is complicated by the fact that the nature and development of royal servitors in the reign of Ivan IV is one of the major themes of this book. We shall argue that in the first half of the sixteenth century, in spite of the great diversity of their origins, wealth and status, the servicemen comprised – at least in embryo – a single social estate (*soslovie*), comparable to the noble estate or order of western European societies. Their tendency to develop a corporate identity was reinforced by the reforms of the 1550s, which restructured local administration by creating separate institutions of self-government for each of the main social groups: servicemen, clergy, townspeople and peasants. As a result of Tsar Ivan's subsequent *oprichnina* policy, however, the incipient noble estate was divided and weakened vis-à-vis the monarchy, and instead of evolving in the direction of a western-style 'estate-representative' monarchy, Russia developed into an autocratic state.

Because of this implicitly comparative line of argument, we shall regularly use the term 'nobility' when talking of the service class as a whole, as a potential 'noble estate' on the Western model. The term 'aristocracy' will be reserved for the privileged élite of princely and boyar families; 'gentry' will where appropriate be used for the less privileged majority of rank-and-file servicemen. In the sixteenth century, the Russian term for these petty servitors was *'deti boyarskie'*, which translates literally as 'boyars' sons'. In reality, in terms of their background, status and lifestyle they were very distant from the aristocratic boyar clans. Most of these ordinary servicemen were based in the provinces where they held their lands, and were organised on a local basis into town or district corporations.

Servitors at the grand prince's court (or 'sovereign's court', as it was known in the sixteenth century) were ranked according to their status. At the top were the duma or conciliar ranks: the boyars and *okol'nichie* who comprised the grand prince's council (commonly described as the 'boyar duma'). Below them were the palace ranks (*dvortsovye chiny*) such as steward (*dvoretskii*), treasurer (*kaznachei*) and equerry (*konyushii*), whose members administered the royal household. The third group comprised members of the 'Moscow ranks', the sovereign's personal guard: the *stol'niki, stryapchie* and *zhil'tsy*.[7] The 'service princes', that is, those princes who did not hold higher ranks, were classified separately from the ordinary gentlemen who served at court (*dvorovye deti boyarskie*). But the court had a territorial basis as well as a hierarchical structure. Courtiers of all ranks, including the princes, belonged to local corporations of servicemen in the districts where their landed estates were located, and thus preserved links with the provinces and with the provincial gentry.[8]

Land was the main source of income for the servitors of the grand prince. In the fifteenth century, most members of the aristocracy held land in the form of hereditary private estates (*votchiny*) which were handed down within families, often in regions where they had been based for generations. Towards the end of the fifteenth century, however, a new form of landholding was introduced. The new estates were known as *pomest'ya*, and their landholders as *pomeshchiki*. These lands were granted to his servitors by the grand prince on condition that they performed military service. This system, which may have been based on a similar Islamic practice adopted by the Mongols,[9] became widespread after the annexation of Novgorod in 1478. Ivan III confiscated the estates of the Novgorod boyars, and also the extensive landholdings of the archbishop and monasteries. He allocated much of this land to his own military servicemen. With the subsequent annexation of other principalities such as Pskov and Ryazan', similar procedures were adopted. Contrary to the impression created by some historians, the distinction between *votchiny* and *pomest'ya*, even in the first half of the sixteenth century, was not too great. *Votchiny* were not necessarily larger than *pomest'ya*. There was no principle of primogeniture in the Russian system of inheritance, so that family estates became fragmented as they were divided among sons on their father's death. Conversely, some *pomest'ya* were very large indeed. And in practice the two types of land tenure were not dissimilar: *pomest'ya* tended to be handed down from father to son; and the *votchiny* of disgraced courtiers were liable to confiscation by the state. Although most *votchiny* were still owned by members of old aristocratic families, and most *pomeshchiki* were rank-and-file servitors, mixed forms of landholding were common. Many aristocrats relied heavily on the incomes from *pomest'ya* which they were allocated in return for their service to the grand prince. The *pomest'e* system created common interests among all strata of servitors, and made most of them dependent, to a greater or lesser extent, on the sovereign's favour.[10]

The introduction of the service-tenure system contributed to the formation of a single integrated army for the newly unified Russian state. The appanage princes kept their own military retainers, but all other servicemen came under the direct command of the grand prince. Since the majority of them now held at least some of their lands on a conditional basis, their incentive to turn up for military service was strong. The Russian army in the early sixteenth century consisted primarily of cavalrymen. Their landed estates, and the peasants who worked on them, not only supplied the nobles with the resources they needed to feed their families, but also provided the horses and equipment they required in order to perform their military service. Depending on the amount of land they held, noblemen were required not only to serve in the army themselves, but also to provide a number of military retainers, often including slaves. The army created on this basis by Ivan III provided a very effective instrument for Russia's territorial expansion in the first half of the sixteenth century.

Notes

1 The best recent accounts in English of Russian history before 1533 can be found in the three relevant volumes of the 'Longman History of Russia' series: Simon Franklin and Jonathan Shepard, *The Emergence of Rus, 750–1200*, London: Longman, 1996; John Fennell, *The Crisis of Medieval Russia, 1200–1304*, London: Longman, 1983; and Crummey, *The Formation of Muscovy*. See also Janet Martin's volume in the 'Cambridge Medieval Textbooks' series: *Medieval Russia, 980–1584*, Cambridge: Cambridge University Press, 1995.

2 On Mongol influence on Russia, see Charles J. Halperin, *Russia and the Golden Horde: the Mongol Impact on Medieval Russian History*, London: Tauris, 1987; and Donald Ostrowski, *Muscovy and the Mongols: Cross-Cultural Influences on the Steppe Frontier, 1304–1589*, Cambridge: Cambridge University Press, 1998.

3 Sigismund von Herberstein, *Notes upon Russia*, vol.1, London: Hakluyt Society, 1851, p.30.

4 Nancy Shields Kollmann, *Kinship and Politics: the Making of the Muscovite Political System, 1345–1547*, Stanford, CA: Stanford University Press, 1987, pp.146–51.

5 See, for example, Sergei Bogatyrev, *The Sovereign and his Counsellors. Ritualised Consultations in Muscovite Political Culture, 1350s–1570s*, Helsinki: Academia Scientiarum Fennica, 2000.

6 The coronation of Dmitrii in 1498 as his grandfather's heir and co-ruler is discussed in the next chapter, in relation to the coronation of Ivan IV in 1547.

7 Later in the sixteenth century two further duma ranks were created, the conciliar courtier (*dumnyi dvoryanin*) and the conciliar secretary (*dumnyi d'yak*); and the 'Moscow courtiers' (*dvoryane mookovokio*) were added to the 'Moscow ranks' (see Chapter 9)

8 This description relates to the court in the mid-sixteenth century, before the introduction of the reforms of the 1550s, which will be discussed in Chapter 4. See V.D. Nazarov, 'O strukture "gosudareva dvora" v seredine XVI v.' in *Obshchestvo i gosudarstvo feodal'noi Rossii. Sbornik statei, posvyashchennyi 70 letiyu akademika L.V. Cherepnina*, Moscow, 1975, pp.40–54; Pavlov, *Gosudarev dvor*, pp.86–139; Bogatyrev, *The Sovereign and his Counsellors*, pp.22–5.

9 Ostrowski, *Muscovy and the Mongols*, pp.48–50.

10 V.B. Kobrin, *Vlast' i sobstvennost' v srednevekovoi Rossii (XV–XVI vv.)*, Moscow, 1985.

Chapter 2

The Young Ruler

The minority of Ivan IV

The boy who would grow up to be known as 'Ivan the Terrible' was born on 25 August 1530. He was the first child of Grand Prince Vasilii III and his second wife, Elena Glinskaya.

Vasilii had divorced his first wife, Solomoniya Saburova, in 1525, after more than twenty years of marriage had failed to produce an heir. The ending of the marriage was controversial: Solomoniya entered a convent, apparently against her will, and some prominent churchmen, including the anti-Josephite monk Vassian Patrikeev, condemned the divorce as contrary to canon law. Rumours circulated in Moscow that soon after becoming a nun Solomoniya had given birth to a son whom she hid away, vowing that when he came of age he 'would revenge the injury done to his mother'.[1] This improbable tale was undoubtedly spread by opponents of Vasilii's divorce; it was subsequently to serve as the basis for various speculative theories about a 'true heir' to the throne whose possible existence supposedly tormented Ivan Groznyi throughout his life.[2] The controversy created by Vasilii's divorce was, however, much less significant than that which was to be aroused by the divorce of Henry VIII of England from Katherine of Aragon in 1533: by 1525 the Russian Church was already subordinate to the state to an extent which was not achieved in England until the break with Rome.

Vasilii's new bride, Elena Glinskaya, came from a family of Tatar origin that had served the grand princes of Lithuania in the fifteenth century. In 1508 the most prominent member of the Glinskii clan, Prince Mikhail L'vovich, transferred his allegiance to Russia. He was accompanied to Moscow by various kinsmen, including his brother Vasilii, the father of Elena. By the time of his daughter's marriage in January 1526 Prince Vasilii Glinskii had died, and Prince Mikhail Glinskii was in prison in the Kremlin, having made an abortive attempt to return to Lithuania. Some sources suggest that the grand prince's choice of bride was determined by personal preference: one chronicler states that he married her because of her lovely face and figure, and Herberstein tells us that Vasilii shaved off his beard at the time of his second marriage, presumably in order to please his new bride. Political considerations may also have played a part, however: the Glinskiis' links with Lithuania could have been considered useful for Russian foreign policy, while the clan's 'outsider' status meant that they seemed to pose little threat to established court factions.[3]

Vasilii's young wife did not immediately produce the longed-for heir. Only after four years of marriage did Elena give birth to her first child. The delay has suggested to some that it may have been Vasilii rather than Solomoniya who was infertile, and that Prince Ivan Fedorovich Ovchina-Telepnev-Obolenskii, whom Herberstein identified as Elena's lover after her husband's death, was the natural father of her two sons (the second, Yurii, was born in October 1532). The safe delivery of a male heir was, however, greeted by Vasilii with great rejoicing: the baby was named Ivan after his grandfather, Ivan III, and he was christened with much pomp at the great monastery of the Trinity and St Sergius, which lay to the north-east of Moscow. Some later sources, with the benefit of hindsight, recorded ominous portents surrounding the infant's birth. According to one chronicle, the wife of the Tatar khan of Kazan' claimed that the new Russian prince had been born with two teeth: 'With one he will devour us, and with the other he will devour you,' she told a Russian envoy.[4]

In December 1533, when his elder son was only three years old, Grand Prince Vasilii died suddenly after a short illness. At first the government was taken over by a small group of boyars appointed by Vasilii. These included Prince Mikhail Glinskii, whose fortunes had been restored by his niece's marriage. In the summer of 1534, however, Prince Mikhail returned to prison, where he died soon afterwards. He had evidently lost out in a struggle for power in which he competed for influence over Elena with her favourite, Prince I.F. Ovchina. From August 1534 until her death in April 1538 Elena was to act as regent for her young son, with the support of Ovchina and other boyars.[5]

The immediate threat to Ivan's succession, on his father's death, had been posed by his uncles, Grand Prince Vasilii's younger brothers, the appanage princes of Dmitrov and Staritsa. The elder of these, Prince Yurii Ivanovich of Dmitrov, had through the long years of Vasilii's childlessness been the heir presumptive, with increasingly realistic hopes of succeeding to the throne. Vasilii appears to have been highly suspicious of his brother Yurii, and did not permit him to marry. The grand prince's divorce, his second marriage, and the birth of his sons dashed Yurii's hopes of the succession. Vasilii's premature death, however, created an unexpected opportunity for Yurii. His brother's elder son was only three years old, and the period of his minority threatened the country with prolonged political instability. It is not clear whether Yurii himself attempted to supplant his nephew, or whether some of the boyars initiated action on his behalf. More likely the ruling group appointed by Vasilii on his death-bed made a pre-emptive strike: within a few days of the grand prince's demise, Yurii was placed under house arrest, and he died in prison in 1536.

Grand Prince Vasilii's other brother, Prince Andrei Ivanovich of Staritsa, posed less of a threat while Yurii Ivanovich was still alive. In 1533 he had been allowed to marry, and his son Vladimir was born soon afterwards. In the first stages of the power struggle after Vasilii's death, Andrei Staritskii appears to have supported the succession of his young nephew. But with the death of his brother Yurii, Andrei became the only adult heir. In 1537, when summoned to Moscow for military service, Prince Andrei, evidently fearing foul play from his sister-in-law Elena, claimed to be too ill to travel. A physician who was sent from Moscow to Staritsa reported that the prince's illness was relatively mild. Mutual suspicions grew. Summoned again to Moscow, Andrei fled from Staritsa and sought support in Novgorod. According to one chronicle, he issued proclamations to the Novgorod servicemen, in which he asserted that 'the grand prince is small, the boyars are running the state, and whom should you serve? If you come and serve me, I shall be pleased to reward you.' Elena's favourite, Ovchina, led troops from Moscow against Novgorod, and promised Andrei safe conduct if he surrendered. Elena, however, did not honour the promise: Prince Andrei was imprisoned, and died in captivity soon afterwards. His wife, Evfrosin'ya, and their small son Vladimir, were also incarcerated. Thus at the time of his mother's death in 1538, the young Grand Prince Ivan had no close adult male relatives on his father's side (see Figure 2.1). The Muscovite rulers' perennial suspicion of collateral heirs, which had led to the deaths of Yurii Dmitrovskii and Andrei Staritskii, continued into the next generation. Yurii Vasil'evich turned out to be a deaf-mute who was never regarded as a threat to his brother, but Prince Andrei Ivanovich's son Vladimir Staritskii came to be seen as a potentially dangerous rival to Ivan and his sons.

A number of letters survive from Vasilii III to Elena Glinskaya, in which the grand prince enquires about the health of their elder son. It is not clear whether Vasilii was an unusually anxious father, or whether

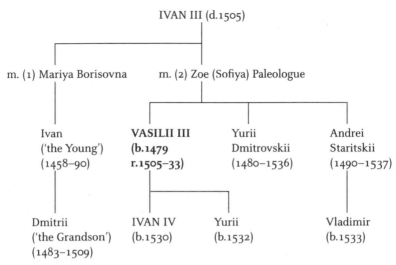

Figure 2.1 The succession to Vasilii III
Note: Reigning grand princes and tsars are indicated in capitals

Ivan was a particularly sickly child. After Vasilii's death, there were frequent rumours that his two small sons had died. These reports contributed to the political instability of the period, and gladdened the hearts of Russia's enemies in Poland and Lithuania.[6] In those days of high infant mortality, it was not surprising that many contemporaries doubted whether the little princes would survive. But in fact it was the adult members of the royal family whose death-rates were high. Elena Glinskaya was still a relatively young woman when she died in 1538, apparently of natural causes. According to gossip she was poisoned, but such rumours were the stock-in-trade of court politics: in 1534 Mikhail Glinskii had been accused of poisoning Grand Prince Vasilii; and the death of Tsar Ivan's first wife Anastasiya, in 1560, was also to be attributed to poison.

Soon after Elena's death her favourite, Ovchina, was arrested and died shortly afterwards in prison: according to Herberstein, he was 'butchered and torn to pieces'.[7] As a result of this court coup, the Shuiskii clan gained power. The Shuiskiis were the senior branch of the Suzdal' princes, and like the grand princes of Moscow they claimed descent from Ryurik. They had entered Muscovite service in the late fifteenth century, and at the time of Elena Glinskaya's death in 1538 the brothers Vasilii and Ivan Vasil'evich Shuiskii and their cousins Ivan and Andrei Mikhailovich Shuiskii were all boyars. Their chief rivals were the Bel'skii princes, who had come to Moscow from Lithuania in the 1480s. The brothers Dmitrii and Ivan Fedorovich were the most prominent members of this clan in the 1530s. In October 1538 the Shuiskiis succeeded in having Prince Ivan Bel'skii imprisoned, but he was released in 1540 as a result of the intercession of Metropolitan Ioasaf. An apparent truce between the two clans came to an end with the re-arrest of Ivan Bel'skii in January 1542 and his execution soon afterwards. In December 1543 it was the Shuiskiis' turn to suffer a reverse, when Prince Andrei Mikhailovich was killed: according to the official chronicler of Ivan's reign, he was thrown to the court kennelmen on the orders of the young grand prince himself. In 1546 Ivan's mother's kinsmen, the Glinskiis, returned to prominence at court. The grand prince was approaching the age of majority, and it has been suggested that all court factions had an interest in resolving their differences in order to choose him a bride and thus restore political stability.[8] The resolution was not an entirely peaceful one, however, since a number of executions took place in 1546 and as late as January 1547, on the very eve of Ivan's coronation and subsequent marriage to Anastasiya, the daughter of Roman Yur'evich Zakhar'in.

Court politics during the minority of Ivan IV, as we have seen, were complex and sometimes bloody. Much is unclear: the sources are defective and often contradictory; and historians have resorted to various types of speculation about the nature of the vested interests at stake. Most pre-revolutionary historians depicted the period as one of personal rivalry and jockeying for power among ambitious courtiers. In the Soviet period, however, scholars such as I.I. Smirnov developed a line of argument which had been pioneered in the nineteenth century by S.M. Solov'ev, that the boyars aimed to hamper the process of creation of a centralised Muscovite state, and to return to the system of relative autonomy for large landholders which had supposedly characterised the 'appanage' period.[9] Smirnov and others depicted the boyars as the reactionary spokesmen of the old class of hereditary landowners (*votchinniki*), who were increasingly locked in conflict with the new class of service landholders (*pomeshchiki*) who supported the centralising and autocratic policies of the Muscovite rulers. From the 1960s onwards, however, Russian historians became increasingly critical of the view that the boyars were opponents of centralisation. The traditional distinction between hereditary and service landholders has also been questioned, most notably in the works of V.B. Kobrin. Recent Russian accounts have returned to the idea that the political conflicts of the 1530s and 1540s were waged primarily for the personal and clan interests of the protagonists. Similarly, the conflicts between the Moscow government and Ivan's uncles, Yurii and Andrei Ivanovich, are now believed to have concerned the succession to the throne itself, rather than the future of the semi-autonomous appanages which the princes ruled.

The American historian Nancy Shields Kollmann also rejects the older Soviet approach to court politics during Ivan's minority. Kollmann stresses the importance of personal and family loyalties rather than the competing class and ideological interests of 'aristocracy' and 'gentry', and she advocates an 'anthropological' approach which places primary emphasis on kinship and marriage ties. In addition, Kollmann argues that Muscovite court politics was based not so much on conflict and competition as on the pursuit of consensus and stability. Finally, developing ideas first put forward by Edward L. Keenan, Kollmann claims that the ideology and ceremonial of autocracy, which impressed so many foreign observers, concealed the reality of oligarchical rule by the boyars.[10] From this point of view, Kollmann contends that the 'boyar rule' in the years of Ivan's minority was 'not an aberration' from 'normal' Muscovite politics.[11] This assertion in particular has recently been challenged by the St Petersburg historian M.M. Krom, who argues that the period of Ivan's minority was one of crisis for the Muscovite political system, which was unable to function normally in the absence of a competent (in this case, adult) ruler. In Krom's view, the prolonged crisis of the 1530s and 1540s demonstrates the importance of the role of the sovereign in the Muscovite political system.[12]

What part did Ivan himself play in the events of his minority? According to official documents, he was the sovereign of Moscow from 1533 onwards, jointly at first with his mother Elena, and from 1538 onwards sole ruler in his own right. Of course an eight-year-old boy could not exercise real political power, as Ivan himself was to recognise in his later writings, which exude resentment of his childhood powerlessness. In a famous passage in his first letter to Kurbskii, Ivan condemned the high-handed behaviour of the boyars in general, and of the Shuiskiis in particular, after the death of his mother. He and his brother, Ivan claimed, were inadequately fed and clothed, and Prince Ivan Vasil'evich Shuiskii had dared to lounge in the royal apartments, 'leaning with his elbows on our father's bed', and ignoring the two little princes who were playing nearby. Some sources attribute a greater role to Ivan in the political conflicts at court from his early adolescence onwards. In his letter to Kurbskii, Ivan himself states that, 'when we reached the fifteenth year of our life, then did we take it upon ourselves to put our kingdom in order, and thanks to the mercy of God, our rule began favourably'. The Nikon chronicle dates his independent action even earlier, crediting the thirteen-year-old grand prince with the murder of Prince Andrei Shuiskii, and adding that 'from then onwards the boyars began to fear the sovereign'. An earlier chronicle, however – probably presenting a more accurate picture – attributed Shuiskii's death to the boyars. According to Kurbskii's 'History', the young Ivan's development as a fearsome ruler went through several stages. At first, from the age of twelve, his victims were dumb animals that he hurled from the upper storeys of houses; at fifteen he turned his sadistic attention to people, beating and robbing his subjects in public places as he rode past with his rowdy young noble companions. Subsequently his counsellors made use of him in order to settle scores among themselves; and only finally did he start to order executions on his own initiative.[13] Kurbskii's chronology is somewhat confused, and his account of Ivan's vicious character is clearly tendentious, but his assertion that the grand prince became an autonomous political actor only at a comparatively late date is generally convincing. There are few signs that Ivan devoted himself to serious statesmanship before 1547, preferring the life of youthful dissipation which was criticised by his mentors such as the priest Sil'vestr. Ivan's direct involvement in court politics may have been limited to securing the return to court of his mother's relatives, the Glinskiis, in 1546.

Older historiography presents the years of boyar rule as a period of virtual anarchy which was quelled only when the young grand prince began to assert himself as autocrat. This picture of the minority was largely created by the later writings of Ivan himself and by official chroniclers who reflected the views of the adult tsar. In the assessment of some recent historians, their depiction of court politics as violent and corrupt is greatly exaggerated. Nancy Kollmann sees the period as one in which the traditional system was subject to great strain, but still survived intact, avoiding anarchy; M.M. Krom concedes that effective government was provided by the boyar duma in association with the leading state officials and the metropolitan, but argues that the absence of an adult ruler weakened Russia's prestige in foreign affairs, and contributed to internal political instability. Whatever the reality of the court politics of his minority, it is important to note that Ivan himself regarded it as a period of disorder and arbitrary rule, for which he blamed the boyars. Having lost his father at the age of three, and his mother at eight, Ivan had no grand princely role-model to follow as he approached the age of majority. He had no personal experience of 'normal' Muscovite politics under an adult sovereign, and developed his own view of 'boyar rule' as an anomalous and undesirable form of government. He was to spend the rest of his reign constantly inventing and reinventing the role of the Muscovite ruler, and attempting to reshape and reformulate his relationship with the boyars.

Coronation, marriage and the fall of the Glinskiis

According to one of the chroniclers, in December 1546 the young Grand Prince Ivan summoned Metropolitan Makarii and all the boyars and informed them that he intended to take a wife. But before he married, Ivan added, he planned to be crowned as tsar and grand prince according to the ritual followed by his ancestors such as Grand Prince Vladimir Monomakh of Kiev.[14] In fact, as we shall see, the coronation of Vladimir Monomakh as tsar was entirely legendary. But there was a Muscovite precedent for the coronation of a ruler, which the chronicler did not, however, choose to mention.

Almost half a century earlier, in 1498, Grand Prince Ivan III had crowned his grandson, Dmitrii Ivanovich, as his co-ruler and heir. This unprecedented step had been taken in the context of the potential dispute concerning the succession which we have already mentioned in Chapter One. The grand prince's designated heir, his son by his first wife, Mariya Borisovna of Tver', had died in 1490, leaving a six-year-old son ('Dmitrii-the-Grandson'). By then Ivan III had a number of sons from his second marriage, to Zoe (Sofiya) Paleologue. The eldest of these, the future Vasilii III, was eleven years old when his half-brother Ivan ('the Young') died in 1490 (see Figure 2.1 above). Although the principle of vertical succession to the grand-princely throne was by now firmly established, and Ivan III's adult brothers were not considered to be serious contenders, there appears to have been uncertainty as to how vertical succession would work in practice, i.e. whether Dmitrii-the-Grandson, as the son of a deceased elder son, had priority over his uncle Vasilii, who was the eldest surviving son of Ivan III. The situation was complicated by the fact that Vasilii and Ivan-the-Young were half-brothers, and the kinsmen of their respective mothers constituted rival supporters of the two potential heirs to the throne.

In 1497 an alleged plot to assassinate Dmitrii was discovered. Vasilii was implicated, and Dmitrii's coronation the following year may thus be seen as a clear statement by Ivan III that the succession had passed by right of primogeniture through the senior line of his descendants. In practice, however, the grand prince's personal preferences – influenced no doubt by court intrigues – played a more important part. In 1499 Vasilii returned to his father's favour, and in 1502 Dmitrii was arrested and imprisoned. When Ivan III died in 1505, it was Vasilii who succeeded him as grand prince; Dmitrii remained in prison, and died there in 1509. Possibly because of the somewhat embarrassing aftermath of the coronation of Dmitrii-the-Grandson, Vasilii III was never crowned, either as co-ruler with his father or as grand prince in his own right. And Vasilii's own premature death when his elder son was still just an infant meant that Ivan IV was not crowned as his father's heir and co-ruler.

Thus when the decision was taken to stage the coronation of Ivan IV in 1547, the earlier coronation of Dmitrii-the-Grandson provided only a partial precedent. In the first place, Dmitrii had been crowned as co-ruler rather than as sole ruler, and the ceremony was based on the imperial Byzantine rite for the coronation of an heir and co-ruler. Secondly, Dmitrii had been crowned with the title of grand prince. Ivan IV, by contrast, was crowned both as sole ruler and as tsar.

Although the chronicler attributed the initiative for staging the coronation to Ivan himself, it is much more likely that it was Metropolitan Makarii – the head of the Russian Church – who took the decision. And since there was no question in 1547 about the legitimacy of Ivan's claim to the throne, the most likely motive for the ceremony was to establish the official right of the Muscovite ruler to use the title of 'tsar', and thereby to enhance both his own status and the international prestige of the country which he governed.

The title 'tsar'' had been used occasionally by Ivan's immediate predecessors. The term was used in Russian to describe the Tatar khans; and in this sense, as we shall see, it was to acquire greater significance for Ivan after his conquest of the Volga khanates of Kazan' and Astrakhan' in the 1550s. But at the time of his coronation its main resonance was as the title of the Byzantine emperors (the imperial title of the Holy Roman Emperors of the west, by contrast, was rendered in Russian as *tsesar'*). It is not surprising that Church leaders such as Metropolitan Makarii were keen to acquire the title of tsar for the Muscovite ruler, since from around the middle of the fifteenth century the religious authorities had increasingly stressed the historical connections and continuities between Byzantium and Moscow. At a time when Tatar suzerainty over Muscovy was weakening, Russian Churchmen looked to Byzantium as the model of an independent Orthodox realm. They advocated the use of the terms *tsar'* and *samoderzhets* as the Russian equivalents of Emperor (*basileus*) and Autocrat (*autokrator*) in the title of the Byzantine ruler.

The best known version of the Russian concept of the continuity between Byzantium and Muscovy is the theory of 'Moscow the Third Rome'. The 'Third Rome' formulation first appears in a letter attributed to the monk Filofei of Pskov, probably dating from the 1520s: 'Two Romes have fallen, the third stands, and a fourth there will not be'. The original Rome had been lost to Orthodoxy as a result of the Great Schism of 1054 between the eastern and western Churches; Constantinople, the second Rome, had fallen to the Turks in 1453; and Muscovy was now the only independent Orthodox Christian realm, whose ruler was therefore obliged to uphold and protect the Church. Although it has often been interpreted as claiming a *translatio imperii* or transfer of empire from Rome to Byzantium and thence to Moscow, it was not the Third Rome theory that provided the official justification for Ivan's adoption of the title of tsar in 1547.

The most important element in the tracing of continuities from Byzantium to Moscow was the legend of Vladimir Monomakh, to which the chronicler had referred in his account of Ivan's decision to be crowned tsar. The text of the Monomakh legend formed part of the 'Story of the Princes of Vladimir', which probably first appeared in the early sixteenth century. It tells how the eleventh-century Byzantine emperor Constantine Monomachus sent royal regalia, including a crown, to Grand Prince Vladimir Vsevolodovich of Kiev. Vladimir, who thus became known as Monomakh (and 'tsar of Great Rus'', according to the legend), was the ancestor of the princes of Vladimir, and hence of the grand princes of Moscow, all of whom were supposedly subsequently crowned with the crown sent from Byzantium by Constantine Monomachus. This crown, later known as the 'cap of Monomakh', was in fact of Tatar origin, and first mentioned (as the 'golden cap') only in the fourteenth century; but the legend provided it with a Byzantine provenance, and also attributed a bogus Kievan pedigree to the title 'tsar'.

Ivan IV's title represented him as tsar of 'all Rus' (*vseya Rusii*)'. This was not in itself an innovation: as we have seen, Ivan III had described himself as sovereign (*gospodin, gosudar'*) of all Rus', with the clear implication that this represented a claim to the Kievan lands which subsequently formed part of Poland-Lithuania. For that reason, the Poles contested the Muscovite rulers' use of the term. Ivan IV's claim to be tsar of all Rus', with the ambitions for territorial expansion which this implied, helps to explain the stress which his coronation ceremony placed on the Monomakh legend, recalling as it did the Kievan antecedents of the Ryurikid dynasty.

The Monomakh legend claimed a symbolic connection between Muscovy and Byzantium which dated back to a period long before its capture by the Turks in 1453, and in that respect the legend had a rather different emphasis from the idea of 'Moscow the Third Rome', which – in spite of the attention which it has attracted subsequently – was a less prominent element of sixteenth-century Russian political ideology. The leading Muscovite ideologists of the mid-sixteenth century were more concerned to fabricate a continuity from early Byzantium via pre-Mongol

Kiev than to claim that Muscovy was the successor to fifteenth-century Constantinople. They placed surprisingly little emphasis on the fact that Ivan IV's grandmother, Zoe Paleologue (the second wife of Ivan III) was the niece of the last Byzantine Emperor. The title of tsar was presented not as a recent borrowing from Constantinople, but as a traditional appellation of the dynasty. Significantly, the 'Story of the Princes of Vladimir' contained not only the Monomakh legend but also a fake genealogy which showed that the Daniilovichi traced their ancestry back not only as far as Ryurik, but even further, to the caesars of ancient Rome. Augustus Caesar had supposedly appointed his kinsman Prus as ruler of what later became the Prussian lands; Ryurik was a descendant of Prus, and Ryurik's descendants in turn included Vladimir I of Kiev, Vladimir Monomakh and the grand princes of Vladimir. Thus the Ryurikids derived their claim to the title of tsar directly from the Roman emperors.[15]

Ivan's coronation took place in the Uspenskii Cathedral of the Moscow Kremlin on 16 January 1547, with Metropolitan Makarii officiating. The ceremony was based on Byzantine models, although in Byzantium the coronation of an emperor was performed by the patriarch. Russia did not acquire its own patriarchate until 1589, and for that reason the patriarch of Constantinople granted only conditional approval of Ivan's coronation as tsar. Makarii invested Ivan with the royal regalia: the jewelled cross, the ceremonial collar known as the *barmy*, and the cap of Monomakh. After the crowning, the archdeacon chanted the *mnogoletie*, a prayer which wished the tsar a long life.[16] Finally, as Ivan left the cathedral, he was showered with gold coins by his younger brother Yurii. (This part of the ceremony was apparently based on a misreading by the Muscovite Churchmen of a description of a Byzantine coronation in which the new emperor threw coins as largesse to the crowds.)[17]

On 3 February 1547, less than three weeks after his coronation, Ivan celebrated his wedding to Anastasiya Romanovna. According to the chronicler, the young grand prince had personally decided against taking a foreign wife, for fear that their temperaments would be too different; with the blessing of the metropolitan and the boyars he made his own choice of a bride from within Russia.[18] In practice, of course, the boyars had great influence over the decision, although we do not know exactly how it was reached. Anastasiya's family, the Zakhar'in-Yur'evs, had become prominent at court in the 1540s, and although her father had died in 1543 she had powerful brothers and cousins who could have helped to secure her the prized royal bridegroom. The tsar's marriage, according to Nancy Kollmann, reflected a new agreement among the boyars concerning the distribution of power at court, which was designed to restore stability after the conflicts of Ivan's minority.[19] Ivan's wedding, however, was to be followed by a major crisis in the summer of 1547.

Fires were a common phenomenon in medieval and early modern Russian towns, as they were in other parts of Europe in an age when buildings were mostly made of wood. But the fires which erupted in Moscow in the spring and summer of 1547 were unprecedented in their scale even in the memory of contemporaries.[20] In April a series of blazes destroyed much of the centre of the capital. Barely had the citizens recovered from the devastation when a new outbreak occurred on 21 June. This fire was even more extensive than its predecessors. Many buildings were burned down in the Kremlin and surrounding areas: the chroniclers provide an eloquent catalogue of the churches which were destroyed, with their precious icons. Thousands of people perished, and Metropolitan Makarii only just escaped from the flames.

The pious chroniclers presented the great fire as divine punishment of the Muscovites for their sins, but the citizens themselves were inclined to look for human agents to blame. Alleged arsonists had been executed after the April disaster, and rumours of fire-raising appeared again in June. This time the finger of suspicion was pointed at the tsar's kinsmen, the Glinskiis, and particularly at Ivan's maternal grandmother, Princess Anna Glinskaya, 'with her children and servants'. The Glinskiis' agents were accused of causing the fire by means of black magic. They allegedly obtained human hearts and steeped them in water, in order to make an infusion with which they sprinkled buildings to set them alight (Princess Anna herself was said to have flown over the city in the guise of a magpie – a traditional characteristic of witches in Russian folklore – in order to burn it down). These accusations were made against the Glinskiis, according to the official chronicler, because they were in favour with the tsar, and because the ordinary people had suffered violence and robbery at their hands. The chronicler adds, however, that it was boyars hostile to the Glinskiis who roused the rabble against them; and this allegation was also made by Ivan IV in his first letter to Kurbskii, in which he claimed that the accusations of the 'traitor-boyars' against the Glinskiis were also directed against himself. Certainly the Glinskiis had made many enemies at court since their return to power; one source claims that Princess Anna Glinskaya and her son Mikhail had ordered the executions which took place in January 1547 on the eve of Ivan's coronation. It is thus not impossible that some of the Glinskiis' rivals may have incited the crowd against them, although it seems more likely that the rumours arose spontaneously among the townspeople. One chronicler records a report that the Glinskiis had ordered the capital to be burned because they were in league with the Crimean khan, who was supposedly heading for Moscow with a large army. Certainly the fear of a Tatar invasion linked to the fires would have heightened the tension in the city and led to suspicions of the existence of a 'fifth column' of traitors.

On 26 June the people of Moscow flocked to the Kremlin. According to the official chronicle, they were summoned by the boyars, who had been instructed by the tsar to investigate the allegations of arson. It seems more likely that, as some other sources suggest, the Muscovites themselves organised the confrontation with the boyars which took place on the square outside the Uspenskii Cathedral. The crowd accused the Glinskiis of burning the city, but only Prince Yurii Vasil'evich Glinskii, the tsar's uncle, was present in the Kremlin that day, Yurii's mother, Princess Anna, and his brother, Prince Mikhail, having fled from Moscow. Prince Yurii tried to take refuge inside the cathedral, but the mob burst in and attacked him. Subsequently the injured man was dragged outside and stoned to death; his body was later displayed at the place of public execution. The boyars who were present in the Kremlin may not have actively incited the people to kill Yurii Glinskii, as the tsar and the official chronicler claimed; but they were unable and probably unwilling to save him. After Prince Yurii's murder the crowd turned their attention to his household: they killed many of his servants and looted his property. A number of military servicemen from the Seversk region were also lynched, on the assumption – apparently incorrect – that they were retainers of the Glinskiis.

Three days later, on 29 June, a large detachment of Muscovites marched to the village of Vorob'evo, outside the capital, where the young tsar had taken up residence after the fire. They demanded that he hand over to them Princess Anna and Prince Mikhail Glinskii, whom they suspected Ivan of harbouring (in fact Prince Mikhail and his mother had taken refuge in the town of Rzhev). In his first letter to Kurbskii, the tsar claimed that the crowd had been incited by the 'traitor-boyars' to come to Vorob'evo in order to kill him for protecting his kinsmen; but it seems more likely that the Muscovites drew a clear distinction between the young tsar and his 'evil counsellors', the Glinskiis, whom they blamed for all the misfortunes that had befallen them. Ivan's response to the unwelcome arrival of his subjects seems to have been somewhat hesitant, especially if he genuinely believed at the time that they had come to lynch him. According to the official chronicle, he ordered the protestors to be seized and executed, but many managed to flee to other towns. An unofficial chronicler, however, states that the tsar was 'amazed and frightened' to see so many people; when he learned that they had been incited to come, he decided to punish only the instigators of the action. (It is not entirely clear how far-reaching the repressions were after this episode.) According to the version of these events which Ivan provides in his correspondence with Kurbskii, his ordinary subjects had been aroused by the boyars against himself and his kinsmen. The incident clearly made a strong impression on the young tsar, and he may well have drawn important lessons from it, concerning the way in which the people of Moscow could be manipulated by one faction of the élite against another. On future occasions, Ivan was to turn the tables by using the crowd against the 'traitor-boyars'.

In spite of Ivan's defence of the Glinskiis against the accusations of fire-raising, their position at court was no longer tenable, and they soon fell from power. In November 1547 Prince Mikhail attempted to flee to Lithuania with his mother, in the company of Prince Ivan Turuntai Pronskii, who had recently been removed from the post of governor of Pskov. Prince P.I. Shuiskii was sent to pursue them, and forced them to return to Moscow, where they told a feeble tale about losing their way when going on pilgrimage. As a result of the intercession of Metropolitan Makarii, the fugitives' punishment was relatively light: their lives were spared, but their property was confiscated and they were obliged to provide deeds of surety that they would not try to flee again. In mitigation for his treason, Mikhail Glinskii cited the fear which the murder of his brother Yurii had inspired in him; but he was stripped of the elevated court position of equerry, in which capacity he had only a few months earlier held a golden dish filled with the gold coins which were showered over his nephew at his coronation. The main beneficiaries of the eclipse of the Glinskiis were the Zakhar'in-Yur'evs, the kinsmen of the young tsar's new wife Anastasiya.

Notes

1 Herberstein, *Notes upon Russia*, vol.1, p.51.

2 See, for example, G.L. Grigor'ev, *Kogo boyalsya Ivan Groznyi? K voprosu o proiskhozhdenii oprichniny*, Moscow, 1998.

3 Kollmann, *Kinship and Politics*, pp.127, 144–5.

4 *PSRL*, vol.34, Moscow, 1978, p.194.

5 M.M. Krom, 'Sud'ba regentskogo soveta pri maloletnem Ivane IV', *Otechestvennaya istoriya*, 1996, no.5, pp.34–49.

6 M.M. Krom, 'Politicheskii krizis 30-40-kh godov XVI veka', *Otechestvennaya istoriya*, 1998, no.5, p.8.

7 Herberstein, *Notes upon Russia*, vol.2, p.93.

8 Kollmann, *Kinship and Politics*, pp.173–5.

9 I.I. Smirnov, *Ocherki politicheskoi istorii russkogo gosudarstva 30-50-kh godov XVI veka*, Moscow, 1958.

10 Kollmann, *Kinship and Politics*, pp.146–51.

11 Nancy Shields Kollmann, 'The Grand Prince in Muscovite Politics: the Problem of Genre in Sources on Ivan's Minority', in Hellie, ed., *Ivan the Terrible*, pp.295, 310.

12 Krom, 'Politicheskii krizis'.

13 *Correspondence*, pp.74–5, 80–81; *PSRL*, vol.13, St Petersburg, 1904 (reprinted Moscow, 1965), p.145; S.O. Shmidt, ed., 'Prodolzhenie khronografa redaktsii 1512 goda', *Istoricheskii arkhiv*, vol.7, Moscow, 1951, p.289; *Kurbsky's History*, pp.10–15.

14 *PSRL*, vol.13, pp.450–51.

15 For a thorough overview of the main ideological currents at this period, see David B. Miller, 'The Velikie Minei Chetii and the Stepennaia Kniga of Metropolitan Makarii and the Origins of Russian National Consciousness', *Forschungen zur osteuropäischen Geschichte*, vol.26, 1979, pp.263–382. For persuasive critiques of older views which attach greater significance to the 'Third Rome' theory, see: Daniel Rowland, 'Moscow – The Third Rome or the New Israel?', *Russian Review*, vol.55, 1996, pp.591–614; and Ostrowski, *Muscovy and the Mongols*, pp.219–43.

16 *PSRL*, vol.13, pp.451–2. There is some debate as to whether Ivan's coronation ceremony included the rite of anointing. For the argument that it did not, see B.A. Uspenskii, *Tsar' i patriarkh; kharizma vlasti v Rossii*, Moscow, 1998, pp.109–13.

17 Ostrowski, *Muscovy and the Mongols*, pp.186–7.

18 *PSRL*, vol.13, pp.450, 453.

19 Kollmann, 'The Grand Prince', pp.310–11; Kollmann, *Kinship and Politics*, pp.124–7, 174–5.

20 For a detailed account of the fires and the subsequent uprising, with a critical review of the sources, see S.O. Shmidt, *U istokov rossiiskogo absolyutizma*, Moscow, 1996, pp.21–143.

Chapter 3

The Conquest of Kazan' and Astrakhan'

Soon after Mikhail Glinskii's abortive flight to Lithuania, Ivan embarked upon his first serious military campaign, against Kazan'. As we have seen, Ivan III and Vasilii III had exerted considerable control over the Volga khanate; and from 1487, when Ivan III placed Magmet-Amin' on the Kazanian throne, the Russian rulers claimed the right to appoint the khans. After the death of Vasilii III in 1533, however, Moscow's influence in the region was weakened, especially when Elena Glinskaya's government was at war with Lithuania in 1534–7. In 1535 a coup in Kazan' overthrew the Muscovite client, Khan Enalei, and restored the previous khan, Safa-Girei. Safa-Girei was a nephew of Saip-Girei, the former ruler of Kazan', who had become khan of the Crimea in 1532. For the next ten years, Crimean influence replaced that of Moscow in Kazan', and both the Kazanian and the Crimean Tatars launched a number of raids on Russian territory. It was of particular concern to the Russians that behind the Crimean khan there loomed his overlord, the Turkish Sultan: in 1541 Turkish troops accompanied Saip-Girei on a major incursion which was driven back only on the River Oka.

Soon after this, the Russians began to adopt a more aggressive policy towards Kazan'. In 1545 they launched an attack on the khanate. This reinforced pre-existing divisions within the Tatar élite, between the advocates of a pro-Russian orientation and those who preferred the Crimean alliance. In 1546 Safa-Girei was overthrown and briefly replaced by the Russian nominee Shigalei, the khan of Kasimov, before being restored to power. On his return to Kazan', Safa-Girei embarked on a purge of his pro-Russian opponents; but the episode demonstrated that the pro-Crimean camp was vulnerable. The non-Tatar peoples of the khanate drew similar conclusions. In December 1546 the Mountain Cheremis, a Finnish people living on the raised right bank of the Volga, sent an envoy to Moscow to offer their support for a new Russian campaign against Kazan'. In response, Ivan IV dispatched a detachment of troops which penetrated

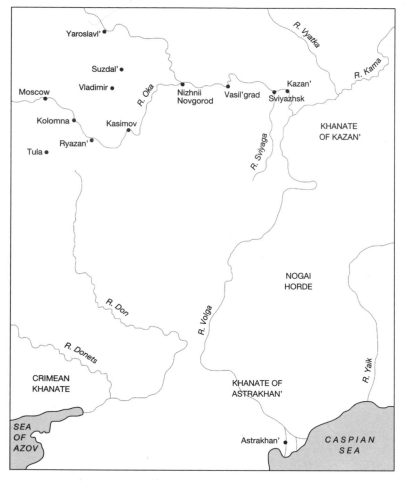

Map 3.1 The conquest of Kazan' and Astrakhan'

the khanate as far as the confluence of the rivers Volga and Sviyaga, about twenty kilometres from Kazan' (see Map 3.1).

The expedition which Ivan personally headed in the winter of 1547–8 was a more serious enterprise, which evidently aimed to attack the fortress of Kazan' itself. The army that mustered at Vladimir was equipped with heavy artillery, but even at this early stage in the campaign the Russians experienced difficulties in transporting their cannon, since the ground was very wet as a result of heavy rain. The weather was unusually mild, and the situation did not improve as the army moved eastward. Just beyond Nizhnii Novgorod thawing ice made it impossible to take the artillery across the Volga; many pieces were lost, and a number of soldiers drowned. Ivan himself returned to Nizhnii Novgorod, shedding 'many tears', according to the chronicler, because of the obstacles he had encountered.[1] The army itself continued the campaign, reaching Kazan' in February 1548 and giving battle to Safa-Girei outside the city. The Russians forced the Tatars to withdraw into the fortress, but in the absence of their artillery they were unable to lay siege to the city and retreated after spending a week encamped outside Kazan'.

A year after this setback, a new opportunity presented itself to the Russians. Safa-Girei died suddenly in March 1549, leaving a two-year-old son, Utemish-Girei, whose mother, the Nogai princess Syuyunbek, acted as regent on his behalf. Now Kazan' was weakened in precisely the same way as Russia had been in 1533, on the death of Vasilii III. The pro-Crimean faction sent a delegation to Saip-Girei to request aid and the appointment of an adult khan, but the envoys were intercepted and killed by Russian cossacks. At the same time, the Kazanians dispatched a mission to Moscow to sue for peace. The Russians, however, considered the situation to be more favourable for warfare, and began to organise another campaign against the khanate. Ivan himself again participated in the expedition. At first it made good progress, and the Russian army arrived at the walls of Kazan' in February 1550 with its artillery intact. The siege engines were set up, but the weather again became unfavourable: according to the chronicler, strong winds and heavy rain made it impossible to fire the cannon and harquebuses, and the downpour prevented the storming of the fortress. The Russians remained outside the city for eleven days before Ivan, fearful that his artillery would become bogged down in the mire, ordered a retreat. An additional reason for the debacle was the failure of the pro-Moscow faction in Kazan' to deliver the assistance they had promised.[2]

On the return journey, the tsar halted at the confluence of the rivers Volga and Sviyaga. God himself, the chronicler assures us, inspired Ivan with the idea of building a fort there, which could serve as a base for future attacks on Kazan'. The construction of the settlement, which became known as Sviyazhsk, began in the spring of 1551 and was carried out with great urgency. This show of Russian strength impressed the indigenous Volga peoples, who sent envoys to petition the tsar to accept them as his subjects. Ivan was of course delighted to do so. He showered the Mountain Cheremis and others with concessions in relation to their payment of tribute, inscribing his assurances in a charter with a golden seal, and bestowing furs and other lavish gifts on their princes. Thus the Russians were able to annexe a considerable proportion of the population and territory of the khanate by peaceful diplomatic means.[3]

These Russian successes caused great concern within Kazan' itself, and after an uprising against the dominant pro-Crimean faction the Tatar leaders approached Moscow to seek an accommodation. The Russians insisted that their client Shigalei be restored as khan, and that Utemish-Girei and his mother be handed over to them. After lengthy negotiations, as a result of which the Kazanians agreed to deliver their Russian prisoners and to make further territorial concessions, Shigalei was installed as khan on 16 August. He was accompanied into Kazan' by 300 service Tatars from the Kasimov khanate and by 200 Russian harquebusiers. At first relations between the Kazanians and their new overlords were amicable, but tensions soon arose over the implementation of the terms of the peace accords. The Russians were unwilling to relax their demands, and this in turn led to the revival of an anti-Moscow faction in Kazan', who tried to obtain backing from the Nogai Horde. Although Shigalei succeeded in suppressing the conspiracy, the Moscow government was concerned that the Crimean khan and the Sultan would support future opponents of its client ruler in Kazan'. The Russians put diplomatic pressure on Shigalei to allow them to station more troops in the city. When the khan refused, they engineered a petition from some of the Tatar princes, supposedly on behalf of the people of Kazan', requesting the tsar to replace Shigalei with a Russian governor 'as in the town of Sviyazhsk'. It seemed that Moscow might be able to annexe the khanate peacefully – a possibility which came closer to realisation when Shigalei, apparently fearing a violent overthrow, left the city on 6 March 1552. Two days later a delegation from Kazan' came to Sviyazhsk to arrange the handover to the Russian governor, Prince S.I. Mikulinskii. At the last moment, however, things went badly wrong. As Mikulinskii prepared to enter Kazan', the inhabitants shut the city gates against him. Opponents of the deal had spread rumours that the Russians planned to massacre the Tatar population. The Kazanian élites were unable to persuade the citizens to admit the governor, and Prince Mikulinskii was obliged to return, somewhat ignominiously, to Sviyazhsk.

When news of the 'treason' of the Kazanians reached Moscow, the decision was taken immediately to launch a punitive expedition against the khanate. Ivan himself, according to the chronicler, insisted on personally heading the campaign. The matter was urgent, since the rebellion threatened to escalate. The Kazan' Tatars sent a delegation to the Nogai Horde to request a new khan, and the Astrakhan' prince Ediger-Magmet was soon installed. More and more bad news reached Moscow from the Volga. The Mountain Cheremis, who had only recently accepted Russian rule, defected and made common cause with the Kazanians. Russian servicemen imprisoned in Kazan' – the advance party of Prince Mikulinskii's ill-fated mission – were killed; and the Tatars attacked Muscovite vessels in the vicinity of Sviyazhsk. The most worrying news of all was received by Ivan in June, when he was mustering his troops at Kolomna. Devlet-Girei, the new Crimean khan, had invaded Muscovy and was attacking Tula 'with much artillery and many Turkish janissaries'. Russian troops were diverted to intercept the invaders, and Devlet-Girei retreated from Tula, abandoning his cannon and camels. The victory over the Crimean Tatars seemed to be a good omen for the success of the campaign against Kazan', and morale was high when Ivan set off in July, fortified by a lengthy missive from Metropolitan Makarii which reminded him that he was undertaking a sacred mission against the 'godless' Tatars.

On 13 August Ivan reached Sviyazhsk, where he prepared for an assault on Kazan' while still holding out hopes for a peaceful resolution. He sent proclamations to the city demanding its immediate surrender, but no response was received, and ten days later the siege of the fortress began. It was to last for six weeks. The Tatars resisted heroically, launching attacks on the Russian troops both from within Kazan' itself and from the surrounding forests. Prince Andrei Kurbskii, who played a major part in the campaign, recalled that because of the frequent enemy sorties during the first three weeks of the siege he was barely able to eat or sleep. After one of these skirmishes resulted in a Russian victory, the tsar had his Tatar prisoners bound to stakes in front of the walls of Kazan', and ordered them to call on their comrades inside the fortress to surrender. If they yielded, the Russians promised, the lives of the prisoners and of the besieged citizens would be spared; otherwise the captives would all be put to death. The defenders, however, began to fire on the prisoners from the ramparts, declaring defiantly, 'We would rather see you killed by our Mussulman hands than slaughtered by the uncircumcised Giaours! [Christians]'.[4] Soon after this incident the Russians began to mine the fortress, under the direction of an experienced foreign sapper named Razmysl. First they destroyed the town's water supply and then, on 2 October, blew up the city walls to enable the final storming of Kazan' to begin. After fierce fighting which lasted for several hours, the Tatars surrendered. When the bodies of the dead had been cleared from his route, the tsar entered the city in triumph, and took up residence in the khan's palace.

Ivan himself appears to have played an active military role in the assault on Kazan' from the outset. The devout official chroniclers depict him remaining in camp and praying in his private chapel, even after the explosions in the mine-tunnels: only at the end of the church service, by which time 'Christian banners' were already flying on the city walls, did the tsar join his troops. The chroniclers' version was evidently designed to convey the edifying message that the victory was a divine reward for Ivan's personal piety, rather than his physical bravery.[5] But the tsar does not appear to have been short of the latter quality: even Kurbskii admits, albeit somewhat grudgingly, that Ivan's presence beside the 'great Christian banner' at the 'Royal gates' of Kazan' served as an inspiration to the Russian soldiers at a crucial point in the battle.

The tsar remained in Kazan' for only a few days after its fall; before he departed, he appointed his senior military commander, the boyar Prince A.B. Gorbatyi-Suzdal'skii, as governor of the city. On his return journey Ivan was met at Vladimir by messengers from Moscow who told him that Tsaritsa Anastasiya had just given birth to their first son, Tsarevich Dmitrii. The celebrations when Ivan reached the capital were therefore doubly joyful: not only had he conquered the infidel stronghold of Kazan', but he now had a male heir to inherit the tsardom. Like his father before him, Dmitrii Ivanovich was christened at the monastery of the Trinity and St Sergius, where his proud parents took him soon after the tsar's return from Kazan'.[6]

The Russians' capture of the fortress of Kazan' did not immediately bring the entire territory of the khanate under Moscow's control. Some of the Tatar princes continued to resist, and they were joined in 1555 by the Cheremis and other indigenous peoples, who refused to pay the Russians the *yasak* (tribute) which they had previously rendered to the khan. (Kurbskii, somewhat unfairly, attributes the revolts to Ivan's decision to return to Moscow so soon after the conquest, before consolidating his victory.) Muscovite troops were repeatedly dispatched to the Volga to suppress the insurgents. Eventually, by the spring of 1557, the conquerors had established their dominion over the peoples of the khanate. The Russian military effort had been assisted by divisions among the indigenous inhabitants of the region: the Chuvash, for example, a Turkic people who lived south of the Volga, supported Moscow; and the rebels received no help from the Nogai, whose prince, Ismail, swore an oath of loyalty to the tsar in 1557.

By this date the Russians had already conquered Astrakhan' as well as Kazan'. In 1554 Moscow formed an alliance with Prince Ismail which led to joint action by the Russians and the Nogai against Yamgurchei, the khan of Astrakhan'. When a large army commanded by Prince Yu.I. Shemyakin-Pronskii sailed down the Volga in the summer of 1554, Yamgurchei fled from Astrakhan' and was replaced by a Russian client, Ismail's nephew Derbysh-Alei. Two years later, however, Derbysh-Alei formed an alliance with the Crimean khan. Another Russian army was sent down the Volga; Derbysh-Alei abandoned Astrakhan', and the khanate came under direct rule from Moscow.

In the decade which followed Ivan's coronation as tsar, therefore, Russia made enormous territorial gains at the expense of the successors of the Golden Horde. Moscow's policy towards the Volga khanates had shifted away from its earlier practice of imposing client rulers on them, and was directed instead towards their direct annexation. The overriding factor in this adoption of a more aggressive policy was undoubtedly the need to counter the danger that Kazan' would become an outpost of the Crimean khanate. But ideological considerations also played a part, although historians have offered different interpretations of these. Some have suggested that Ivan IV aimed to conquer the states of the Chingisid rulers (the descendants of Genghis Khan) in order to claim the inheritance of the Golden Horde and thereby legitimise his adoption of the title of tsar (khan). But the advocates of this notion adduce little evidence in its support. Nor do they provide convincing arguments for the related idea that the 'secular authority' in mid-sixteenth-century Moscow, in contrast to the religious leaders, promoted the concept of continuity with the Golden Horde rather than with Rome, Byzantium and Kiev.[7] Much more convincing is the argument that Moscow's ideological motives for the conquest reflected her growing national self-consciousness and self-confidence, together with her new imperial aspirations, and a desire to launch a crusade against the infidel – ideas which stemmed primarily from Church leaders.[8]

Arguments in favour of the Russian conquest of Kazan' can be found in only a few sources which predate the fall of the city in October 1552. The Lithuanian nobleman Ivan Peresvetov, in his 'Great Petition' to the tsar of 1549, advised him to attack Kazan' because of its prosperity (Peresvetov described it as an 'earthly paradise') and its dangerous proximity as a hostile power. The inhabitants of the khanate, Peresvetov recommended, should be killed or taken captive and forcibly baptised. The religious argument was stressed even more strongly by Metropolitan Makarii in the series of letters which he addressed to the tsar during the campaigns of 1549 and 1552. These called on the Russians to fight 'for the holy churches and our holy Orthodox faith against the godless sons of Hagar [the Moslems]'.[9]

The initial policy of the Russian conquerors after the fall of Kazan' corresponded closely to this advice. The official chronicle tells us that the tsar ordered the Tatar women and children to be taken captive, and the armed men put to death 'because of their treason'. An Orthodox church was erected in Kazan' even before Ivan's departure from the city; mosques were destroyed; and a programme of forced conversion was introduced, on the advice of the priest Sil'vestr. The last two khans of Kazan', the infant Utemish-Girei and the Astrakhan' prince Ediger-Magmet, were baptised in Moscow in early 1553, and given the Christian names of Alexander and Simeon respectively. In 1555 the Archbishopric of Kazan' was created, and Abbot Gurii of the Selizharov Monastery was appointed as the first Archbishop of Kazan' and Sviyazhsk. The tsar's instructions to Gurii, however, recommended that the conversion of the Tatars should take place on a voluntary basis. The change of policy was partly a response to the opposition which the original programme of forced baptisms had provoked in the khanate, and which was reflected in the uprisings of 1553 onwards. The policy of voluntary conversion, however, achieved only limited success.[10]

In spite of the initial setbacks which their annexation encountered, the conquest of the Tatar khanates on the Volga was celebrated as a major event, and as a triumph for Orthodox Christianity over the Moslem infidel. It was exploited in various ways to boost the status and prestige of Muscovy in general and of the tsar in particular. On his return to Moscow from Kazan' Ivan was welcomed by the metropolitan, and a great religious procession was held, followed by a three-day celebration in the Faceted Palace of the Kremlin. The victory was marked by the painting, probably in 1552–3, of the huge icon of the Church Militant (the Blessed Host of the Heavenly Tsar), in which Ivan follows the Archangel Michael in leading the Russian troops, in the form of the heavenly host, back from Kazan' to Moscow. In the Bible, the Archangel Michael overthrows Satan in the last days; in this icon, therefore, imagery borrowed from the Book of Daniel and from Revelation imbued the victory over the Tatars with an apocalyptic significance in the cosmic battle between good and evil. It also equated the Muscovites with God's chosen people, Israel, since the representation of Moscow resembled that of Jerusalem. Imagery similar to that in the icon of the Church Militant was used in frescoes and murals in the Kremlin when it was redecorated after the fire of 1547; it was also found in battle standards of the same period. The theme of the Host of the Heavenly Tsar was used to glorify not only the ruler, but also the Russian army, and especially the military élite of boyars and commanders, depicting them as enjoying the special protection of the Archangel Michael, in particular.[11]

An association between Ivan and the Archangel Michael was an important theme of the age. In his first letter to Kurbskii, the tsar referred to Michael as 'the champion of Moses, of Joshua the son of Nun and of all Israel'; he was also the protector of Constantine the Great, 'and from that time forth even unto the present day he has aided all pious tsars'. Indeed, Michael had long been associated with the Muscovite dynasty: the cathedral of the Archangel Michael in the Kremlin was the burial place of the grand princes of Moscow. Metropolitan Makarii, in one of the letters he addressed to the tsar during his march on Kazan' in the summer of 1552, called on the archangel to assist Ivan against the Tatars, just as he had helped Old Testament warriors such as Abraham, Joshua, Gideon and Hezekiah.

The identification of Russia as the 'New Israel' and of Moscow as the 'New Jerusalem', which we find in the 'Church Militant' icon, was very common in the sixteenth century: much more common, in fact, than the 'Third Rome' image.[12] The term *'tsar'* was used in Russian for Old Testament kings, and in Ivan's coronation ceremony Metropolitan Makarii had drawn a parallel between the tsar and King David – and, by extension, between Makarii himself and the Prophet Samuel. In fact one can go further and note that the term *'tsar'* may also refer to God (at a somewhat later date not only was God described in Russia as the 'heavenly tsar', but the tsar was also referred to as the 'earthly God').[13] The metropolitan's prayer at Ivan's coronation brought all three connotations together:

O Lord our God, King of Kings (*tsarstvuyushchim tsar'*) and Lord of Lords, who by Samuel the Prophet did choose thy servant David and anoint him to be king (*vo tsari*) over thy people Israel ... look down on thy faithful servant Grand Prince Ivan Vasil'evich, whom thou hast deigned to raise up as tsar over thy people ...[14]

Thus God, King David and Ivan are all described as 'tsars' within a single sentence which – no doubt quite consciously – drew parallels between the three, and identified the Russians with God's chosen people. Old Testament imagery was extensively deployed in the decoration of the Golden Palace in the Kremlin after 1547, in scenes representing the victory of the 'armies of the Lord' under warrior-heroes such as Moses, Joshua and Gideon. The depiction of Old Testament figures in an allegorical and symbolic way, in order to glorify Moscow and its new young tsar, was one of a number of controversial innovations in Russian art sponsored by Metropolitan Makarii in the 1550s.[15]

The 'New Jerusalem' image also, of course, reflected New Testament ideas. The Cathedral of the Intercession on the Moat (subsequently better known as St Basil's) on Red Square was built between 1555 and 1561 to commemorate the victory at Kazan'. The cathedral was intended to represent Jerusalem (some believed that its architecture was modelled on that of the Church of the Holy Sepulchre) and its largest chapel was dedicated to Christ's entry into Jerusalem on Palm Sunday. After its consecration in 1560, the annual Palm Sunday procession was extended beyond the Kremlin walls to the Jerusalem chapel. In this ceremony, which depicted Christ's entry into Jerusalem and prefigured his Second Coming, the tsar (on foot) led the metropolitan, mounted on a horse. In the interpretation of the American scholar Michael Flier, it symbolised the role of the Orthodox tsar in leading Orthodox Christianity (embodied by the metropolitan, representing Christ riding on a donkey) to its historic destiny; it also reinforced the notion of Moscow as the New Jerusalem. Flier has argued that when the procession was extended to St Basil's it became an annual celebration of Ivan's victory over Kazan'. It re-enacted the procession of 1552, in which the tsar had removed his military attire on the outskirts of Moscow, in order to dress in his royal garments and walk on foot to the Kremlin. According to Nancy Kollmann, Ivan's humble behaviour in the 1552 procession physically acted out his supposed relationship with God, and demonstrated publicly that the tsar 'functioned as God's lieutenant on earth and shepherd of his flock'.[16] The annual re-staging of the procession on Palm Sunday linked the Kazan' victory not just with Christ's historical entry into Jerusalem, but also with the future Second Coming, when the Orthodox tsar would lead his people to their salvation in the New Jerusalem. Since the late fifteenth century, the Orthodox faithful had been expecting the imminent end of the world (7000 years since the Creation having elapsed in 1492) and apocalyptic ideas and imagery were common currency of the age.

The conquest of Kazan' provided an additional justification for the Russian ruler's adoption of the title 'tsar'. The annexation of the khanate was stressed in some of the diplomatic correspondence in which Ivan claimed his new imperial status; and Ivan's letter of 1557 to the patriarch in Constantinople, requesting confirmation of his title, referred not only to his coronation, but also to the conquest of Kazan' and Astrakhan'. 'Tsar of Kazan'' and 'Tsar of Astrakhan'' were added to Ivan's already long list of titles; and the regalia of Kazan' were added to his crown jewels. In the dating of his letters, the years since his conquest of Kazan' and Astrakhan' were added to those of his accession and coronation in Russia (his second letter to Kurbskii of 1577, for example, is dated: 'the

43rd year of our reign; and of our tsardoms: the 31st of the Russian, the 25th of the Kazanian and the 24th of the Astrakhanian').

The symbolic significance of the conquest of Kazan' and Astrakhan' for the prestige of the Muscovite ruler was therefore enormous. In the seventeenth century some Russians evidently believed that it was the conquest of the khanates that had led Ivan to call himself tsar. Grigorii Kotoshikhin, a former official in the Chancellery for Foreign Affairs, wrote in 1667 that Ivan had become tsar as a result of conquering Kazan', Astrakhan' and Siberia. It seems unlikely, however, that this statement reflects a residual idea in the Foreign Office that the title of tsar could be legitimised only by succession from the Chingisid khans of the Golden Horde, as Donald Ostrowski suggests.[17] It is more probable that by the seventeenth century the title of 'tsar' was firmly associated with the concept of empire, understood as a multi-ethnic, multi-religious supra-state created by the conquest of existing sovereign states. To a much greater extent than through the 'gathering of the lands of Rus'', Muscovy became an empire in this sense as a result of the 'gathering of the lands of the Golden Horde'.[18]

The idea that Ivan acquired the title of tsar as a result of his conquest of Kazan' can also be found in some folklore texts recorded from the eighteenth century onwards. The late eighteenth-century 'Kirsha Danilov' version of the song about Ivan and his son, for example, states that

> The Terrible Tsar Ivan Vasil'evich
> Was crowned tsar and sovereign lord
> Because he captured the tsardom of Kazan' . . .

Similar claims are made in some versions of the song about the capture of Kazan', which was one of the most popular of all Russian historical folksongs. The song focuses on the mining of the Tatar fortress: Ivan accuses the sappers of treason when the fuses in the mine-workings seem to have failed; but a young Russian gunner stands up to the tsar and points out that the underground fuses burn more slowly than the control fuse laid in the open air; and he is proved correct when a spectacular explosion destroys the besieged citadel. Although the episode with the sapper appears to have been fictional, it is nevertheless clear that graphic details of the conquest of Kazan' left an enduring imprint on the popular memory, and that its symbolic significance was recognised by the Russian people over a period of many centuries.[19]

The conquest of the khanate of Kazan' was also celebrated in literary sources. The official chronicles contain long and detailed narratives of the military expeditions and the eventual victory. The 'Chronicle of the

Beginning of the Tsardom' includes an independent tale about the events of April 1551 to November 1552; and the literary work entitled 'The History of Kazan'', probably dating from the 1560s, is an ultra-patriotic and triumphalist account of the conquest.[20] A major theme in these accounts was the claim that in conquering Kazan' and Astrakhan' Ivan was regaining territory which had belonged to early Rus' before the Tatar invasion, and hence formed part of the 'patrimony' of his ancestor, Prince Vladimir I of Kiev. Astrakhan' was even declared to have been ancient Tmutorakan', which Vladimir had bequeathed to his son Mstislav – although the fortress of Tmutorakan' was located on the Black Sea, while Astrakhan' is on the Caspian. Thus the conquest of Kazan' and Astrakhan', in Muscovite imperial ideology, was entirely consistent with the idea of continuity with Kiev and Rome – an idea which is made quite explicit in a passage in the 'History of Kazan'' which not only depicts Russia, after the defeat of the Tatars, as having been restored to the glory it had enjoyed under the Orthodox Grand Prince Vladimir, but also describes Moscow both as the 'second Kiev' and as the 'third new great Rome'.

The significance of the conquest of Kazan' and Astrakhan', of course, was not exclusively or even primarily symbolic. Moscow now controlled the whole of the Volga basin, and this created the potential for further expansion of her influence into Siberia and the North Caucasus, and for trade across the Caspian Sea to Persia and Central Asia. This trade soon became truly international in character. As early as 1557 the Russia Company of English merchants sent its agent Anthony Jenkinson to Moscow with instructions to make an exploratory journey down the Volga, in the hope of proceeding further to China. Jenkinson reached Astrakhan' in the summer of 1558, and was distinctly unimpressed by the new fortified town which the Russians had built on an island at the mouth of the Volga, downriver from old Astrakhan'. He described the region as stricken by famine and plague, which particularly affected the local Tatars and the surrounding Nogai. New Astrakhan' was full of merchants, but their goods were, in the Englishman's opinion, 'poor and beggerly'. Jenkinson crossed the Caspian, and travelled as far as Bukhara, in Central Asia, but he was unable to continue to either China or Persia, because of the 'great wars' in the region.[21] In spite of Jenkinson's pessimistic report, the Company decided to undertake trade with Persia through Russia, and a number of expeditions were carried out between 1561 and 1581, with the English merchants often acting as diplomatic and commercial agents for the tsar.

Russians, too, benefited from the annexation of the khanates. After the uprisings of 1553–6 the remaining Tatar population of Kazan' was deported from the city, and Russian merchants were encouraged to settle there. Land confiscated from the khan and from rebel Tatar nobles was allocated to Russian servicemen, and the newly created archbishopric of Kazan' was given generous land grants, trade privileges and fishing rights. Moscow's control of the Volga basin enabled the government to promote the settlement of the new frontier region by peasants from the centre. But in addition to its policies of repression and colonisation the Russian government allowed a considerable degree of autonomy to its newly annexed territories on the Volga. They were administered by a special central department, the Chancellery of the Kazan' Palace; the landowner-ship rights of loyal members of the Tatar élite were recognised, and they were incorporated into the Muscovite nobility; and the Tatar and other non-Russian peasants of the region retained their free status, and continued to pay the traditional dues (*yasak*) in cash or kind, rendering them now to the tsar rather than to the khans. According to the German scholar Andreas Kappeler, who has studied the process of formation of the Russian multi-ethnic empire over several centuries, the methods of incorporation pioneered by the Muscovite government in relation to the khanate of Kazan' served as the model for the 'nationalities policy' of subsequent tsars.[22]

Notes

1 *PSRL*, vol.29, Moscow, 1965, p.55.

2 Florya, *Ivan Groznyi*, pp.35–6.

3 For a detailed account of events from the building of Sviyazhsk to the tsar's triumphant return to Moscow after the conquest of Kazan', see *PSRL*, vol.29, pp.59–116.

4 *Kurbsky's History*, pp.42–5, 48–9.

5 Florya, *Ivan Groznyi*, pp.42–3.

6 *PSRL*, vol.13, pp.522–3.

7 Michael Cherniavsky, 'Khan or Basileus: an Aspect of Medieval Political Theory' [1959], reprinted in Michael Cherniavsky, ed., *The Structure of Russian History: Interpretive Essays*, New York: Random House, 1970, pp.72–3; Omeljan Pritsak, 'Moscow, the Golden Horde and the Kazan Khanate from a Polycultural Point of View', *Slavic Review*, vol.26, 1967, pp.582–3; Ostrowski, *Muscovy and the Mongols*, pp.186–7.

8 Andreas Kappeler, *The Russian Empire. A Multiethnic History*, Harlow: Longman, 2001, pp.26–7.

9 *Sochineniya I. Peresvetova*, Moscow, 1956, pp.182–3, 245; A.A. Zimin, *I.S. Peresvetov i ego sovremenniki*, Moscow, 1958, pp.377–8; Jaroslaw Pelenski, *Russia and Kazan: Conquest and Imperial Ideology (1438–1560s)*, The Hague: Mouton, 1974, pp.177–213.

10 On Russian religious policy towards Kazan', see Pelenski, *Russia and Kazan*, pp.251–75; Michael Khodarkovsky, 'Four Degrees of Separation: Constructing Non-Christian Identities in Muscovy', in A.M. Kleimola and G.D. Lenhoff, eds., *Culture and Identity in Muscovy, 1359–1584*, Moscow: ITZ-Garant, 1997, pp.257–64; Kappeler, *The Russian Empire*, pp.27–8.

11 Rowland, 'Biblical Military Imagery'.

12 Rowland, 'Moscow – the Third Rome'.

13 B.A. Uspenskii, *Izbrannye trudy*, vol.1, Moscow, 1994, pp.143–7.

14 *PSRL*, vol.29, p.150.

15 See, for example, David B. Miller, 'The Viskovatyi Affair of 1553–54: Official Art, the Emergence of Autocracy, and the Disintegration of Medieval Russian Culture', *Russian History/Histoire Russe*, vol.8, 1981, pp.293–332.

16 Michael S. Flier, 'Breaking the Code: the Image of the Tsar in the Muscovite Palm Sunday Ritual', in Flier and Rowland, eds., *Medieval Russian Culture*, vol.2, pp.213–42; Kollmann, 'Pilgrimage, Procession and Symbolic Space', pp.178–9.

17 Ostrowski, *Muscovy and the Mongols*, p.177.

18 For the latter term, see Kappeler, *The Russian Empire*, chapter 2.

19 Maureen Perrie, *The Image of Ivan the Terrible in Russian Folklore*, Cambridge: Cambridge University Press, 1987, pp.66–72, 181–8.

20 *PSRL*, vol.29, pp.59–116; *Kazanskaya istoriya*, ed. G.N. Moiseeva, Moscow, 1954; Pelenski, *Russia and Kazan*, pp.104–35.

21 Richard Hakluyt, ed., *Voyages* (Everyman's Library Edition [1907]), London: Dent, vol.1, 1967, pp.438–64.

22 Kappeler, *The Russian Empire*, pp.28, 53. See also Andreas Kappeler, 'Die Moskauer "Nationalitätenpolitik" unter Ivan IV', in Hellie, ed., *Ivan the Terrible*, pp.267–8.

Chapter 4

Reformers and Reforms

The reasons for reform

The decade which followed Ivan's coronation witnessed not only significant foreign-policy successes, with the Russian conquest of the Volga khanates of Kazan' and Astrakhan', but also an extensive programme of domestic reforms. What were the reasons for these reforms, and what implications did they have for the power of the tsar?

Ivan's adoption of the title of tsar had significantly enhanced the prestige of the Russian monarchy, both at home and abroad. Having become a 'God-crowned' tsar, the Muscovite ruler was raised to an inaccessible height above his subjects, including the 'princelings' (the descendants of the ruling princes of north-east and south-west Rus'). But this was only the first step towards the assertion of his autocratic power. It had to be reinforced by real moves towards the consolidation of Russian statehood and the creation of a new state apparatus. In the middle of the sixteenth century Russia stood at a crossroads. It was unclear which direction the political development of the country would take, and what principles would govern relations between the tsar and his subjects. To a considerable extent the outcome depended on the balance of power in the country and on the political will of its leaders.

At the end of the 1540s the Russian government faced an acute need for political change and the introduction of reforms affecting the most diverse aspects of state and society. During the years of 'boyar rule' the authority of the central government had significantly declined. The bitter struggle for power among the various boyar groupings had destabilised the social and political situation in the country, and had led to the growth of abuses by officials. As a result, dissatisfaction with the authorities had increased in many sectors of the population. The uprising against the Glinskiis in Moscow in the summer of 1547 had been the most dramatic expression of popular protest concerning maladministration by the boyars, but there is evidence of unrest in other places at around the same time. Such symptoms of social strife forced the government to face up to the need to take urgent decisions. It was essential to resolve the political crisis, to strengthen the power of the state, and to guarantee legality and social stability. The need for social consolidation and the strengthening of state order was especially acute in view of Russia's adoption of a more aggressive foreign policy, against the Tatars in particular.

But changes were made necessary not only and not even primarily by such short-term concerns. The introduction of reforms was a response to longer-term problems of Russia's development. The old system of administration, which had been established in the appanage period, no longer served the needs of the more centralised state, and it required fundamental restructuring.

The reforms were not, however, prompted only by the requirements of the state. In spite of the harsh forms assumed by the centralisation which the Russian government had imposed in the late fifteenth and early sixteenth centuries, the process of unification had led social groups such as the nobility, townspeople and peasantry to begin to acquire a sense of their common identity as estates of the new Russian realm. There is much direct and indirect evidence to suggest that these groups were gradually becoming aware of their own particular interests. Let us examine the position of each of these groups in turn.

As the country became more centralised and its foreign-policy aims became more complex, the nobility acquired increasing significance in the state. This process could not be halted even in the years of 'boyar rule'. But the consolidation of the nobility into a single social estate was hampered by a number of factors. In the middle of the sixteenth century, in respect of their obligation to pay state taxes the rank-and-file servicemen were still in an inferior position to the large landowners who enjoyed tax privileges. Unlike the aristocratic boyars, who were subject to the judgment of the tsar, the ordinary nobles (the provincial servicemen) came under the jurisdiction of the *namestniki* (governors) and were often powerless in face of their arbitrary actions. The servicemen suffered especially from abuses by the *namestniki* in the years of 'boyar rule', as many contemporaries testify. The boyar governments of court favourites who succeeded one another in power rewarded their supporters with lavish grants of hereditary and service estates. The smaller landholders were often subject to violent attacks by their influential neighbours. The large-scale landowners lured their peasants away from them, and sometimes simply seized their estates. The impoverishment of the servicemen became a widespread phenomenon, and many of the gentry entered the service of powerful lords as slaves. All of this had a very negative impact not only on the position of the nobility, but also on the military capacity of the Russian army, since cavalrymen recruited from the service class constituted the backbone of the armed forces at that time.

The mood of the ordinary nobles was clearly expressed by Ivan Peresvetov. The scion of an Orthodox Lithuanian petty-noble family, Peresvetov had entered Russian service in the late 1530s and had shared the experiences of many nobles of that period. His estate had been destroyed by the 'strong men', so that he could neither support himself independently nor render military service to the state. In his writings,[1] Peresvetov angrily and passionately denounced the boyars' misrule during Ivan's minority. He persistently advised the tsar to put an end to the omnipotence of the magnates and to rule the country 'ruthlessly' (*grozno*), basing himself on the ordinary 'warriors' (servicemen). His ideal political system was the Ottoman Empire, which derived its strength from the support of the rank-and-file military servicemen and from the general concern of the Turkish authorities to maintain the welfare and military capacity of the armed forces. Peresvetov painted a very different picture of the situation in Byzantium. There, power had lain in the hands of the magnates, whose abuses had led to the impoverishment of the realm and the decline of its defence capability. This, he argued, had been the main reason for the conquest of the once mighty Orthodox empire by the Turks. Peresvetov thought that the fate of Byzantium, where, in spite of its Christian faith, there had been no true justice (*pravda*), ought to serve as a lesson to the young Russian state.

It may be worth noting here that Peresvetov in his writings uses the term '*groznyi*' – conventionally, although somewhat misleadingly, translated into English as 'terrible' – to describe the nature of the power of his ideal ruler. The great Turkish sultan, Mehmet II, ruled through both fear (*groza*) and wisdom in order to introduce justice in his realm, and in this respect Peresvetov held him up as a model for Ivan: 'without such fear one cannot introduce justice into a tsardom'. (In sixteenth-century Russia the term '*tsar*' was used for the Turkish sultans as well as for the Tatar khans.) In his 'Great Petition' Peresvetov described Ivan as a 'dread (*groznyi*) and wise sovereign'; and although there is no clear evidence that the epithet *Groznyi* was regularly used to designate Ivan in his own lifetime (it appears most frequently in folklore recorded at a later date), the concept of the tsar's power as 'terrible', with the positive connotations of 'dread and awe-inspiring' rather than the negative ones of 'cruel and sadistic', undoubtedly dates to the mid-sixteenth century.

Peresvetov considered that the introduction of a judicial reform would help Russia to find a solution to its crisis. Officials should be paid a salary by the state, and placed under the strict supervision of the tsar. Those found guilty of abuses would be subjected to harsh punishment, including the imposition of the death penalty. Peresvetov called for the establishment of a single court for all members of the military-service class, a reform which would have been in the interests of the majority of ordinary nobles. He thought that the main criteria for the appointment of servicemen to civil and military posts should be their personal qualities and contributions, and not their social status. In the interests of the nobility, he proposed that the tsar should introduce a system of regular money payments to the servicemen from the state treasury, and that the entire financial system of the country should be reorganised in order to resolve this problem. In spite of the utopian character of many aspects of Peresvetov's proposals – it was hardly possible to impose the entire political system of the Ottoman Empire upon Russia – many of the notions put forward in his works resonated with Tsar Ivan's own ideas. Some scholars – admittedly without much justification – are even inclined to attribute the authorship of these writings to *Groznyi* himself. Peresvetov's statement of his views was not a 'voice crying in the wilderness'; similar ideas about the need to introduce fair systems of justice and taxation were also expressed by other leading figures of the time.[2]

It was not only the nobility who were interested in improving their situation, but also the great majority of the urban and rural population – the townspeople and the peasants of the so-called 'black-ploughing' (state) lands. The political unification of the country, with the disappearance of separate principalities, and liberation from Tatar overlordship, had created favourable conditions for the development of towns. In the first half of the sixteenth century there was a marked growth in the number of towns and in the size of the urban population. Within the latter there was an increase in the sector directly employed in crafts and trade. At the same time, the urban population was increasing much more rapidly than the rural population. The towns witnessed the continued development of the corporate organisations of the privileged large-scale merchantry – the 'guests' (*gosti*) – who exerted considerable influence in the localities and headed the institutions of urban self-government. All of this contributed to the formation of a single social estate of townspeople. But there were various obstacles to this development. One of these was the continued existence within the towns, alongside the property of the urban communes, of the so-called 'white quarters' (areas exempt from the payment of taxes) which belonged to boyars, bishops and monasteries. In an attempt to avoid the onerous tax burden, many townspeople went to live in these privileged areas. The rich and influential owners of the 'white quarters' frequently lured traders and craftsmen on to their lands, and sometimes even transferred them forcibly. This imposed considerable economic losses on the urban communes and impeded the melding of the townspeople into a single social estate. Like the petty servicemen, moreover, the urban population suffered greatly from abuses by the *namestniki*, especially during the years of 'boyar rule'.

Reforms in the spheres of local government, justice and finance were also in the long-term interests of the state peasants, especially in the north of the country, where the traditions of peasant self-government were particularly well established and where economic development had enjoyed its most visible successes. The peasantry of the state lands, and its prosperous élite in particular, suffered from the maladministration of the *namestniki* and *volosteli* (the governors of rural territories who, like the *namestniki*, had the right to 'feed' themselves at the expense of the local population). All the evidence suggests that the peasants sought to free themselves from their tutelage. Certainly, when introducing its reforms of local administration in the 1550s, the government claimed that it was responding to petitions from the peasants complaining about abuses of power by the *namestniki* and *volosteli*.

The élites too had an interest in reform, if only from considerations of self-preservation. The widespread popular disturbances in Moscow and other towns, and the harsh reprisals which the Muscovites had inflicted on the hated court favourites in 1547, must have forced members of the boyar and princely aristocracy to think seriously about their future. The magnates urgently needed reforms which would strengthen their dominant position as the privileged ruling group in the Russian state.

Thus the introduction of reform was in the interests of many different sectors of Russian society, and it represented a response to fundamental structural problems. This helps to explain the breadth and depth of the changes which were implemented in the middle of the sixteenth century. At no other time in the early history of Russia were so many important reforms carried out as in the ten-year period from the late 1540s to the end of the 1550s.

Adashev and Sil'vestr

Who instigated the reforms, and which specific political groups devised the plan to transform the country? It is difficult to provide clear and unambiguous answers to these questions. Some historians have described the transformations of the 1550s as the 'reforms of the Chosen Council'. But in the documents of the middle of the sixteenth century we do not come across a government with that name. The term 'Chosen Council' (*Izbrannaya Rada*) itself is of later – and non-Russian – origin. It was first used by Ivan the Terrible's political opponent Prince Andrei Kurbskii in his 'History of the Grand Prince of Muscovy'. This polemical work was written by Kurbskii when he was living in emigration in the Grand Duchy of Lithuania. It was intended in the first instance for readers there, which explains the wealth of Polish and west-Russian terms which it contains. The word *rada*, which is derived from the German *Rat* (council), was initially borrowed by Polish, and passed from there into the Ukrainian and Belorussian languages. The term *rada* was not found in Muscovite Rus', where the words *duma* and *sovet* were used instead.

The sources provide us with only very fragmentary and contradictory evidence about the character and membership of the government of reformers (the 'Chosen Council'). Nor is there any unanimity amongst historians on this issue. Traditionally, the term 'Chosen Council' was used in the historical literature to refer to a group of reformers which was created around the young Tsar Ivan. Its leaders were the nobleman Aleksei Fedorovich Adashev and the priest Sil'vestr from the Blagoveshchenskii Cathedral in the Kremlin. Adashev and Sil'vestr were indeed outstanding and talented figures who played a very active part in the implementation of the reforms of the mid-sixteenth century.

Aleksei Adashev came from a noble family from Kostroma. By sixteenth-century standards this clan was comparatively modest, and it did not form part of the traditional élite of aristocratic boyar families. The very fact of the elevation and entry into ruling circles of such a relatively low-born person as Adashev testifies to his outstanding personal qualities. Later on, Ivan Groznyi was to observe acerbically that he had raised Adashev up from a dungheap. The notion of Aleksei Adashev as a 'lowly' man who made a brilliant career does, however, require some qualification. He was the son of Fedor Grigor'evich Adashev, an eminent diplomat who was a well-known figure at the Muscovite court. In 1538–9 F.G. Adashev went to Turkey as the head of a Russian embassy, charged with an important diplomatic mission. According to some accounts, he took with him his son Aleksei, who was then only a boy. There was nothing unusual in this: noblemen carrying out service to the crown were often accompanied by their young sons, who thereby served a kind of apprenticeship. The young Aleksei Adashev had the opportunity to become directly acquainted with the institutions and customs of the

Ottoman Empire, and this undoubtedly served him well in his future political activity. In 1547 F.G. Adashev obtained the duma rank of *okol'nichii* (subsequently he was granted the higher rank of boyar). Young Aleksei Adashev also came to court, where he was given the rank of *stryapchii*. He began his career, therefore, not from the bottom rung, but as the son of an *okol'nichii*, a member of the highest state council, the boyar duma. Later A.F. Adashev himself entered the duma, first as a conciliar courtier (*dumnyi dvoryanin*) and then as an *okol'nichii*. Subsequently his brother Daniil was also to acquire the rank of *okol'nichii*.

A.F. Adashev played an active role in a number of very different spheres of political activity. As a close counsellor of the tsar he was undoubtedly a major actor in the discussion and revision of reform proposals. Adashev was one of the most energetic statesmen charged with the conduct of the government's domestic and foreign policy. He served not only as a leading diplomat (conducting the diplomatic preparations for the campaign against Kazan' and for the Livonian War) but also as an administrator, the head of the central administrative institutions, the chancelleries (he was head of the Grand Treasury and also, perhaps, of the Petition Chancellery – which dealt with various kinds of complaints by the public against the authorities – and of various other institutions). It is also thought that Adashev took part in the compilation and editing of the official chronicle and of other major works, such as the 'Royal Genealogy' (the official genealogical book of the princely and boyar families) and the 'Royal Register' (a book which contained systematic records of the appointments held by members of the ruling élite of the service class).

The tsar's other leading adviser, the priest Sil'vestr, was a brilliant and remarkable figure. Unlike A.F. Adashev he was not a young man when he first became one of the tsar's closest advisers – at the end of the 1540s he was well over fifty years of age. We know that before moving to Moscow Sil'vestr had served as a priest in Novgorod. It is possible that he owed his transfer to the capital to the patronage of Metropolitan Makarii, who had at one time been Archbishop of Novgorod. But it seems that Sil'vestr gained entry to the upper circles of government primarily because of his own personal qualities. He did not hold any high office within the Church hierarchy, having been neither a bishop nor an official confessor to the tsar. According to established tradition, the role of confessor to the tsar was usually played by senior clerics (archpriests) of the Blagoveshchenskii Cathedral. But the evidence suggests that Sil'vestr was not an archpriest, but merely an ordinary priest in the cathedral.[3] Nonetheless, Sil'vestr possessed enormous spiritual authority and he perhaps exerted greater influence on Tsar Ivan than any other member of the clergy. It seems that he enjoyed a considerable reputation as a spiritual adviser. Not only the tsar, but also a number of eminent boyars turned to him for guidance. In his conversations with the tsar, Sil'vestr did not restrict himself to the usual preaching of Christian morality, but formulated general principles of behaviour which should influence an Orthodox ruler. He called on the tsar to rule the country 'by justice and kindness', that is, to maintain strict order and legality, but at the same time to display mercy to his subjects and listen to wise counsel. Sil'vestr firmly and persistently reminded the tsar about his special responsibility for the country in the eyes of God, and about the inevitability of the Last Judgment. The young and impressionable Tsar Ivan listened to his tutor's sermons with reverence and awe. Subsequently, when he had come to hate Sil'vestr and Adashev, the same Tsar Ivan would recall how the priest Sil'vestr had tried to 'scare him with childhood bogeymen'. Sil'vestr's sermonising activity was not confined to the interior of the royal palace. His name is also associated with the composition of a famous Old Russian work, the *Domostroi* (*Household Management*: literally, 'the building of the house'), which from the standpoint of Christian morality provides all sorts of practical advice on how to organise one's family and manage one's household.[4]

The sources invariably mention Adashev and Sil'vestr together as political allies. But they were united not only by political ties but also, it seems, by close personal ones. In spite of their superficial differences – in age and in social status – these two figures were in many ways very similar. Both had come into the highest ruling circle primarily because of their personal qualities rather than their social origins. Neither of them had had – nor did they evidently aspire to – a formal career: Sil'vestr remained an ordinary priest, and although Aleksei Adashev was a much more influential figure than his father, unlike him he did not achieve the rank of boyar. Both Adashev and Sil'vestr were distinguished by their profound religiosity and personal piety. Both were characterised by their strength of will and by their firm adherence to principle in upholding their opinions.

Adashev and Sil'vestr indisputably exerted a significant influence on the course of political events in Russia in the middle of the sixteenth century. Nevertheless, their true role as the organisers and initiators of reform is not entirely clear. We do not know for sure whether the proposals for change emanated specifically from these two men, whether they enjoyed sufficient power and political influence to guide the course of events, or whether they were the leaders of some particular party of reformers.

The traditional point of view, that Adashev and Sil'vestr had a decisive influence on affairs of state and on the character of Tsar Ivan, has been subjected to criticism by a number of scholars.[5] Doubts have even been expressed (in the works of A.N. Grobovsky and A.I. Filyushkin) about the very existence of a 'Chosen Council' government headed by Adashev and Sil'vestr. Such doubts are indeed well founded. Our notions of Adashev and Sil'vestr as all-powerful figures come primarily from later sources, such as the correspondence of *Groznyi* and Kurbskii, and the additions to the Illustrated Code (the official chronicle). We may seriously doubt whether such 'low-ranking' individuals as Adashev and Sil'vestr, who occupied a very modest position in the official hierarchy, could have acted independently, without taking into account the opinion of the high-born boyars and the upper echelons of the Church. It is impossible to form any clear picture of the membership of the so-called Chosen Council. Scholars' opinions on this issue are often contradictory. For example, Kurbskii has traditionally been regarded as one of the leading figures in the Chosen Council, but even his membership of this government has been disputed by a number of historians, such as D.N. Al'shits and R.G. Skrynnikov. The very status of the supposed Chosen Council government is entirely unclear. Many scholars identify it with the later 'Privy Council' (*Blizhnyaya duma*) – a council of those members of the boyar duma who were closest to the tsar and whose advice he constantly sought. But one of the main figures in the Chosen Council, Sil'vestr, was a priest in holy orders, who could in no way have been a member of such a purely secular body as the Privy Council. These considerations lead us to share the doubts of historians such as A.N. Grobovsky and A.I. Filyushkin concerning the very existence of the so-called Chosen Council as a specific government of reformers. It is more likely that Kurbskii used the term, the 'Chosen Council', as a collective literary image of the tsar's 'good' or 'chosen' counsellors, such as Adashev and Sil'vestr, in contrast to the 'evil' counsellors who induced Tsar Ivan to establish his autocratic tyrannical regime.

Tsar Ivan's closest associates in the period from the end of the 1540s to the mid-1550s did not comprise only Adashev and Sil'vestr. Other influential figures were the tsar's wife's kinsmen, the Zakhar'in-Yur'ev boyars, who held high-ranking positions at court. The documentary evidence suggests that their activity was primarily concerned with the management of the royal household. But we may assume that they too were not indifferent to ideas about a general reform of state institutions. It was thanks to their patronage that many talented individuals were able to enter the ruling élite – for example, Ivan Mikhailovich Viskovatyi,

1550

who became head of the department of foreign affairs, the Ambassadorial Chancellery. According to R.G. Skrynnikov, it was the Zakhar'in administration which initiated the implementation of reforms at the end of the 1540s, while Adashev's group, the 'Chosen Council', merely continued with these changes when it acquired the dominant position in the second half of the 1550s.[6] But the view that it was the Zakhar'ins who initiated the implementation of reforms is more of a supposition than a proven fact.

It remains an open question precisely which political groups were responsible for planning the introduction of reforms at the end of the 1540s. We know virtually nothing about the real balance of political forces at the beginning of the reform period, nor about the nature of discussions in the higher levels of government concerning specific proposals for change. In the last analysis, however, this is not what determined the fate of the reforms and defined their course and direction. As we have argued, the reforms were a response to real problems, and reflected the interests of very diverse social groups. The introduction of reforms in the middle of the sixteenth century became possible as a result of the achievement of consensus within the ruling élite as a whole, and it was this development, rather than conflicts among various vaguely defined court factions, which was the main factor in the political situation at this period. Recent researchers have noted that members of very diverse groups within the ruling élite played an active part in the implementation of reforms: the 'princelings', the untitled (old Moscow) boyars, and the nascent chancellery bureaucracy. It is revealing that at the very beginning of the reform process there was a significant increase in the membership of the boyar duma, the highest ruling body in the land: it more than doubled in comparison with its size at the end of the period of 'boyar rule'.

The need for the moral and political renewal of society was also recognised by the leadership of the Church. One of the instigators and most active implementers of reform was Metropolitan Makarii, an outstanding ecclesiastical and political figure. As we have seen, it was he who had the idea of having Ivan crowned tsar in 1547. Two years later he took charge of the work of the so-called 'Council of Reconciliation' which initiated the reform process in the country.

When speaking of the leading figures in the political reforms of the mid-sixteenth century, we should not, of course, overlook Tsar Ivan himself, the head of state. It is not easy, however, to assess the extent of Ivan's personal participation in the preparation and implementation of the reforms. We cannot always distinguish what the tsar himself did, from the results of the activity of his advisers. Unfortunately, the surviving sources do not provide us with sufficient firm evidence of his political views in the period under consideration; we know much more about the ideology of the later Ivan Groznyi, after he had become a 'counter-reformer'. But it is difficult to imagine that such an imperious and energetic man, with such exceptional qualities as Ivan possessed, could have remained a mere observer of the changes which were being carried out in his realm. The sources have preserved details of his passionate public outbursts at the 'Council of Reconciliation' and the 'Council of a Hundred Chapters', in which he denounced the moral vices of the secular and ecclesiastical authorities, and called upon society to mend its ways. Apparently the young tsar, who vividly remembered the abuses committed by the boyars in the years of his minority, was greatly impressed by the idea of the moral reconstruction of society, and the introduction of order and legality into the land for which he was accountable to God. Reformist ideas were very popular amongst the leading figures of the age, and a number of people (Aleksei Adashev and others) were prepared to assume responsibility for the implementation of reform. The very fact that Ivan drew such people into his inner circle, and allowed them to develop an active reformist policy, indicates his prominent role in the enactment of the reforms, in their initial stage at least.

The reforms of the 1550s

On 27 February 1549 a conference was convened in the tsar's palace. It comprised members of the Church hierarchy headed by Metropolitan Makarii (the so-called Sacred Council), and members of the boyar duma. Some of the nobility were also invited. The broadly representative character of this assembly, which was designated the 'Council of Reconciliation' by later scholars, has encouraged some historians to regard it as the first Assembly of the Land.[7] At this council, however, there were no representatives of the 'third estate' – the townspeople. Tsar Ivan himself addressed the council with a programme for resolving the political crisis and introducing internal reforms. The tsar harshly accused the boyars of committing abuses during his minority, and he threatened that in future those guilty of such offences would be severely punished. But at the same time he promised that he would not punish the boyars for their past actions, and he called on all his subjects to be 'reconciled'. He declared his firm intention to put an end to lawlessness in the country, and to carry out serious reforms in the fields of administration and justice. All of these proposals reflected the interests of the various social estates which were in process of formation.

The matter was not confined to declarations by the tsar. The programme of reforms which he announced was actively implemented. On 28 February, the very day after the convocation of the assembly, and in accordance with its decisions, an important law was passed which freed the nobles from the judicial authority of the *namestniki*, admittedly with the exception of the most severe criminal offences – murder and robbery. Like the members of the aristocracy, the ordinary servicemen now acquired the right to appeal directly to the judgment of the tsar. The resolution of 28 February 1549 was a major landmark in the formation of a special judicial system for the servicemen and the consolidation of the entire nobility into a single social estate. The 'Council of Reconciliation' also took the important decision to prepare a new Law Code to replace the Code of 1497, which was outdated in many respects.

The new ('Royal') Law Code, which was introduced in June 1550, was much more extensive and systematic than its predecessor.[8] Its appearance marked a far-reaching stage in the development of Russian law. The elaboration of the new Code was dictated by the need to introduce legal norms which corresponded to the changed socio-political situation in the country and which met the needs of the new era. The Code significantly improved the system of regulation of judicial proceedings, limited the powers of the *namestniki* and extended the rights of elected representatives of the local population in administrative and judicial affairs. It introduced for the first time a system of punishments for officials who abused their powers. The Code established strict forms of state supervision over the activities of officials, which was to be exercised by members of the newly formed bureaucratic apparatus of the chancelleries – the secretaries (*d'yaki*). Taking into consideration the interests and demands of various sectors of society, especially the nobility and the townspeople, the compilers of the Code introduced a number of important new statutes (articles).

In the interests of the servicemen, who demanded the fair distribution of state taxes, the Code included Article 43, which announced the abolition of tax exemptions for large-scale secular and religious landowners. In 1551 the government carried out a re-registration of the documents which granted privileges to the monasteries.

With the aim of retaining the peasant population on the service and hereditary estates of the servicemen, the Code of 1550 reaffirmed the provision of the previous Code which restricted the peasants' right to leave their landlords to one period in the year – the week before and the

week after 'the autumnal Yurii's Day' (the feast of St George the Dragon-Killer, which was celebrated on 26 November). In the interests of guaranteeing the military capability of the servicemen, the Code included measures which forbade the large boyar landowners from enslaving nobles who were capable of rendering military service to the tsar.

The Code also took into account the special interests of the townspeople. Article 91 forbade those townspeople who were members of the urban communes from settling on the private tax-exempt urban property of the large landowners. In practice this meant that the government recognised the exclusive rights of the inhabitants of the urban commercial districts (the *posadkie lyudi*) to engage in craft and trade activity in the towns.

Article 98 of the Code had far-reaching significance. This stated that all new laws which were issued after the acceptance of the Code of 1550 would have to be reported to the tsar and confirmed by the boyar duma. The boyars' approval, therefore, was recognised as an essential component of the legislative process. In effect Article 98 established the position of the aristocratic boyar duma as the supreme governmental institution alongside the tsar.

The Code clearly reflected the nature and direction of the reforms undertaken by Ivan's government in the middle of the sixteenth century. All the indications are that one of the main aims of the reforms was the achievement of a political consensus amongst the various social groups in the country, in order to overcome the consequences of the social and political crisis which had been provoked by 'boyar rule'. The Code reflected not only the vital interests of the nobility and the townspeople, but also the political claims of the boyar magnates to be the ruling élite of the state.

Important Church reforms were carried out in the middle of the sixteenth century. At the Church councils of 1547 and 1549 there took place a general canonisation of Russian saints; many locally revered saints (those of Novgorod, Pskov, Tver', Yaroslavl', Ryazan' and other regions) were recognised as Russian national saints. The creation of a single Russian 'pantheon' of saints contributed not only to the strengthening of the authority of the Russian Orthodox Church, but also to national integration. Under the direction of Metropolitan Makarii, a grandiose anthology was compiled of works of Christian literature (mainly the lives of the saints) which were recommended for everyday reading. The 'Great Menology' consisted of twelve huge volumes designed to be read on a monthly basis. It had been started in Novgorod during Makarii's period of office as Archbishop, and it was continued in Moscow. The preparation of the collection, which involved the labours of a large number of translators, scribes and artists, lasted for about twenty years.[9]

In 1551 there assembled in Moscow a Church council which has gone down in history as the 'Council of a Hundred Chapters', because its concluding document, the so-called *Stoglav*, consisted of a hundred chapters. The tsar presented the council with a long list of questions concerning the improvement of the morals of the clergy and the correction of abuses in the Church. The council's conclusion was headed: 'The tsar's questions and the council's responses concerning multifarious Church matters.' It is difficult to determine exactly who was the true author of the 'tsar's questions' (there is no unanimous opinion among historians on this issue). It is clear, however, that the tsar and his entourage had a prominent role in the resolution of Church affairs. Metropolitan Makarii played a significant part in the organisation and conduct of the council.

One of the most complex problems which the council faced was the issue of the standardisation of Church rituals. In the period of separate principalities many differences had accumulated in relation to the performance of rituals. The Novgorodians, for example, followed the Byzantine tradition of crossing themselves with three fingers and proclaimed the 'Alleluia' three times, whereas the Muscovites crossed themselves with two fingers and sang the 'Alleluia' twice. And although the triple observance was more canonically correct, the leadership of the Church under Metropolitan Makarii, not wanting to provoke a split in the Church, took the Moscow ritual as its basis. This decision was also influenced by the fact that the 'God-crowned' Russian tsar himself made the sign of the cross with two fingers. In the sixteenth century, as Moscow increasingly came to regard itself as the 'Third Rome', it was no longer prepared to accept Byzantine canons as the ultimate authority. All of this bore witness to the unification of the Russian state and Church under the auspices of the Russian Orthodox tsar.

The council marked an important stage in the formation of the clergy into a separate social estate.[10] One of the council's decisions gave the Church hierarchs the right to exercise judicial authority over all the clergy who lived within their dioceses. The resolutions of the council promoted the creation of special organs of self-government for the clergy. The institution of elected 'priestly elders' became widespread, and occupied an important place in the internal life of the clergy. It was these elders, chosen by the priests themselves from their own ranks, and not officials appointed by the tsar or the bishops, who supervised the clergy's way of life, the fulfilment of Church rituals and the collection of taxes from the clergy. In addition, the priestly elders acquired the right to take part in the episcopal court and to appeal against its verdicts.

The government devoted particular attention to issues concerning the organisation of military service and the material remuneration of the servicemen. This was not surprising, in view of the fact that at that time Russia was beginning to pursue a much more aggressive foreign policy.

One of the first measures implemented in the series of reforms of the mid-sixteenth century was the restriction or, rather, the introduction of a degree of regulation of the institution of precedence. Precedence (*mestnichestvo*) was a peculiar system of making appointments to military and court duties in which the primary consideration was not the serviceman's personal capabilities but his social origin and the 'positions' (*mesta*) which his ancestors had held during their service careers. Members of the aristocracy kept a sharp lookout to make sure that their appointment to any service position corresponded to the eminence of their lineage, and that members of other clans did not occupy more elevated service positions. The service status of their descendants, and the honour of their clan as a whole, depended directly on such matters. The frequent quarrels over precedence damaged the efficiency of state service, especially during military campaigns. Even the threat of royal disgrace, however, could not make the boyars cease their squabbles over precedence. As the saying went in Russia at that time, 'The tsar rewards us for service with lands and money, but not with "birth" (eminent lineage)'. But in spite of the negative aspects of precedence, there was no question of abolishing it completely in the mid-sixteenth century. Precedence not only served the interests of the boyar aristocracy, which owed its position at the apex of the social ladder largely to the workings of that institution, but it also suited the monarchy itself. A serviceman's honour within the system of precedence depended not only on his origins, but also on the actual service rendered by his ancestors. Service appointments were made by the supreme authority of the ruler, and the system of precedence provided the sovereign with the opportunity to encourage the aristocracy to serve at court. But at the same time the highly confused relationships of precedence required some regulation. To this end a law was passed in 1550 which somewhat limited the sphere of operation of precedence disputes.[11] The first provision of the act related to the service positions of the young scions of aristocratic families who could not be appointed to high-status duties because of their age. It was decided that, in the case of young aristocrats, service in minor posts was not dishonourable and could not be considered to be a precedent. Another provision regulated the order of precedence among the commanders of various regiments: in particular, the second-in-command of the Grand (main) Regiment was not permitted to engage in precedence disputes with the commanders-in-chief of the other regiments. The introduction of the law on precedence benefited the system of state service, but it was also in the interests of the boyar aristocracy itself, which was concerned with preserving the tradition of precedence to which it owed its status at the top of the social ladder, and which enabled it to retain its monopoly over the highest positions at court, in the army and in the state administration.

Also in 1550, an important reform was introduced which was designed to regulate the composition and structure of the sovereign's court (the circle of people who comprised the tsar's entourage and who had the preferential right to occupy the highest positions in the state), and to facilitate the court service of its members.[12] Under this so-called 'Thousander Reform', a thousand of the 'best servants' were selected from amongst the members of the old court, which had greatly expanded as a result of the annexation of other lands and principalities by Moscow. In addition to their existing service and hereditary estates which were scattered in various districts, they received special service estates near Moscow. The size of these estates depended on the serviceman's rank. Now that they lived close to the capital on their Moscow estates, the members of the sovereign's court could whenever necessary appear at court and receive a service appointment. The revitalised court contained, as a rule, the most eminent and wealthy men. This fact disproves the view that the Thousander Reform had a pro-gentry and anti-boyar character. In fact the reform promoted the further consolidation of the upper echelon of the service class into a special and privileged ruling group.

But, while endowing members of the ruling élite, and the aristocrats in particular, with rights and privileges, the monarchy at the same time required of them the obligatory performance of state service. In 1556 a 'Code on Service' was approved which specified that one mounted soldier had to be provided without fail for a specified amount of service and hereditary land (from every 100 chetverts, that is approximately 150 hectares).[13] The significance of the Code on Service was that it in effect equalised service from *pomest'ya* (lands granted on condition of service) and *votchiny* (hereditary landholdings). This was the final stage in the process of the creation of a single service class, all of whose members were obliged to perform state service. At the same time, the princely and boyar aristocracy did not comprise a separate group of independent landed magnates, but constituted only the uppermost and most privileged stratum of the servicemen.

Alongside the consolidation of the ruling élite of the service class (the sovereign's court), in the middle of the sixteenth century the service-men's provincial organisations – the 'service town' – began to form, and this acquired a fairly distinctive hierarchical structure. At this time we can see the elevation of the nobility above the other social estates as a privileged class. We have already noted that ordinary nobles acquired the same right as the boyars to appeal directly to the tsar's court of justice. In the mid-1550s large-scale inspections of the armed forces of the nobility took place. In order to assess the personal composition and military preparedness of the nobles of the various 'service towns', special documents were compiled – the so-called *desyatni*. In the course of these measures a single system was established for the remuneration of the nobility with service lands and money. All members of the noble estate, and also their sons who were capable of performing state service, acquired the right to service lands in accordance with specific norms. The size of the land grants depended on the serviceman's origins and his personal merits.

In the middle of the sixteenth century there occurred the final shaping of the *pomest'e* system, which constituted the basis of the material provision of the military servicemen. In order to assess the size of the land fund, a general survey of the districts of the country was undertaken in the 1550s. The survey was accompanied by a reform of land taxation, and a single system of land tax was introduced. The common unit of taxation was the 'large plough', the size of which depended on the category of landholder. On the lands of the state peasants a 'plough' comprised 500 chetverts of land in a single field (approximately 750 hectares); on monastery lands – 600 chetverts (900 hectares); and on the lands of the nobility, 800 chetverts (1200 hectares). Thus the most favourable calculation of the size of the 'plough' applied to the lands of the servicemen: for the same amount of land the nobles paid tax on the basis of a smaller number of ploughs than the peasants or monasteries. This was in the interests both of the embryonic noble estate and of military service to the state.

An important feature of the reform of the Russian army was the creation in 1550 of a special force of *strel'tsy* (harquebusiers). Detachments of *strel'tsy* numbering several thousand men were stationed at the royal residence of Vorob'evo, near Moscow, as the personal bodyguard of the tsar and his family. Unlike the nobles, who fought as cavalrymen, the *strel'tsy* were an infantry formation. Their main weapons were heavy firearms – harquebuses; in addition, they were armed with swords and pole-axes (halberds). But there was another important difference between the *strel'tsy* and the nobles. Whereas the latter belonged to the category of servicemen 'by paternity', that is, their service was determined by their origins and was hereditary, the *strel'tsy* belonged to the category of servicemen 'by choice', that is, by special selection. The *strel'tsy* were mostly recruited from men of the tax-paying classes – the townspeople and the state peasantry. The *strel'tsy* regiments were a permanent, although not an entirely regular, force. As well as performing military service the *strel'tsy* engaged in crafts, trade and other forms of economic activity in the towns. The combination of the *strel'tsy* detachments with the cavalry regiments of the noble servicemen provided a strong base of support for the Russian monarchy, and enabled it to implement its foreign policy initiatives of the 1550s.

The middle of the sixteenth century marked a new stage in the development of the institutions of state administration. This period saw the completion of the process of the formation of chancelleries (*prikazy*) – the institutions of the central state apparatus.[14] Even earlier, in the fifteenth and early sixteenth centuries, there had existed a fairly numerous category of officials – secretaries (*d'yaki*), who were ordered or 'commanded' (*prikazyvalos'*, whence the name *prikazy*) to carry out a certain task; but specific, permanently functioning institutions, specialising in one aspect or another of state administration, did not yet exist. The first chancelleries to acquire the character of permanent institutions were departments of the royal household, the Grand Palace and the Treasury, from within which the other chancelleries subsequently came to be formed. The principal innovation of the mid-sixteenth century was the establishment of a system of chancelleries with general state functions. It was at this time that the Ambassadorial Chancellery was created, to conduct diplomatic relations with other states. It was headed for twenty years by the secretary Ivan Mikhailovich Viskovatyi, a talented diplomat and outstanding statesman. The structure and sphere of influence of other important general state chancelleries were also defined: for example, the Military Chancellery, which controlled the organisation of nobles' service; the Chancellery of Landed Estates, which administered service-tenure and hereditary landholding; the Banditry Chancellery, which coordinated the activity of the local institutions charged with the detection and capture of bandits; and the Harquebusiers Chancellery, which administered the *strel'tsy* regiments.

In the 1550s there appeared the chancellery of the 'Grand Income', which became the main financial department of the country. Special chancelleries with territorial jurisdiction were also formed – the so-called *Chetverti*, which were concerned with tax-collection and administration in specific geographical areas. The chancelleries of pre-Petrine Russia did not become truly bureaucratic and standardised institutions (there remained a degree of vagueness about the distribution of functions amongst them, and personal factors were very important), but the formation of the chancellery system in the middle of the sixteenth century had enormous significance for the centralisation of the country. An important consequence of the reform of the administrative apparatus was the restriction of the role of the departments of the royal household and the strengthening of institutions of state power. This demonstrates the extent to which Russia had evolved from a patrimonial principality to a centralised state. As the role of the household departments diminished and the system of state chancelleries developed, greater significance was acquired by the boyar duma, which coordinated the activity of the chancelleries. The latter became as it were the branches of a single administrative structure subordinate to the boyar duma. A system was established whereby on all contentious issues (matters which did not have precedents in previous judicial practice) the secretaries could not take independent decisions without the agreement of the boyar duma (without the verdict of 'all the boyars').

Reforms of local government were also implemented in the middle of the sixteenth century, and these had far-reaching social and political consequences. The administration of the enormous territory of the unified country was a very complex task, and the government did not yet possess a sufficiently developed and diversified bureaucratic apparatus to establish effective control over the provinces. For this reason the Muscovite authorities were obliged to involve representatives of the population in affairs of local government and justice. From the end of the fifteenth century onwards, the government had begun to issue special documents to the localities, which prescribed the obligatory participation of elected members of the local communities in the law-courts of the *namestniki*. The first document of this type was the Beloozero statutory charter (*ustavnaya gramota*) of 1488. The Law Code of 1550 contained a demand for the compulsory participation of 'judicial men' – a kind of juror – in the trials conducted by the *namestniki*. The Code placed the *namestniki* under the firm control of the local government bodies. The elected representatives of the local population were charged, in particular, with responsibility for ensuring that the *namestniki* did not take bribes. Thus at the end of the fifteenth century and in the first half of the sixteenth century there was a clear trend towards the limitation of the power of the *namestniki* in favour of the local elected institutions.

The formation of estate-representative institutions in the localities had begun in the second third of the sixteenth century. At the end of the

1530s the *guba* reform began to be introduced (the word *guba* refers to a specific administrative area which corresponded to the territory of a *volost'* or an *uezd*). Criminal matters were removed from the competence of the *namestniki* and transferred to the administration of the elected *guba* institutions, which were responsible for the detection and detention of bandits on the territory under their jurisdiction. At the head of these new institutions of power there stood the *guba* elders, who were elected by the local nobility. The *guba* agencies were the first institutions of local self-government by the social estates, and their introduction marked an important step towards the consolidation of the nobility as an estate. The intense struggle for power among the boyar factions which unfolded in the 1530s and 1540s, however, prevented the continuation of this reform.

The further development of the system of estate-representative institutions dates to the period of the reforms of the mid-sixteenth century. An important event in this period was the abolition in 1555–6 of the old system of 'feeding' (*kormlenie*), that is, the power of the *namestniki* who obtained as remuneration for their service the right to 'feed themselves' (to extort specific sums) at the expense of the local population.[15] The abolition of the 'feedings' facilitated the transfer of power in the localities to the elected agencies of estate self-government.

In the middle of the 1550s the implementation of the *guba* reform was concluded. *Guba* agencies were established all over the country. In addition to the detection of bandits, the *guba* elders were given jurisdiction over very diverse matters of administration in the localities, including landholding matters. As elected representatives of the nobility, the *guba* elders were guided in their practical activity primarily by the interests of their own class. In the *guba* elders the provincial nobility acquired an institution which defended their interests. Together with the urban *prikazchiki* (also an essentially noble agency of power) they became the main administrative figures in local government.[16]

The abolition of the system of 'feedings' led to a marked decline in the role of the boyar aristocracy in local government affairs. Contrary to a widespread opinion among historians, however, this reform cannot be considered to have been a purely anti-boyar measure. It was not only members of the princely and boyar aristocracy who had had the right to receive 'feeding' in the posts of *namestniki* and *volosteli*,[17] but also a fairly broad category of people (numbering several hundred), predominantly members of the sovereign's court. As compensation for the lost revenue from 'feeding', a new type of tax was extracted from the population – the so-called 'feeding moneys', which were distributed to the servicemen who had had the right to 'feeding'. The receipt and distribution of the 'feeding moneys' was conducted by the special *Chetverti* chancelleries, and the people who received money from the *Chetverti* came to be called *chetvertchiki*. The significance of the reform lay in the fact that it converted the remuneration of the élite servicemen who had had the right to 'feeding' on to the basis of a monetary salary from the state. At the same time, the *chetvertchiki* received their salary on a regular basis – every year – whereas the great majority of the ordinary provincial nobles received their monetary salary only once every few years.

The power of the *namestniki*, it is true, was retained in several major frontier towns even after the official abolition of 'feeding'. But it had more of a formal than a real administrative significance. The retention of *namestniki* in such cities as Novgorod, Pskov and Smolensk, through which foreign envoys passed, can be explained to a considerable extent by the requirements of external representation: it was important that negotiations with envoys were conducted by eminent persons who occupied a high position in the official hierarchy. The Novgorod *namestniki* played a particularly important role in diplomatic relations: all negotiations with Sweden were traditionally conducted not in Moscow, but in Novgorod. The Swedes considered the downgrading of negotiations with Sweden to the level of the Novgorod *namestniki* to be an affront to their dignity, and this gave rise to conflicts between the two states. The *namestniki* of the major frontier towns also retained their military significance, particularly at times when troops were being mustered in these towns. The administrative role of the *namestniki*, however, was insignificant. The records of the Novgorod secretaries' office in the middle of the 1550s show that it was the secretaries who carried out all the routine work of administration in the city. The government of the lands newly annexed to Russia – the Kazan' and Astrakhan' regions – was entrusted to *voevody*, who wielded not only military but also administrative power over the population. The establishment of a new form of local government by the *voevody*, however, was not to occur until later, at the end of the sixteenth and beginning of the seventeenth centuries. In spite of the retention of some elements of administration by the *namestniki* and the introduction in some regions of the new form of local powerholding by the *voevody*, in the main territory of central Russia, where service and hereditary landholding by the nobles were well developed, the leading role in local government and administration passed to the elected institutions of estate self-government.

It was not only the nobles who acquired rights of self-government and real power in the localities in the mid-sixteenth century. As we have already noted, in the course of the implementation of the Church reforms the parish clergy also obtained rights of self-government through the 'priestly elders', and they acquired relative independence from the secular authorities. An innovation of major social and political significance was the so-called *zemstvo* (rural and urban community) reform of the 1550s.[18] It was implemented in 1556, when the abolition of 'feeding' took place. According to the provisions of this reform, in regions where there was no service landholding, power passed into the hands of the *zemstvo* elders and their assistants – the *zemstvo* sworn-men (*tseloval'niki*), secretaries and so on – who were elected by the peasants and townspeople. The elected *zemstvo* institutions were endowed with fairly extensive administrative, financial and judicial powers. They carried out the collection of taxes and, in particular, they collected the 'feeding moneys' which went to pay the servicemen's salaries. The *zemstvo* elders were usually chosen from the 'best', that is, the most prosperous, peasants and townspeople. They staunchly defended the interests of the emerging 'third estate' in the localities, primarily the peasant and urban élite. *Zemstvo* self-government developed particularly strongly on the lands of the state peasantry of the north of the country, who were free from direct dependency on noble landholders. In the north, traditions of communal self-government were particularly well developed, and peasant entrepreneurship and trade had become most extensive.

Thus as a result of the reforms of the mid-sixteenth century the various social estates began to acquire clearly defined rights and to develop their own institutions of self-government. This process affected very diverse groups of Russian society – the nobility, the clergy, the peasantry and the townspeople. At the same time the government took measures to safeguard the rights and privileges of the ruling aristocratic élite of the service class. The formation of this élite was facilitated by the aforementioned reforms of the sovereign's court and by the confirmation of the position of the boyar duma as the highest governmental institution.

In essence, the reforms of the middle of the sixteenth century were designed to bring about a consensus of interests between the state and the emergent social estates. They paved the way for the development of the Russian state as an estate-representative monarchy.[19] Of course, the level of development of the estates and their representative institutions was much lower than in the countries of western Europe, and the estates themselves were still only at an embryonic stage. The process of development of estate representation was made significantly more complex by the intervention of the state and by attempts to place the estate-representative institutions under the control of the central authorities. The formation of a single service class was accompanied by the confirmation in the mid-sixteenth century of the principle of compulsory service to the monarch. The activity of the *guba* elders was strictly controlled from Moscow by the Banditry Chancellery, and the activity of the institutions of *zemstvo* self-government was associated with so-called 'collective responsibility' (*krugovaya poruka*), that is, a system in which all members of the community provided mutual guarantees for one another in relation to the payment of state taxes and other obligations. The establishment of *zemstvo* self-government was accompanied by an increase in the tax burden. Nevertheless, with the economic growth of the country, the development of estate rights, and the formation of self-government institutions at various levels, Russia was making a very real move in the direction in which the countries of western Europe were heading – the establishment of a representative monarchy in which the power of the ruler was limited by the estates. However, this failed to come to fruition. As a result of various political factors, the country was diverted from the designated course of reform and went down a very different path of development.

Notes

1 *Sochineniya I. Peresvetova.*

2 For examples, see Zimin, *I.S. Peresvetov i ego sovremenniki.*

3 N.N. Rozov, 'Biblioteka Sil'vestra (XVI vek)', *Issledovaniya istochnikov po istorii russkogo yazyka i pis'mennosti*, Moscow, 1966, p.192; I.V. Kurukin, *Sil'vestr. Politicheskaya i kul'turnaya deyatel'nost' (istochniki i istoriografiya).* Avtoreferat dissertatsii na soiskanie uchenoi stepeni kandidata istoricheskikh nauk, Moscow, 1983.

4 For an English version, see *The Domostroi. Rules for Russian Households in the Time of Ivan the Terrible*, ed. and trans. Carolyn Johnston Pouncy, Ithaca: Cornell University Press, 1994.

5 For detailed accounts of the historiography of this issue, see the works of A.N. Grobovsky (A.N. Grobovsky, *The 'Chosen Council' of Ivan IV: a Reinterpretation*, New York: Gaus, 1969; A.N. Grobovskii, *Ivan Groznyi i Sil'vestr (Istoriya odnogo mifa)*, London, 1987); and the recent monograph by A.I. Filyushkin (A.I. Filyushkin, *Istoriya odnoi mistifikatsii. Ivan Groznyi i 'Izbrannaya Rada'*, Moscow, 1998). For a reassertion of the older view concerning Adashev's importance, see Bogatyrev, *The Sovereign and his Counsellors*, p.138.

6 R.G. Skrynnikov, *Tsarstvo terrora*, St Petersburg, 1992, pp.108–9.

7 L.V. Cherepnin, *Zemskie sobory Russkogo gosudarstva v XVI–XVII vv.*, Moscow, 1978, pp.68–78.

8 *Sudebniki XV–XVI vekov* (Podgotovka teksta R.B. Myuller, kommentarii B.A. Romanova), Moscow and Leningrad, 1952, pp.111–342.

9 See Miller, 'The Velikie Minei Chetii'.

10 This issue has recently been thoroughly researched by B.N. Florya: see B.N. Florya, *Otnosheniya gosudarstva i tserkvi u vostochnykh i zapadnykh slavyan*, Moscow, 1992, pp.78–80.

11 *Zak. akty*, pp.29–30.

12 *Tysyachnaya kniga 1550 g. i Dvorovaya tetrad' 50-kh godov XVI v.*, ed. A.A. Zimin, Moscow and Leningrad, 1950; Veselovskii, *Issledovaniya*, pp.77–91; Pavlov, *Gosudarev dvor*, pp.86–100.

13 *Zak. akty*, p.38.

14 A.A. Zimin, 'O slozhenii prikaznoi sistemy na Rusi', *Doklady i soobshcheniya Instituta istorii AN SSSR*, vyp.3, Moscow, 1954; A.K. Leont'ev, *Obrazovanie prikaznoi sistemy upravleniya v Russkom gosudarstve*, Moscow, 1961.

15 *Zak. akty*, pp.37–8.

16 The institution of urban *prikazchiki* appears in the towns at the turn of the fifteenth and sixteenth centuries. In spite of the fact that they were representatives of the grand-princely (royal) administration, they were usually appointed from the ranks of the local nobility. The urban *prikazchiki* were like military commanders in the towns – they managed the layout of the town's fortifications, the construction of roads, etc. In the course of time, they also acquired other broader functions of administrative control.

17 As distinct from the *namestniki*, who were appointed to govern the towns and districts (*uezdy*), the *volosteli* were representatives of the central authorities in the *volosti* (administrative-territorial units within the districts). It was usually aristocratic servitors who were appointed as *namestniki*, but the *volosteli* were predominantly men from non-aristocratic noble clans.

18 N.E. Nosov, *Stanovlenie soslovno-predstavitel'nykh uchrezhdenii v Rossii: Izyskaniya o zemskoi reforme Ivana Groznogo*, Leningrad, 1969.

19 This tendency was first noticed and demonstrated by N.E. Nosov (Nosov, *Stanovlenie soslovno-predstavitel'nykh uchrezhdenii*, p.9).

Chapter 5

From Consensus to Conflict

The 'boyar revolt' of 1553

The first symptom of political crisis was provided by the events of 1553, which historians have described as a 'boyar revolt'. At the beginning of March that year Tsar Ivan became seriously ill. The question arose of who should succeed to the throne in the event of his death. Ivan wanted the boyars to swear an oath of loyalty to his son, Tsarevich Dmitrii. But quarrels and disputes arose amongst them. The main source which describes these events is the famous 'interpolations' (additions) to the official chronicle, the so-called Illustrated Code.[1] They were made in distinctive handwriting in the margins of this ceremonial chronicle, which is richly decorated with miniatures, and they represent a kind of editorial amendment. Historians disagree on whether these interpolations are in Ivan Groznyi's own handwriting, or whether they were written by one of his trusted secretaries. It is undoubtedly true, however, that they appeared as a result of Tsar Ivan's direct intervention. According to the interpolations, the boyars organised a 'great revolt', refusing to swear loyalty to the infant Tsarevich Dmitrii. Only after the tsar had appealed to the boyars 'with a harsh speech' did the latter 'take fright', and they were obliged to kiss the cross to the heir. Historians have long since pointed out that this late source is blatantly tendentious. It contains a number of purely factual absurdities. For example, how could the tsar, who, according to the text of the interpolations, was so ill that he was no longer able to recognise the people around him, have been able to address speeches – and incessant ones at that – to the 'mutinous' boyars?

If we ignore the ideological issues and the later literary accretions, the general course of events in March 1553 may be depicted as follows. On 1 March the tsar really did fall so seriously ill that the issue of the succession arose. The heir to the throne was Ivan's only son, Tsarevich Dmitrii, who was then just five months old. It was essential to get the boyars – the members of the boyar duma – to swear an oath of loyalty to the tsarevich. The first to take the oath were the tsar's closest counsellors, the members of the 'Privy Council', including the tsar's wife's relatives, the Zakhar'in boyars, and the tsar's favourite, Aleksei Adashev. A general session of the boyar duma was arranged for the following day. It was there that disagreements arose amongst the boyars. There were fairly serious grounds for disputes and doubts about taking the oath to the tsarevich. Many boyars feared that if the throne passed to the infant Dmitrii all power in the country would end up in the hands of the Zakhar'in clan. The mood of a considerable section of the duma was expressed by Aleksei Adashev's father, the *okol'nichii* Fedor Grigor'evich Adashev, who declared that he was willing to serve Tsarevich Dmitrii, but not the Zakhar'ins. At the same time, Fedor Adashev recalled the problems which had been created by the boyars during Ivan IV's minority. It is not possible to detect any 'treason' in Fedor Adashev's words. On the contrary, he expressed a concern which was shared by many, about the danger of a return to the days of 'boyar rule'. One faction of the members of the duma, fearing an increase in the influence of the Zakhar'ins if Tsarevich Dmitrii were crowned, spoke in favour of another candidate for the throne – the tsar's cousin, the appanage prince Vladimir Andreevich Staritskii (see Figure 5.1).

Several boyars had entered into secret negotiations with Vladimir Staritskii, suggesting that he become tsar. The idea of occupying the Russian throne did not displease Prince Vladimir, and the appanage prince was encouraged in his ambition by his energetic and strongminded mother, Princess Evfrosin'ya Staritskaya. During the tsar's illness the Staritskiis carried out a review of their vassal servitors and began to reward them with generous monetary payments. It is not entirely fair, however, to consider these actions as preparations for a military *coup d'état*. It is quite possible that the Staritskiis had merely decided to take measures to guarantee their safety in case of their possible arrest, if the situation had developed in an unfavourable way for them. (Similar precedents had taken place in the not too distant past – the arrest by Elena Glinskaya of Prince Vladimir's uncle, the appanage prince Yurii Dmitrovskii, and the persecution of his father, Prince Andrei Staritskii.) Nevertheless, when they heard about the military preparations which Vladimir Staritskii had undertaken, Tsar Ivan's closest boyars, who were primarily the kinsmen of Tsaritsa Anastasiya, decided not to let him into the tsar's apartments. It is revealing that the tsar's mentor Sil'vestr stood up for Staritskii and roundly condemned the Zakhar'ins' actions. The

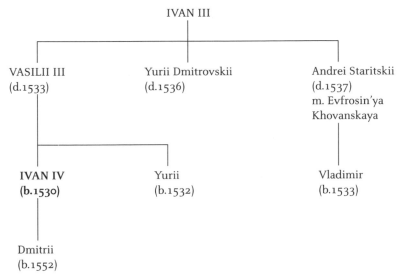

Figure 5.1 The dynastic crisis of 1553
Note: Reigning grand princes and tsars are indicated in capitals

priest's demand that Prince Vladimir should be allowed to see the tsar was rejected, and this, the authors of the interpolations observed, caused enmity between the Zakhar'ins and Sil'vestr. When he was invited into the palace to take the oath, Prince Vladimir Staritskii at first refused outright to kiss the cross to the infant Dmitrii, and it was only on the insistence of the Privy Council boyars that he was obliged to swear loyalty to the tsar's heir.

In view of the fact that so much of our information is of a late date and of a tendentious nature, it is difficult to state with confidence whether a 'boyar revolt' really took place in 1553, as Tsar Ivan claimed, or whether the affair was confined merely to disputes and discussions, which seems more likely.

The main cause of the quarrels and doubts about swearing an oath to Tsarevich Dmitrii was not the boyars' dissatisfaction with the policy of the ruling dynasty, but the tender age of the heir, and fears that the position of one of the boyar clans, the Zakhar'ins, would have been excessively strengthened, which would inevitably have led to new upheavals and strife. It was primarily this consideration which pushed several boyars towards the idea of swearing loyalty to Prince Vladimir. But by no means all of the boyars came out as supporters of Staritskii:

a significant sector of the boyar duma had unanimously taken the oath to the tsar's heir on the first day of Ivan's illness. There was no mention of the Staritskiis in the speech made by Fedor Adashev, who expressed the views of many of the boyars. One important detail is worth noting: it was only after his illness that the tsar received news of the intention of several boyars to swear loyalty to Vladimir Staritskii instead of to the heir. Consequently Tsar Ivan had no reason to rise from his bed and admonish the 'mutinous' boyars with 'harsh words'. These 'words' were the product of the later literary imagination of Ivan Groznyi and his entourage.

In his first letter to Kurbskii, Ivan Groznyi depicts Aleksei Adashev and Sil'vestr as the chief 'conspirators' in the events of 1553. The tendentious character of this claim is self-evident. The version expounded in the letter to Kurbskii blatantly contradicts what Tsar Ivan himself had stated in the additions to the Illustrated Code: according to the text of the interpolations, Aleksei was in the first group (the Privy Counsellors) that swore loyalty to the tsar's heir. During the squabbles 'around the bed' he apparently advocated ideas similar to those expressed by his father, which, as we have observed, were not subversive. As for Sil'vestr's behaviour during the events of 1553, we can judge only on the basis of a single piece of evidence – his dispute with the Zakhar'ins on whether Vladimir Staritskii should be allowed into the tsar's apartments. But the priest's action can hardly be interpreted as an unambiguous expression of sympathy for the appanage prince and his plans to seize the throne. According to the interpolations, Sil'vestr merely reminded the tsar's servants, the Zakhar'ins, of the great eminence of the tsar's closest blood relative. 'Why do you not let Prince Volodimir [Vladimir] in to see the tsar?', Sil'vestr demanded of the boyars. 'A brother [that is, the tsar's cousin] is more benevolent [closer] to the tsar than you boyars.'[2]

Thus we can detect no 'boyar revolt' in the form of open insubordination to the tsar and his family on the part of the boyar duma during the tsar's illness. The quarrels and disagreements within the boyar duma were the consequence not of a confrontation between the tsar and his 'unruly' boyars, but of a split within the duma itself, a rivalry for power among various court groupings, which intensified at a time of dynastic crisis.

The dynastic crisis came to an end without any visible political upheavals. In the last resort all the boyars, as well as the appanage prince Vladimir Staritskii, swore the oath of loyalty to the infant tsarevich. The tsar made a speedy recovery, and it seemed that the conflict had been resolved. But nonetheless the March events left a deep imprint on the mind of Tsar Ivan, who recalled them with great agitation many years later. And there were good reasons for this.

According to the logic of the subsequent interpretation of these events provided by Ivan Groznyi himself, after his recovery and reassumption of power the tsar should have punished those who had disobeyed his royal wishes – the boyars who had hesitated over the oath to the infant heir – and he should have promoted those who had zealously supported the rights of the heir to the throne during the crisis. But in fact things happened the other way round. Not only did the hesitant courtiers not suffer for their 'treachery', but many of them were elevated in rank. Aleksei Adashev received the duma rank of *okol'nichii*, and his father was promoted from *okol'nichii* to boyar. Even members of the aristocracy who had declared themselves to be supporters of the Staritskiis (Prince S.V. Rostovskii, Prince D.F. Paletskii and others), entered the duma. By contrast, the position at court of the Zakhar'in boyars was seriously weakened after 1553.[3] In 1554 the most influential members of the Zakhar'in clan, Danila Romanovich Yur'ev and Vasilii Mikhailovich Yur'ev, lost important court positions: the former was deprived of the post of steward (*dvoretskii*) of the Grand Palace, and the latter of steward of the Tver' Palace. Ivan Petrovich Golovin, a kinsman and supporter of the Zakhar'ins, lost the position of treasurer. In all probability it was Aleksei Adashev and Sil'vestr who persuaded the tsar to limit the power of the Zakhar'ins, whose activity had provoked widespread discontent in boyar circles. By having the hated Zakhar'in boyars removed, the tsar's advisers hoped to preserve the political consensus within the ruling circle that had been achieved in the course of the reforms. In practice, however, it proved impossible to restore the equilibrium which had been lost in 1553.

By bringing about the dismissal of the Zakhar'ins from their important positions at court, Adashev and Sil'vestr made dangerous enemies of them and of Tsaritsa Anastasiya herself. This contributed to the intensification of conflicts at court and to an increase in intrigues. In his letter to Kurbskii the tsar reproached Adashev and Sil'vestr for inciting hatred towards the tsaritsa by comparing her to disreputable queens of old.

But the most important factor was that Tsar Ivan himself clearly remained unhappy with the course of events. Things had happened against his will. Ivan had been obliged to make concessions to his counsellors and boyars, and this was not in his character. But the problem was not confined to an affront to the tsar's self-esteem. The roots of the developing crisis went much deeper.

The power of the Muscovite ruler

Just over a year after the events of March 1553 the Rostovskii princes were exposed as traitors. According to the chronicle account, in July 1554 Prince Nikita Lobanov-Rostovskii was detained on the Lithuanian border and despatched to Moscow. Under interrogation he admitted that he had been sent to Lithuania by the boyar Prince Semen Rostovskii to report that the latter intended to cross over into the service of the king of Poland-Lithuania. Prince Semen and his associates were arrested and interrogated. The investigation of the affair was entrusted to an authoritative boyar commission which included representatives of various political interests: the highest category of princes (Prince I.F. Mstislavskii and others), the tsar's kinsmen (the Zakhar'in Yur'ev boyars) and the tsar's advisers and favourites, including Aleksei Adashev. As a result of the investigation it was revealed that in the summer of 1553 Prince Semen had held secret talks with the Polish envoy Stanisław Dowojno, in the course of which he had handed over state secrets, and had also tried to dissuade him from concluding peace with Moscow, because 'the tsardom has become impoverished, and the tsar will not be able to hold on to Kazan'. The prince had asked the envoy to provide him with asylum in Lithuania.

In the course of the investigation details were also revealed of the behaviour of the boyars and the Staritskiis during the tsar's illness in 1553. Prince Semen admitted under questioning that emissaries from Prince Vladimir Staritskii and his mother Princess Evfrosin'ya had come to his house with a proposal that he enter their service and exert influence on fellow boyars. Prince Semen and a number of other boyars and noblemen had been inclined to accept this suggestion, since they considered that it was better to serve the Staritskiis than to permit the Zakhar'ins to become all-powerful. Rostovskii's accomplices were the boyars Prince Petr Shchenyatev, Prince Ivan Turuntai Pronskii, Prince Dmitrii Nemoi Obolenskii, Prince Petr Serebryanyi, Prince Semen Mikulinskii, the princes Kurakin and others, as well as a number of nobles. Semen Rostovskii's testimony demonstrates that in 1553 the Staritskiis had succeeded in attracting to their side a fairly significant group of boyars and noblemen who were unhappy with the dominance of the Zakhar'ins at court.

For his grave crime against the state (treason in the interests of a foreign power) the tsar and the boyars sentenced Prince Semen to public execution. But as a result of the intercession of Metropolitan Makarii and the Church authorities the death sentence was commuted and the disgraced boyar was sent to Beloozero, where he was imprisoned.

In spite of the revelation about the stance of the Staritskiis and a number of boyars, there was no widespread reprisal following the Rostovskii affair. It is possible that Tsar Ivan had wanted to punish the boyars for their disloyalty during his illness, but at that time the necessary legal basis for this did not exist. Although the Code of 1550 did refer to political (state) crimes such as 'sedition' (conspiracy, revolt) and the deliberate surrender of a city to the enemy, it did not distinguish between political crimes and other serious offences, and neither was there a special section on the defence of the 'sovereign's honour'. Such legal norms were developed only later, under the influence of the *oprichnina*. A clear classification of political crimes as crimes directed against the supreme monarchical power and against the life of the sovereign and his family is first found in sources dating from the end of the sixteenth century (the records of the oaths of loyalty to Boris Godunov).[4] This concept of political crime was definitively affirmed in the Law Code (*Sobornoe Ulozhenie*) of 1649, where there is a special chapter (the second) devoted to 'The sovereign's honour and how to safeguard the sovereign's health'. In the period before the *oprichnina*, legislation did not in practice distinguish between crimes directed against the state and crimes directed against the life of the ruler himself. In the middle of the sixteenth century the judicial prosecution of political cases was regulated by the norms of customary law and ancient tradition. Custom dictated that the boyars had to participate in the trial. Punishment was imposed primarily for the actual commission of a crime, not simply for the intention to commit one. Moreover, the accusation had to be made in public. Bound as he was by existing laws and by tradition, Tsar Ivan could not subject the boyars to prosecution simply for their 'conversations' expressing doubts about the wisdom of passing the throne to the infant Dmitrii and discussing the possible candidature of Prince Vladimir Staritskii. An important factor which inhibited the imposition of a repressive policy was the ancient right of the Church authorities to intercede with the ruler for the pardoning of those in disgrace. This did not permit the tsar to punish troublesome figures entirely according to his own wishes. The intercession of the clergy and members of the boyar duma meant not only that Prince Semen Rostovskii's life was spared but that he was able subsequently to return to state service. There is no evidence of repression of Prince Semen's associates and kinsmen, the princes Lobanov-Rostovskii and Priimkov-Rostovskii. The tsar became more and more aware of the degree to which his power was limited. The policy of consensus between the monarchy and the boyar aristocracy, implemented by Adashev and his colleagues, ceased to satisfy Ivan, as did the teachings of Sil'vestr that the

sovereign should rule not only by 'fear' but also by mercy, making concessions and listening to the wise counsel of his courtiers. Ivan was
becoming increasingly frustrated by the tutelage of his closest advisers.

There is reason to believe that soon after the events of 1553 Ivan had
begun to ponder the relationship of Russian political reality to the ideals
of autocratic tsarist power. How far had the reforms which had been
implemented in the country (and which had undoubtedly contributed to
the strengthening and centralisation of the Russian state) enhanced the
personal power of the ruler? According to Kurbskii, after recovering
from his illness Tsar Ivan had gone to visit a number of monasteries
to pray, and had held a conversation with his father's former adviser,
the monk Vassian Toporkov (Vassian was the nephew of Joseph of
Volokolamsk, the outstanding Church figure of the late fifteenth and
early sixteenth centuries and one of the first proponents of strong autocratic power in Rus'). In reply to a question from the tsar about how it
was possible to combine merciful rule with the obedience of one's subjects, Vassian had replied, 'If you want to be an autocrat, do not retain
advisers who are wiser than you are, for you as tsar are superior to them
all.' In Kurbskii's opinion, this conversation had a fateful effect on Tsar
Ivan's character, turning him from a well-intentioned monarch into a
dread tyrant.[5] Kurbskii's account is very plausible, although he had clearly
shifted the emphasis, in line with his view that Ivan's personality under-
went a marked change around this time. In reality the monk's advice fell
on ground which was already well prepared. His answer was in many
ways predetermined by Ivan's question, which reflected a critical and
even ironic attitude towards the teachings of Sil'vestr, who, in the tsar's
opinion, advocated the reconciliation of the irreconcilable: merciful rule
and the necessity of retaining the obedience of one's ungrateful subjects.
Ivan Groznyi's ideology, directed towards strengthening the autocratic
power of the tsar, was reflected most clearly in his later writings (such as
his letters to Kurbskii and to foreign rulers). A constant theme in all of
Ivan's literary works is one single big idea – that of unlimited autocratic
power, independent of any earthly authorities.[6] In *Groznyi*'s view, the
origin of the tsar's power was not earthly, but divine, and only the tsar,
as 'God's chosen one', could be held responsible for the fate of the country and exercise the exclusive right to 'reward the good and execute the
wicked'. None of his subjects was entitled to proffer him advice, insofar
as all of them, from the most elevated boyars to the rank-and-file servicemen, were 'the sovereign's slaves'. Tsar Ivan wrote ironically about the
political systems in European states, where the king's power was limited
by the estates and by parliaments. It must be said that the Russian court

was fairly familiar with events in other European countries and their social structure; this was particularly true of neighbouring states. Of course, this information was interpreted in a particular way. 'The Godless pagans [that is, the non-Orthodox rulers of Europe]', the tsar declared, 'do not rule their states themselves, but rule them according to the dictates of their subjects.' In Russia, by contrast, Ivan said haughtily, it was the autocrats who governed the state, and not the boyars and magnates. In a letter to the Polish king Stephen Bathory (Polish kings were of course elected at the *sejms*), Tsar Ivan wrote of himself that he was the sovereign 'by God's will, and not by the turbulent desires of humanity'. In the same way he addressed the English queen Elizabeth, pointing out that her power was limited not only by the nobility but also by the 'trading peasants' (representatives of the 'third estate', the 'commons') who were not concerned about the interests of the state, but only about their own profits. Ivan Groznyi did not want to be dependent in any way either on the boyars or on the merchants.

But in essence these ideas of Ivan's were not new. The first Russian tsar was simply developing ideas about the 'divinely ordained character' and unlimited nature of monarchical power which had arisen much earlier. Such ideas had already been formulated in the Byzantine Empire, on the basis of the Eastern Orthodox Christian tradition which recognised the 'vertical' direction of relations between the sovereign and his subjects and the divine origin of the power of the monarch, and which also rejected the contractual (legal) principle as a 'human' and not a divine institution. It is significant that in Byzantium a system of vassalhood had not developed as it had in the countries of western Europe; nor had a contractual legal consciousness, nor the 'politicisation' of social estates. In spite of the fact that the socio-political development of early Rus' had taken a rather different direction from that of the Byzantine Empire, the former was part of the Eastern Christian world, and the political and legal ideas of Byzantium were always revered in Rus'. Moreover, for a number of reasons (such as the enormous size of its territory, the constant external threat, and the economic weakness of its towns) the power of the monarch played a very significant role in Russia, and the state dominated society to a much greater extent than it did in the European monarchies. As we have seen, the Imperial envoy Sigismund von Herberstein had reported in the reign of Vasilii III that the power of the Muscovite grand prince over his subjects exceeded that of all other rulers.

The symbolic demonstration of the tsar's power and glory was a striking feature of the 1550s. We have already noted the ways in which the conquest of Kazan' was celebrated in art and architecture as well as through ritual and ceremony. The court itself presented a lavish spectacle. Richard Chancellor, the first English envoy to Moscow, was dazzled by the amount of gold and jewels on show when he was received at Ivan's court in 1553: 'our men beganne to wonder at the Majestie of the Emperour,' he reported. The tsar also displayed himself publicly to his subjects, for example at the ceremony of the blessing of the waters at Epiphany and in the Palm Sunday procession, both of which were witnessed by Anthony Jenkinson in 1558.[7] Ivan's frequent pilgrimages to holy places such as the Trinity Monastery presented him to his people outside Moscow as a pious and accessible ruler.[8]

As we have seen, Ivan's coronation as tsar in 1547 enhanced his status as a divinely appointed ruler on the Byzantine model. The Russian scholar Boris Uspenskii has argued that in Muscovy the sacralisation of the ruler went even further than in Byzantium. The Russian coronation ceremony of anointment took the form of a second sacrament of baptism, and thereby endowed the tsar with a special charisma which identified him with Christ. In Byzantium, Uspenskii asserts, the anointing of the Emperor corresponded to that of the Old Testament kings; whereas the Russian anointment (based perhaps on a misunderstanding of the Byzantine ceremony) compared the tsar with Christ, who was anointed by the Holy Spirit at his baptism. Uspenskii believes that the sacrament of anointment was not performed during Ivan's coronation, but was devised in the mid-1550s and incorporated into a version of the coronation ceremony which was sent to Constantinople in 1557 with Ivan's request for the patriarch's confirmation of his title.[9] Thus, even if Ivan himself was not anointed at his coronation in 1547, the concept of a special charisma associated with the tsar had come into existence in Russia by the end of the 1550s.

The idea of divinely ordained autocratic tsarist power, unlimited by any earthly institutions, found itself at variance with Russian reality. The removal of the Zakhar'ins from power led to an increase in the influence of Adashev and Sil'vestr over political matters. The strengthening of their position was helped to a considerable degree by the fact that the policies which they pursued were broadly supported by the princely and boyar aristocracy and by the élite of the nobility. In the second half of the 1550s there was a marked influx of members of aristocratic clans into the boyar duma. The supporters of Adashev and Sil'vestr included many distinguished and high-born boyars: Prince A.B. Gorbatyi-Suzdal'skii, the hero of the capture of Kazan'; Prince D.I. Kurlyatev-Obolenskii; Prince A.M. Kurbskii-Yaroslavskii (Andrei Kurbskii, who was descended from the Yaroslavl' princes) and others. The policy of implementing reforms continued after 1553. Moreover, it was in the middle of the 1550s that major reforms such as the abolition of 'feeding' and the passing of the Code on Service were introduced, as well as the implementation of the *guba* and *zemstvo* reforms. As we have noted, these reforms were intended to achieve social cohesion. They contributed to the development of the social estates and their corporate self-government, and indicated the possibility that Russia's political development might take the direction of a representative monarchy. Such a path would not have run counter to state centralisation. In many countries of western Europe a representative monarchy, in which the power of the ruler was to some extent restricted by the estates, marked a particular stage in the evolution of centralised states – the stage which preceded absolutism.

But that particular path of political development did not appeal to Ivan IV. The need to share power with the boyars and to take into account the interests of the emerging social estates was interpreted by the tsar as an affront to the supreme power of an autocratic 'God-crowned' ruler. In the last resort, it was this consideration, and not simply the 'psychological incompatibility' of the personalities of Tsar Ivan and his advisers, which was the main cause of his conflict with Adashev and Sil'vestr and of their dismissal.

The beginning of the Livonian War and the dismissal of Adashev and Sil'vestr

In the 1550s Russia achieved very significant foreign-policy successes in the east and south. In addition to the annexation of Kazan' and Astrakhan', Bashkiriya became part of the Russian state, and the Nogai Horde and the Siberian khanate were drawn into Russia's orbit when their rulers acknowledged themselves to be vassals and tributaries of the tsar. Of the major successors of the Golden Horde, only the Crimean khanate remained outside the Russian sphere of influence. Crimea was a threatening and dangerous opponent of Russia on her southern frontiers, since behind the Crimean khans there stood the mighty Ottoman Empire. Nonetheless, in the mid-1550s Russia undertook a number of major military operations against the Crimea. These failed to lead to the destruction of the Crimean Horde, but for the first time in the history of Russo-Crimean relations Russian troops did not restrict themselves to defending their frontiers, but went on to the attack. Thus in the middle of the sixteenth century a major shift took place in the balance of power between Russia and the Tatar khanates. To a considerable extent this occurred as a consequence of the reforms of the Russian army and the consolidation of the military-service class which had resulted from these changes. A large share of the credit also belonged to Russian diplomacy, and in the first instance to the architects of the state's foreign policy – Aleksei Adashev and the head of the Ambassadorial Chancellery, the secretary Ivan Viskovatyi.

These successes enabled Russia to pursue a more aggressive policy in the west. The Russian government turned its gaze to the Baltic region, through which passed the major trade routes linking the countries of western and eastern Europe. The mid-sixteenth century saw the development of commercial relationships and the growth of towns and manufacturing in the states of western Europe, and there was also a marked growth in their interest in Russian goods – agricultural and forest products such as grain, tallow, wax and furs. Russia in her turn was developing an ever greater need for manufactured goods such as weapons and metal from western Europe. An important event in the development of Russia's trade links with western Europe was the appearance in 1553 of an expedition headed by Richard Chancellor at the mouth of the Northern Dvina (at the point where it entered the White Sea). Two years later, a special 'Muscovy Company' was formed in England with the aim of trading with Russia. It obtained significant trade privileges from the Muscovite government. This helped to establish regular Russian commerce with England and other west European countries. The harsh natural environment, however, significantly impeded trade through the White Sea. The Baltic Sea was much more convenient for trade relations between Russia and Europe.

Since early times Rus' had controlled the eastern shores of the Gulf of Finland, which were inhabited by various Baltic and Finnic peoples, as well as by eastern Slavs. The Muscovite government made an attempt to organise regular trade with the West through the Baltic. A shipping wharf was built in 1557 at the mouth of the River Narova, in the hope that foreign trading vessels would frequent it, but the plan was not successful. The most important commercial ports on the Baltic (Riga, Revel' and Narva) were in the hands of the Livonian Order of German knights, who had occupied the Baltic lands in the thirteenth century. The Livonians did everything they could to hamper the development of direct trade contacts between Russia and the West. Russian merchants were forbidden from travelling freely to the countries of western Europe, and western European merchants were prevented from coming to Russia. They could make commercial deals in the Baltic ports only through local traders. Their role as commercial middle-men brought huge profits to the Livonian authorities and merchants, but harmed the interests of the Russian state. All attempts by the Russian government to influence the situation by diplomatic means met with failure, and it became clear that the problem could not be resolved without military pressure on the Order. The situation seemed favourable for Russia. The Livonian Order was at that time suffering from a serious political crisis. By the middle of the sixteenth century it had in effect lost its internal unity and had acquired the form of a fairly amorphous political conglomerate, comprising the Order's own possessions, bishoprics and towns. As a result of the Reformation, most of the nobles and townspeople had become Protestants, while the Livonian knightly monks headed by their Master remained loyal to Roman Catholicism and were under the jurisdiction of the Pope. The weakness of the Order became more and more apparent, and the Russian government decided to take advantage of this.

A pretext for exerting political pressure on the Order was provided by the issue of the so-called 'Yur'ev tribute'.[10] At one time the bishopric of the city of Dorpat (previously the town of Yur'ev, founded by Russian princes and seized by the Knights in the thirteenth century) had paid tribute to the city-state of Pskov. The requirement to pay the 'Yur'ev tribute' was repeated in treaties between Dorpat and Muscovy, but by the middle of the sixteenth century the tribute had not been exacted for many years. The payment of tribute by the Dorpat bishopric was one of the central issues in the negotiations which Adashev and the Ambassadorial Secretary Ivan Viskovatyi conducted with the Livonian envoys in 1554. The Russian diplomats argued not only that the payment of the tribute had been established almost three centuries earlier, but also that it represented a form of compensation to the tsar's ancestors for the Livonian knights' occupation of Rus' lands. Muscovite statesmen were subsequently to develop their claim that Livonia was the age-old patrimony of the Russian rulers, and that the 'Yur'ev tribute' was evidence of their longstanding rights to the Baltic lands.

The Russian diplomats let the Livonians know that they had broken the previous treaties and they demanded not only that the tribute should be paid in future, but also that they should receive compensation for its non-payment in previous years. If the Livonians refused to pay the tribute, the Russian envoys declared, 'the tsar would come for it himself'. These threats produced the required effect. The Livonian authorities were obliged to make concessions – they promised to pay the tribute owed by the Dorpat bishopric and even agreed to a certain relaxation of the terms of trade for Russian merchants in Livonia. It turned out, however, that

Livonia had no intention of fulfilling the terms of the treaty. In spite of the fact that the amount of the 'Yur'ev tribute' was not too onerous, the Livonians demonstratively attempted to avoid paying it. The Livonian envoys who came to Moscow in 1557 not only failed to bring the tribute with them, but also tried to persuade the Russian government to cease demanding it. It became clear that it would not be possible to get the Order to meet its treaty obligations without military pressure. At the beginning of 1558 Russian troops were ordered by Ivan IV to attack the territory of the Order, with the aim of exerting pressure on Livonia. Military action against the Order began in May 1558 when Russian troops took the town of Narva by storm. After this a major military campaign was undertaken against Livonia. As a result, Dorpat and a large number of other towns were captured. The entire eastern sector of present-day Estonia came under the control of the Russians (see Map 5.1).

Meanwhile, Russia took offensive action against the Crimean khanate. In 1558 and 1559 Russian troops succeeded in inflicting a number of serious defeats on the forces of the Crimean Horde. Among the military commanders who distinguished themselves against the Crimea was Aleksei Adashev's brother, Daniil Adashev.

It is widely believed by historians that Ivan himself initiated the policy of open aggression in the Baltic, whilst Adashev and Sil'vestr considered that the conflict with the Crimean khanate was the main priority in foreign policy, and opposed the Livonian War. It was this disagreement over foreign policy priorities which, in the opinion of many historians, led to the rift between Tsar Ivan and his advisers. In reality, however, things were rather more complicated.

As we have seen, it was Aleksei Adashev, who was in practice in charge of Russian foreign policy, who conducted the negotiations with the Livonian envoys, obtaining concessions from the leaders of the Order as a result of diplomatic pressure. The breakdown of these talks led to the commencement of military operations in Livonia. At the same time Adashev was displaying a degree of caution in the conduct of his Baltic policy. There was good reason for this. A war against the Livonian Order on its own presented no real threat to the Russian state. A much greater danger arose from the prospect that a war for Livonia might develop into a broader international conflict involving the participation of a number of European states against Russia. Adashev had this danger in mind when he endeavoured to prevent the creation of an anti-Russian coalition and Russia's involvement in a war against her powerful neighbours. The main threat was posed by the Polish-Lithuanian state, which had

Map 5.1 The Livonian War

economic and political interests of its own in the Baltic region, and which, like Russia, was attempting to establish its influence there. With the commencement of military operations in Livonia, Adashev attempted to achieve peace with Poland and Lithuania at any price. In order to guarantee the neutrality of Poland-Lithuania in the Russo-Livonian conflict, the Russians proposed that Lithuania should conclude an offensive alliance with them against the Crimean Horde, whose incursions caused damage not just to Russian possessions, but also to those of Poland-Lithuania.[11] Adashev's plans, however, turned out to be unrealistic. The leaders of Poland-Lithuania were reluctant to see Russia's position strengthened in both the east and the west, and they not only failed to conclude this alliance but, on the contrary, secretly incited the Crimean Tatars to undertake a war against Russia. It was a major mistake on Adashev's part to offer the Livonian Order a six-month armistice (from May to November 1559) to consider the Russians' demand that Livonia place itself under a Russian protectorate. It was during this time, on 31 August, that the Order concluded an agreement with Lithuania that Livonia should come under the protection of the Grand Duchy of Lithuania. Now, in the event of the continuation of military action in Livonia, Russia would have to fight not only the weak Order but also the mighty Polish-Lithuanian state. The Livonian authorities took advantage of Moscow's armistice to muster their military forces and hire mercenaries. The Knights' armies managed to inflict significant losses on Russian troops near Dorpat.

News of the failures in Livonia reached Ivan IV at Mozhaisk. En route from Mozhaisk to Moscow harsh exchanges took place between the tsar and his advisers. Adashev and Sil'vestr considered that in the circumstances it would be dangerous and futile for Russia to become involved in a war against Poland-Lithuania. It seems that they insisted on the cessation of military operations in Livonia and the re-orientation of Russia's foreign policy towards the conflict with the Crimea. Tsar Ivan took a different view. In his later writings he harshly reproached his advisers, saying that if it had not been for their 'malevolent obstruction' (opposition to the tsar's will), then 'with God's help all of Germany [that is, Livonia] would have become Orthodox [come under the rule of the Russian tsar]'. Ivan could not forgive Adashev for his diplomatic blunders. It was this which led to his dismissal and that of Sil'vestr.

In the spring of 1560 Aleksei Adashev was appointed as one of the commanders of the army which was setting off for Livonia. Sending Adashev, one of the most active figures in government, on a campaign far from Moscow meant that in practice he had been dismissed from any participation in court life and diplomatic negotiations. After Russian troops captured the Livonian town of Fellin the tsar ordered Adashev to remain there as governor. The Kostroma nobleman Osip Polev, who had been appointed second-in-command in Fellin, became involved in a precedence dispute with Adashev. Previously Polev would have been disgraced for infringing the honour of a man who was the tsar's close adviser and a member of the boyar duma. But times had changed. Polev's precedence claims were recognised as valid. He remained in the town as commander-in-chief and Adashev was transferred to Dorpat under the command of the town's governor, Prince Dmitrii Khilkov. There is evidence that Adashev begged Khilkov to give him some kind of responsibility. But each time the governor refused, evidently reluctant to compromise himself by helping the disgraced grandee.[12] Clear evidence that Adashev was in disgrace was provided by the confiscation of his hereditary estates in the Pereyaslavl' and Kostroma districts; in their stead he was granted service lands in the Novgorod region. The priest Sil'vestr was dismissed from court at the same time as Adashev. He was obliged to leave Moscow and take the tonsure in the Kirillo-Belozerskii Monastery.

It seems likely, however, that the main cause of Ivan IV's rift with his former favourites was not so much their disagreements over foreign policy, but rather the tsar's dissatisfaction with the results of Adashev's and Sil'vestr's domestic policy, which had not led to any real increase in power of the Orthodox ruler over his subjects.

On the eve of the *oprichnina* terror

The end of the 1550s was an important watershed in the development of the Russian state. The dismissal of Adashev and Sil'vestr was not merely a reshuffle of court groupings, but marked a change of political direction. No significant new reforms were introduced after the end of the 1550s. Tendencies towards repressive policies became noticeably stronger. Around the tsar there gathered a circle of men who advocated harsh and decisive measures both in internal policy (confrontation with the opposition) and in external relations (offensive military operations in Livonia). In them Tsar Ivan found kindred spirits and a base of support. With the removal of Adashev and Sil'vestr, the leading role at court again came to be played by Tsaritsa Anastasiya's kinsmen, the Zakhar'in boyars, and their supporters. New men also came to the fore. An increasingly prominent figure at court was Aleksei Danilovich Basmanov-Pleshcheev, who had proved himself an outstanding military commander (in particular during the capture of the Livonian fortress of Narva). He was to become one of the leaders of the *oprichnina*.

The death of Tsaritsa Anastasiya on 6 August 1560 triggered the introduction of repressive measures by the tsar against his entourage. According to some sources, Anastasiya had a benevolent influence on her husband. For example, Jerome Horsey, an agent of the English Muscovy Company, noted in his memoirs that 'he [Ivan IV] being young and riotous, she [the tsaritsa] ruled him with admirable affability and wisdom'.[13] Such sources, however, are of a relatively late provenance. It is difficult to judge just what Tsar Ivan's personal relations with his first wife were like. Undoubtedly Anastasiya's death was a great loss for Ivan. She had given him six children in the space of only eight years (1549–57): three daughters, all of whom died in infancy, and three sons. Their first-born son, Tsarevich Dmitrii, whose claim to the throne had caused so many disputes during Tsar Ivan's illness in 1553, drowned in the River Sheksna in June that year, while the tsar and his family were returning from a pilgrimage to the Kirillo-Belozerskii Monastery. In March 1554 Ivan and Anastasiya acquired a new heir, Tsarevich Ivan, who died in 1581. Tsarevich Fedor, the future tsar, was born in May 1557.

It is difficult to reach any firm conclusions about Anastasiya's role in the political life of the country. No doubt she was not indifferent to the conflict between her kinsmen the Zakhar'ins and Adashev and Sil'vestr. The latter tried by every means to discredit the tsaritsa and her 'brethren' in the eyes of the public, and it is not surprising that when rumours were spread that the tsaritsa had been bewitched, the shadow of suspicion fell on the former government leaders. This created a pretext for the convening at the end of 1560 of an assembly of representatives of the clergy and boyars to pass judgment on Adashev and Sil'vestr. Our information about the activity of this assembly comes primarily from the writings of Ivan Groznyi and Andrei Kurbskii, which provide tendentious and contradictory versions of events. The opponents of Adashev and Sil'vestr clearly tried to accuse them of Anastasiya's death. But the sources do not permit us to form any clear or precise impression of the proceedings of the assembly, or its decision about the sentence which was pronounced against the tsar's former advisers. We can, however, note one important feature of the assembly – the accused were not present during its sessions; in other words, they were tried *in absentia*. A trial held in the absence of the accused ran counter to the traditions of justice in Rus', and marked an important watershed in the establishment of new principles of judicial procedure in political trials. A new concept was introduced of political crime as a crime directed primarily against the life of the ruler himself and members of his family.

Soon after the assembly the disgraced Aleksei Adashev became seriously ill (a 'fiery ailment' befell him) and died. Prince Andrei Kurbskii wrote that in accordance with the decision of the assembly, Sil'vestr, who had become the monk Spiridon in the Kirillo-Belozerskii Monastery, was exiled to the remote northern Solovetskii Monastery. This is not, however, confirmed by other sources. It is most probable that the tsar's former mentor remained at Kirillo-Belozerskii and died there at the end of the 1560s.[14] Having been liberated from the tutelage of his former advisers and having broken with tradition in the field of judicial procedure, the tsar acquired freedom of action in his battle to affirm his political ideal – an autocratic mode of rule.

The beginning of the 1560s was marked by major foreign policy successes. In 1561 the envoys of the Constantinople patriarch Ioasaf brought to Moscow a document conveying the decision of the ecumenical church council to recognise the Moscow ruler's title of tsar. In its attempt to prevent the formation of a broad anti-Russian coalition, the Russian government concluded an alliance with Denmark and a 20-year truce with Sweden. A number of successful military ventures were undertaken against the Crimean khanate. At the same time an embassy was sent to the Crimea with the aim of achieving peace. A favourable international situation had been created for offensive action against the main enemy – the Lithuanian state. In November 1562 Tsar Ivan set out at the head of a large army on a campaign against Polotsk, which was the key to the river route along the Western Dvina, and the most important fortress shielding the Lithuanian capital of Vil'na. On 15 February 1563, after a relatively short siege, the garrison of the fortress surrendered. The capture of Polotsk marked the greatest success for Russia in the Livonian War, and the regaining of such an important part of the ancient 'patrimony' of Kievan Rus' was celebrated with elaborate rituals, culminating in a great victory procession when the tsar returned to Moscow.[15] In Ivan's eyes his foreign policy successes confirmed that right had been on his side in his quarrel with his former advisers.

Just over a year after Anastasiya's death, Ivan remarried. According to the official chronicle the tsar had been prostrate with grief at his wife's death; an unofficial chronicler, however, claims that Ivan's reaction to the loss of the tsaritsa was to indulge in an orgy of promiscuous behaviour. Within a week of Anastasiya's funeral, the metropolitan and boyars begged Ivan to remarry – an indecently hasty request which some historians have interpreted as confirmation of the rumours about the tsar's debauched response to his bereavement. The search for a new tsaritsa began, and on 21 August 1561 Tsar Ivan entered into his second marriage. His bride was Kuchenei, the daughter of the Circassian prince of Kabarda in the Caucasus; after her baptism she took the name Mariya Temryukovna. In order to safeguard the rights of his heir, the seven-year-old Tsarevich Ivan, in the event of his death, Ivan IV arranged for the formation of a regency council for his son, comprising seven boyars as his guardians. The members of the council were the tsar's kinsman, the eminent boyar Prince Ivan Fedorovich Mstislavskii; the boyars Danila Romanovich and Vasilii Mikhailovich Yur'ev-Zakhar'in; Ivan Petrovich Yakovlev-Zakhar'in; the Zakhar'ins' relative Fedor Ivanovich Umnoi Kolychev; and two younger men, the tsar's favourites Prince Andrei Petrovich Telyatevskii and Petr Ivanovich Gorenskii.[16] It was not difficult to see that the membership of the regency council was dominated by the kinsmen of the previous tsaritsa – the Zakhar'in boyars. Their supremacy at court could not fail to provoke widespread dissatisfaction among the aristocracy. It was noteworthy that the regency council (which was in effect the ruling circle) did not include either the tsar's blood relative Prince Vladimir Andreevich Staritskii or any members of such eminent princely and boyar clans as the Bel'skiis, Glinskiis, Shuiskiis or Vorotynskiis. All of this indicated a deep division within the ruling élite. The anger of the princely aristocracy was provoked by a Resolution (law) on princely hereditary estates which was passed on 15 January 1562. Compared with a Resolution of 1551 it significantly restricted the rights of the princes to dispose of their family estates, and increased the intervention of the state in matters pertaining to hereditary landownership.[17] The new law categorically forbade the princes from selling or exchanging their ancient family lands. Escheated estates (i.e. those whose owners had died intestate without heirs) had to be assigned to the Treasury. Only the closest heirs (sons) had an unconditional right to inherit family estates. The brothers or nephews of a deceased prince, by contrast, could inherit his lands only with the tsar's permission. The inheritance of family estates by widows and daughters was significantly restricted.

The coming to power of the Zakhar'ins, the *de facto* removal from power of the highest ranking princely aristocracy, and the anti-princely land legislation all contributed to the growth of opposition to the tsar amongst the boyars. In response the government began to resort more and more frequently to political repression.

In the summer of 1561 the tsar had some kind of confrontation with his kinsman Prince Vasilii Mikhailovich Glinskii. It is possible that the boyar was suspected of planning to flee to Lithuania. In fact the conflict was soon resolved as a result of the intercession of Metropolitan Makarii. An undertaking was obtained from the prince that he would not commit further treason against his sovereign and would not depart for Lithuania. In January 1562 another kinsman of the tsar's, the eminent boyar Prince Ivan Dmitrievich Bel'skii, was arrested on a charge of treason on behalf of the Lithuanian state. When he was arrested he was found to have a letter from the king guaranteeing him safe passage to Lithuania. In spite of the fact that Bel'skii had not merely come under suspicion of treason but was caught red-handed, he managed to avoid the death penalty which was prescribed in such cases. As a result of the metropolitan's entreaties, he was freed from custody. Two 'surety deeds' were obtained from him. The guarantors (half-a-dozen boyars and more than a hundred noblemen and officials) gave a pledge that if the prince fled abroad they would pay the Treasury 10,000 roubles – an enormous sum in those days. In addition, Bel'skii himself provided a sworn written undertaking that he would faithfully serve Tsar Ivan. The tsar decided against executing the eminent boyar, and was satisfied with the fact that he had bound him with a firm guarantee.

Also in 1562 another two prominent princes fell into disgrace – Mikhail and Aleksandr Ivanovich Vorotynskii. The sources do not provide any clear indication of the reasons for their disgrace. Russian diplomats abroad explained that 'Prince Mikhail had insulted the sovereign'. It is possible that the authorities suspected the brothers of planning to go over to the king's service, transferring their appanage lands, which lay on the border between Russia and Lithuania. The Vorotynskiis had good reason for dissatisfaction with the policies of Tsar Ivan's government. The law on princely estates was approved in 1562, not long before they fell into disgrace. The provisions of this law deprived them of the right to obtain their brother Vladimir's share of the family appanage lands after his death (according to the law, the escheated portion of the appanage had to revert to the Treasury). Prince Mikhail Vorotynskii and his family were imprisoned in Beloozero, where he spent three and a half years in exile. Prince Aleksandr suffered less. He and his family were exiled to Galich, but were freed in six months after providing guarantees to the boyars and nobility.

After the dismissal of Adashev and Sil'vestr a 'great persecution' of their supporters and kinsmen began. In the autumn of 1562 one of the most outstanding statesmen of the mid-sixteenth century, the boyar Prince Dmitrii Ivanovich Kurlyatev, fell into disgrace. He had been close to Adashev and Sil'vestr. The official chronicle notes vaguely that the boyar had paid the price for 'treasonous acts'. Some additional details about the reasons for Kurlyatev's disgrace are provided by the inventory of the tsar's archive. This mentions a letter from Kurlyatev, addressed to the tsar, in which the prince pleaded in his defence that he 'had taken the wrong road'.[18] In order to understand the meaning of this document it should be noted that until July 1561 Kurlyatev had served as governor of Smolensk, a city on the Lithuanian border. Evidently while stationed there the prince had tried to cross the border, but had been detained and had claimed he had lost his way. The fact that he had been accompanied by his servants aroused the government's suspicion and was used as evidence against him. The episode provided the authorities with a convenient excuse to deal with a troublesome boyar. Kurlyatev was forced to become a monk and was confined in a remote monastery in the Kargopol' district, where, if Kurbskii is to be believed, he was subsequently strangled. His wife and children were tonsured at the same time as he was. Such persecution not only of an accused person, but also of members of his family, was a violation of traditional judicial procedures.

Kinsmen, friends and neighbours of Adashev and Sil'vestr were subjected to repression. It seems that the pretext for the persecution was the alleged treason of the governors of Starodub. In 1563 the tsar received a message from the governor of Smolensk, the boyar M. Ya. Morozov, relaying the claims of a captured Lithuanian, to the effect that the governors of Starodub supposedly 'wanted to surrender the town' to the Lithuanian army. The officials were arrested, and the assistant governor, Ivan Fedorovich Shishkin-Ol'gov, a kinsman of Adashev-Ol'gov, suffered a particularly harsh fate. According to Kurbskii, he was executed along with his wife and children. At about this time others who suffered disgrace and execution included Aleksei Adashev's brother, the *okol'nichii* Daniil Fedorovich Adashev, and his son; Daniil Adashev's father-in-law, Petr Ivanovich Turov; and Aleksei and Andrei Postnikov Satin, whose sister was married to Aleksei Adashev.

One of the most important political trials of the first half of the 1560s was the 'treason trial' of the Staritskiis. In the context of the worsening internal political conflict, the tsar was seriously afraid of the possibility that the opposition forces might unite around Vladimir, the appanage prince. The excuse to attack the Staritskiis was provided by Savluk Ivanov, the secretary of the Staritsa appanage, who denounced his master. Ivanov had been imprisoned by Prince Vladimir for some minor offences. From prison he managed to send the tsar a message in which he told him that Vladimir and his mother, Princess Evfrosin'ya Staritskaya, were conspiring against him. The government took the denunciation seriously. In the course of the investigation Ivan IV requested from the archive details of a case that had occurred ten years before – that of the treason of Prince Semen Rostovskii. As we have seen, this included important information about the contacts between the Staritskiis and the boyars at the time of the tsar's illness in 1553. Among the boyars most heavily compromised in the Rostovskii case were the relatives of Princess Evfrosin'ya, the Kurakin and Shchenyatev boyars.

In the summer of 1563 the tsar summoned Metropolitan Makarii and the entire Sacred (Church) Council for the trial of the Staritskiis. It seems that the boyars did not have the right to take part in a judicial examination which affected members of the tsar's family. According to the chronicle account, at the Council Tsar Ivan made accusations against Princess Evfrosin'ya and Vladimir Staritskii, but pardoned them as a result of pleas from the metropolitan and the Church authorities. After this Princess Evfrosin'ya allegedly begged the sovereign to allow her to take the veil. The tsar granted her request and she became a nun in the Voskresenskii Goritskii Monastery at Beloozero, which she had founded. It seems unlikely, however, that the energetic and strong-willed Evfrosin'ya took the veil voluntarily. It is more probable that she was forced. Significantly, the tsar ordered several noblemen to keep her under surveillance in the monastery. After a short period of disgrace Prince Vladimir was pardoned and allowed to return to his appanage estate. But to safeguard himself against any possible intrigues on the part of the Staritskii princes, Tsar Ivan carried out a complete reorganisation of the membership of the appanage court, taking Vladimir's boyars, noblemen and officials into his service, and appointing his own people to replace them. In addition, the tsar made Vladimir 'exchange' a number of his appanage possessions, taking away from him the town of Vyshgorod and its surrounding district, and several wealthy crown *volosti* in the Mozhaisk district, and giving him instead the town of Romanov on the Volga.

The trial of the Staritskiis and the government's anti-appanage measures helped to strengthen the tsar's autocratic power and to weaken the boyar opposition. But the government was unable to halt the development of a political crisis.

On 31 December 1563 Metropolitan Makarii died. Makarii had enjoyed great authority and influence both in government circles and amongst the opposition. Tsar Ivan himself took his views into account. Makarii was an advocate of strong autocratic power. At the same time he tried by all possible means to bring about reconciliation in the tsar's disputes with his subjects, making use of his traditional right to intercede with the tsar on behalf of disgraced courtiers. It was as a result of his intervention that the princes Semen Rostovskii and Ivan Bel'skii had managed to avoid the death penalty. The tsar took heed of the views of the metropolitan and the Church hierarchy, and his conflict with the Staritskiis was resolved relatively peacefully, without bloodshed.

In February 1564 a new metropolitan was appointed. Afanasii was an elder from the Chudov Monastery, and before becoming a monk he had been an archpriest in the Blagoveshchenskii Cathedral and the tsar's confessor. But the new metropolitan did not enjoy the influence and authority of his predecessor and was unable to halt the development of political confrontation within the country.

Within the tsar's entourage men who advocated more severe repression of the opposition were becoming increasingly influential. The leader of this group was Aleksei Danilovich Basmanov-Pleshcheev. In time these new royal favourites would succeed in driving the Zakhar'in boyars from power.

The defeat of Russian troops by the Lithuanians on the River Ula in January 1564 contributed to the intensification of repression of the boyars. The tsar laid the blame for the defeat on his boyars and commanders. On 30 January Yurii Ivanovich Kashin and Mikhail Petrovich Repnin, two leading boyars from the princely clan of the Obolenskiis, were executed in Moscow. According to Kurbskii's 'History', Ivan invited Prince Repnin to a drunken feast and ordered him to join the tsar and his courtiers in wearing a comic mask and dancing with the *skomorokhi* (minstrels). When Repnin indignantly refused, he provoked the monarch's wrath and disfavour, and a few days later Ivan ordered his soldiers to kill the prince as he stood at the altar during a church service. Kurbskii's account appears to be apocryphal, but it does reflect the essence of the relationship between the tsar and his subjects at that time – any defiance of the will of the autocratic ruler had come to be regarded as a criminal act, deserving of punishment.

Another member of the princely clan of the Obolenskiis, Dmitrii Fedorovich Ovchinin Obolenskii, paid with his life for insulting the honour of the tsar and his favourite, Aleksei Basmanov's son, Fedor (he allegedly accused them of having a homosexual relationship). A little later, in the autumn of 1564, Prince Petr Ivanovich Gorenskii-Obolenskii tried to flee to Lithuania, but he was seized on the border, sent to Moscow under guard and executed. The reason why this close associate of the tsar came to betray his sovereign was probably his disagreement with the repressive policy being pursued by the government, from which his kinsmen, the Obolenskii princes, had suffered. It is revealing that alongside Petr Gorenskii his close relatives Princes Nikita and Andrei Chernyi-Obolenskii were also executed. The repressions of 1564 affected not only members of the Obolenskii clan – amongst those executed at this time was an eminent prince from the Starodubskii clan, the boyar Dmitrii Ivanovich Khilkov.

At the end of April 1564, evidently fearing that he would fall into disfavour with the tsar, Kurbskii fled to Lithuania. Kurbskii was an outstanding general who had been close to Tsar Ivan; in 1563 he had been given the post of governor of Yur'ev-Livonskii, with responsibility for the administration of Russian territory in Livonia. From beyond the frontier he sent Ivan a letter in which he angrily condemned the tsar for shedding 'innocent Christian blood' and threatened him with the Last Judgment. The tsar sent a lengthy reply. The correspondence between them was to continue for some time. Now that its authenticity is again generally accepted, after Edward Keenan's scepticism, it remains a major source of Russian social and political thought in the 1560s and 1570s. The positions of the two protagonists are clearly stated at the very beginning of the correspondence. Tsar Ivan set out his basic ideas about power in his first letter to Kurbskii. All of Ivan's subsequent writings basically only repeated and developed the ideas expressed in this letter, which was sent to Kurbskii in the summer of 1564. Thus the ideology which guided Ivan in the second half of his reign had been formulated even before the introduction of the *oprichnina*. Ivan's first letter to Kurbskii was a true manifesto of autocracy in Russia. Ivan persistently advanced the idea of the divine origin of the tsar's power, which could not be limited by any earthly institutions. He provided a justification for his inherent right to rule the country autocratically, and to 'reward and punish' his 'slaves' (subjects) according to his own discretion. The tsar did not in any way attempt to justify his actions to his 'slave' Kurbskii but, on the contrary, he endeavoured to demonstrate in every way that the prince's actions were treasonous. In Ivan's eyes Kurbskii's defection from a tsar whose power was granted by God was not only an act of personal betrayal but also treason to the cause of Orthodoxy. In his letter, however, Ivan went far beyond a personal polemic with Kurbskii. The main issue which preoccupied the tsar was the relationship of the ruler with his subjects, and in the first instance with the aristocrats who were closest to him. Ivan asserted that Russian autocrats, unlike other European monarchs, had from the outset ruled their state themselves, without their boyars and magnates. Ivan also appealed to ancient history, seeking examples there of how the overweening power of the magnates had led to the fall of entire empires. But Tsar Ivan was not simply writing an abstract political tract. He was primarily concerned with the events of the recent past. The tsar could not forgive the boyars for their 'many treasons' and especially for their behaviour during his illness in 1553. Ivan wrote with particular indignation about his former counsellors Adashev and Sil'vestr, who had in effect deprived him of power in the interests of a boyar oligarchy. His hatred for his former advisers was so great that in his letter, in complete disregard for the truth, he turned them into the chief organisers of a boyar conspiracy whose main aim was to kill his infant heir and transfer the throne to Prince Vladimir Staritskii. The notion of large-scale boyar treason was one of the main leitmotifs of that first letter to Kurbskii. The natural conclusion Ivan drew from these reflections was that it was necessary to put a firm stop to boyar self-will and to reaffirm autocratic monarchical rule. This could be achieved in the current circumstances only by intensifying repression.

In the 1560s defections to Lithuania took place on a much greater scale than before. The flight of Kurbskii was perhaps the most striking political event of the pre-*oprichnina* period. But having said this, we should not lose sight of the fact that Kurbskii's 'treason' was only one link in a long chain of defections abroad by Muscovite servicemen.

The scanty and intermittent data in the sources do not permit us to trace the full pattern of Russians fleeing abroad in the 1560s, nor to establish the exact chronology and sequence. The sources provide the fullest information about escapes to Lithuania by eminent boyars and generals, but it should be noted that it was not only boyars and princes who fled abroad, but also many ordinary members of the service class (nobles and officials). Moreover, men from the lower ranks of the sovereign's court, together with provincial nobles, comprised the overwhelming majority of those who attempted to go abroad in order to escape the tsar's wrath, and they played a prominent part in the Russian political emigration in Lithuania.

A leading Russian fugitive was Timofei Ivanovich Pukhov Teterin, from the Mozhaisk nobility, whose father and grandfather had served as state secretaries. Timofei had reached the rank of captain of harquebusiers, serving with distinction on the front lines during the Livonian War, but at the beginning of the 1560s he fell into disgrace for some offence. He was forced to become a monk and was exiled to the remote Antoniev-Siiskii Monastery. Around 1563 he managed to escape to Lithuania, where he engaged in lively anti-Muscovy activity. From Lithuania he sent letters to the Russian boyars, in which he sarcastically mocked Muscovite customs and called on them to defect. Subsequently he was to play an active part in Lithuanian military operations against Russian troops. His treason prompted widespread persecution of his relatives. It appears that several were executed soon after Timofei's defection, and others later, during the *oprichnina*. In the memorial lists of Ivan's victims we encounter the names of 17 members of the Teterin clan who were executed before and during the *oprichnina*. Timofei's case also involved some of his associates, including Andrei Kashkarov.

This evidence is inconsistent with the traditional view that the repressions of the 1560s were directed exclusively against the boyar aristocracy.

At that time, opposition sentiments were widespread amongst the service class. A serviceman's defection to Lithuania led to the persecution of his relatives and acquaintances, and this in its turn led to further defections. Evidence of the scale of flights abroad by servicemen is provided by the significant increase in the number of so-called 'deeds of surety' in the 1560s. The imposition of surety deeds was used by the authorities as an important way to tackle the escape of servicemen across the border. An individual who was convicted or suspected of defection might be pardoned for his offence by the sovereign. But in order to avoid a repetition of his crime, the fugitive was obliged to swear an oath and to make guarantee payments, for which special types of document were drawn up – deeds of surety, which were ratified by the signatures of the guarantors. Before the middle of the sixteenth century there were few such deeds of surety, but their numbers increased noticeably during Ivan's reign. About ten deeds of surety have survived from the first half of the 1560s, but in practice, judging by the evidence of the inventory of the tsar's archive, considerably more were issued. The nature and format of the deeds also changed – in particular, the number of guarantors increased significantly. Thus in the ten extant deeds alone the names of more than 1,000 guarantors are mentioned. The majority of these were members of the nobility, primarily the élite, connected with the sovereign's court. By compiling these deeds of surety the tsar hoped to bind the servicemen on the basis of collective responsibility. But in the context of the sharp intensification of conflict between the tsar and his subjects this practice provoked unforeseen consequences which were undesirable from Ivan's point of view – in practice they served to unite the forces which opposed him.[19] The profound conflict between Ivan and his entourage threatened to have grave consequences. Having lost the support of a significant part of the ruling group, Tsar Ivan was unable to govern the country by the customary methods, on the basis of established legal norms. He found a way out of the political crisis by introducing the *oprichnina*.

Notes

1 *PSRL*, vol.13, pp.522–6.

2 *PSRL*, vol.13, p.524.

3 V.D. Nazarov, 'Iz istorii tsentral'nykh gosudarstvennykh uchrezhdenii v Rossii serediny XVI veka (k metodike izucheniya voprosa)', *Istoriya SSSR*, 1976, no.3, pp.82–3, 86–7; Skrynnikov, *Tsarstvo terrora*, p.117.

4 *Akty, sobrannye v bibliotekakh i arkhivakh Rossiiskoi imperii Arkheograficheskoyu ekspeditsieyu imperatorskoi Akademii nauk*, vol.2, St Petersburg, 1836, p.41; *Sobranie*

gosudarstvennykh gramot i dogovorov, khranyashchikhsya v Gosudarstvennoi kollegii inostrannykh del, vol.2, Moscow, 1819, p.192.

5 Kurbsky's History, pp.82–3.

6 Poslaniya Ivana Groznogo, ed. D.S. Likhachev and Ya.S. Lur'e, Moscow and Leningrad, 1951; Correspondence.

7 Hakluyt, Voyages, vol.1, pp.280 (Chancellor), 424–7 (Jenkinson).

8 Kollmann, 'Pilgrimage, Procession and Symbolic Space'.

9 Uspenskii, Tsar' i patriarkh, pp.14–21, 109–13.

10 I.P. Shaskol'skii, 'Russko-livonskie peregovory 1554 g. i vopros o livonskoi dani', Mezhdunarodnye svyazi Rossii do XVII v., Moscow, 1961, pp.376–99.

11 B.N. Florya, 'Proekt antituretskoi koalitsii serediny XVI v.', Rossiya, Pol'sha i Prichernomor'e v XV-XVIII vv., Moscow, 1979; I. Gralya, Ivan Mikhailov Viskovatyi: Kar'era gosudarstvennogo deyatelya v Rossii XVI v., Moscow, 1994, pp.232–3.

12 PSRL, vol.34, p.181.

13 Rude and Barbarous, p.264.

14 Rozov, 'Biblioteka Sil'vestra', p.206; I.V. Kurukin, 'Novye svedeniya monastyrskikh arkhivov o Sil'vestre', Voprosy istochnikovedeniya i istoriografii istorii dosovetskogo perioda, Moscow, 1979, p.67; Grobovskii, Ivan Groznyi i Sil'vestr, pp.135–6.

15 See Nancy Shields Kollmann, By Honor Bound: State and Society in Early Modern Russia, Ithaca: Cornell University Press, 1999, pp.194–6.

16 Skrynnikov, Tsarstvo terrora, pp.142–4.

17 Zak. akty, pp.32–3, 55–6.

18 Opisi Tsarskogo arkhiva XVI veka i arkhiva posol'skogo prikaza 1614 goda, Moscow, 1960, p.36.

19 Veselovskii, Issledovaniya, p.124.

Chapter 6

The Introduction of the *Oprichnina*

The tsar's departure from Moscow

The train of events which led to the establishment of the *oprichnina* regime is described quite fully and thoroughly in the official Russian chronicle, and also in the accounts of foreign contemporaries such as the Livonian noblemen Johann Taube and Elert Kruse.[1] On 3 December 1564 Tsar Ivan and his entire family left Moscow to go on pilgrimage. Such departures were frequent and familiar occurrences. But on this occasion the tsar's preparations for the journey were very unusual. He took all his treasury with him, and his armed retinue was exceptionally large. In addition, the tsar ordered the boyars and nobles who accompanied him 'to travel with their wives and children'. Usually when Muscovite rulers departed from the capital for even a short time, they appointed a special boyar commission to administer affairs in Moscow. This time the tsar left Moscow without nominating anyone to replace him. Only those he trusted most were informed of his plans. All of this could not fail to arouse feelings of alarm and foreboding in the Muscovites.

The tsar's 'journey' lasted for almost a month, until he arrived at the well fortified settlement of Aleksandrova Sloboda, situated about 100 kilometres north-east of the capital. This was an estate which belonged to the crown, and Ivan had been there more than once for 'entertainment' (hunting). But this time the tsar had decided to base himself there for more serious purposes.

It was on 3 January that Moscow received news from its ruler. The tsar's messenger K.D. Polivanov brought two letters to the capital. In the first, addressed to the ruling élite, Ivan accused the boyars, nobles and officials of 'treasonous deeds': for example, of evading military service and embezzling money from the treasury. He condemned the magnates not only for damaging the interests of the state, but also for abusing his ordinary subjects, especially during the years of his minority. The tsar also expressed his anger against the clergy, who had allegedly 'covered up' the improper actions of the servicemen. In the conclusion to this message he announced that he was abdicating, because he no longer wanted to 'endure many treasons'. In the second letter, addressed to the ordinary inhabitants of the capital ('to all the Orthodox Christians of the city of Moscow'), Ivan declared that 'he had no anger against them [the citizens]'. When the tsar's letters were read out to the population, they provoked widespread unrest in Moscow. The ordinary people – the artisans and merchants – declared their willingness to avenge themselves on the 'traitors' and tearfully begged the tsar to 'show them his mercy, not to leave the tsardom and abandon them to be ravened by the wolves [i.e. the boyars and other officials]'. It should be noted that in the view of the Russian people of that period there was probably no more terrible prospect than that of being left without a ruler: the country was threatened with the danger of being plunged into anarchy and turmoil, and of falling victim to foreign conquest (remember that Russia was then at war with her western neighbours in the struggle for the Baltic). Tsar Ivan, however, had no intention of renouncing power. His appeal to the people over the heads of the boyars and officials was a shrewdly calculated political manoeuvre; with his condemnation of the magnates as exploiters of his ordinary subjects, the tsar clearly aimed to secure the support of the great majority of the population of the capital. This ploy produced immediate results. Faced with the threat of widespread protest by the citizens, the magnates were obliged to capitulate. They asked the head of the Church, Metropolitan Afanasii, to beseech the tsar to remain on the Muscovite throne.

A delegation of boyars and members of the clergy set off for the Sloboda to declare their obedience and to beg the tsar to return to the capital. The delegates found the Sloboda to be a well fortified military camp with a large contingent of heavily armed troops. The new arrivals were brought before the tsar under guard, like real enemies of the state. Having obtained the support of the ordinary people and surrounded himself with a strong armed guard, Tsar Ivan was completely in control of the situation. In his negotiations with the representatives of the clergy and the boyars he acted in an openly triumphal manner. He repeated his accusations against the powerful élites, and then 'graciously' agreed to remain on the throne, but on an important condition: that he might at his own discretion prosecute and punish 'traitors' (in effect, all troublesome individuals), and confiscate their property. In practice this meant that the tsar acquired complete freedom of action in investigating his political opponents. From then onwards the clergy were in effect deprived of their traditional right to intercede for those who were in disgrace, and the practice of passing judgment on accused persons *in absentia* was legitimised, as were all other extra-judicial forms of punishment of suspected traitors, along with members of their families. In order to guarantee these extraordinary powers in the country, the tsar announced his decision to establish a special political regime – the *oprichnina*.

Thus, in spite of the dramatic form which it assumed, Ivan's departure from Moscow for Aleksandrova Sloboda was not mere play-acting, as some historians have suggested, but a well thought-out political act, meticulously planned. The decision to take such an important step, which represented a major departure from the entire traditional system of relationships between the ruler and his subjects, caused Ivan great physical and emotional stress. According to Taube and Kruse, when the tsar returned to Moscow from his six-week 'journey', he was unrecognisable: 'he had lost all the hair from his head and his beard'.

The decree on the *oprichnina*

In February 1565, when Ivan returned to the capital, the decree on the *oprichnina* was made public. The original text has not been preserved, but its content is fully conveyed in the chronicle.[2] According to the decree, the country was to be divided into two parts: the *oprichnina*, a peculiar kind of royal 'appanage', where the tsar was the full proprietor and powerholder; and the *zemshchina*, the rest of the country, which was transferred to the administration of the *zemshchina* boyar duma.

The word '*oprichnina*' is derived from the root '*oprich*' (apart). The term *oprichnina* was not, however, a new one: in the appanage period it had indicated the special land allocation (the 'dower') of widowed princesses. Indeed, superficially the *oprichnina* of Ivan Groznyi resembled the former appanages in many ways. Significantly, it is sometimes referred to in the sources as 'the sovereign's appanage'. In reality, however, it had many unique features. In terms of the size of its territory alone, Ivan's *oprichnina* was strikingly different from the former appanages, and especially from the widows' dowers. The *oprichnina* was large, and included the richest lands, and those with important strategic significance.

In order to provide for the economic needs of the *oprichnina*, its territory included wealthy towns and districts – Dvina, Kargopol', Velikii Ustyug, Vologda, Beloozero, Galich, Staraya Russa, and a number of crown *volosti* around Moscow and in other districts (see Map 6.1). The *oprichnina* included all the most important regions for salt extraction (such as Staraya

Map 6.1 The territory of the *oprichnina*

Russa and Soligalich) which in practice meant that it had a monopoly of trade in this important commodity.

The *oprichnina* decree envisaged the allocation of special territories on which the landholdings (both *pomest'ya* and *votchiny*) of the tsar's *oprichnina* servitors (the *oprichniki*) would be situated. These were mostly districts which occupied an important strategic position on the western and south-western approaches to the capital, close to the frontier (such as Mozhaisk, Vyaz'ma, Kozel'sk, Maloyaroslavets and Medyn'). In these districts the service form of landholding predominated, and the service landholders (*pomeshchiki*) were men who had recently been resettled there from various parts of the country. Not having strong traditional corporate links, the noble landholders of these districts were heavily dependent on the power of the state, and it is significant that Ivan IV's government directed its attention to such men in the first instance when forming the corps of *oprichniki*. In the central regions of the country, where hereditary landownership was long established, the original territory of the *oprichnina* included only Suzdal' district, the hereditary base of the Shuiskii princes and other descendants of the princely house of Suzdal'-Nizhnii Novgorod. The 'sovereign's appanage' also included Belev, Likhvin and part of Peremyshl' district, which had previously formed part of the appanage possessions of the Vorotynskii and Odoevskii princes, and had been confiscated from them not long before the introduction of the *oprichnina*. (The policy of the *oprichnina* in relation to princely landholding will be discussed in more detail on p.144.)

The *oprichnina* also included part of the territory of Moscow itself (the districts of the Arbat, Znamenki, Vozdvizhenki, and Chertopol'skaya Street). Only *oprichniki* were permitted to live there, and the *zemshchina* nobles were evicted from their homes. In addition, three *strel'tsy* districts in the Vorontsovo Pole area were incorporated into the *oprichnina* territory in Moscow, and the *strel'tsy* quartered there were recruited into the tsar's personal bodyguard. The centre – or capital – of the *oprichnina* was Aleksandrova Sloboda, which was transformed into a mighty fortress.

The rest of the country, the *zemshchina*, was placed under the jurisdiction of its own boyar duma. According to the decree, the *zemshchina* boyars and other officials (the heads of the central administrative institutions, the chancelleries) were to fulfil the functions of governance, the administration of justice and military command on the core territory of the Muscovite state 'in the old way' (that is, as before). However, the freedom of the *zemshchina* boyars in administrative matters was limited. The decree required the boyars to report on all important matters, both military and civil, directly to the tsar. Thus the main reins of governance of the country as a whole, and not just of the *oprichnina*, remained in Ivan's hands.

From the very outset, the *zemshchina* was in an inferior position by comparison with the *oprichnina*. The tsar's *oprichniki* servitors could enter the territory of the *zemshchina* unopposed, on the pretext of tackling sedition. The tsar could at his discretion take into the *oprichnina* towns and districts other than those identified in the decree of 1565. Indeed, the territory of the *oprichnina* was subsequently significantly extended by the incorporation of other regions – Kostroma, Yaroslavl', Rostov and other districts, and the Bezhetsk and Obonezhsk *pyatiny* of Novgorod district. In order to finance the *oprichnina* (for instance, the tsar's court, and the equipment of the corps of *oprichniki*), the tsar imposed on the *zemshchina* a tax of 100,000 roubles, an enormous sum for those days. In addition, lands and property confiscated from 'traitors to the sovereign' who had been executed or disgraced were to be transferred to the coffers of the *oprichnina*.

In order to protect the life of the sovereign and to combat treason, Ivan created a special corps of *oprichniki*, who constituted the tsar's personal bodyguard. At first, according to the *oprichnina* decree, it was intended that the corps should contain a thousand noblemen, but as new territories were added to the *oprichnina* it constantly increased in size. Taube and Kruse provide a vivid account of the process of recruitment of men into the *oprichnina*. On his return to Moscow, Tsar Ivan ordered that all the nobles from Suzdal', Vyaz'ma, Mozhaisk and the other towns incorporated into the *oprichnina* should be summoned to the capital. A separate review was organised for the noblemen of each town, and selection took place in the presence of the tsar himself. Each noble was asked detailed questions about the origins of his clan, his wife's clan and his connections with other clans. Only men with no ties of kinship or friendship with the *zemshchina* nobles or with the princes and boyars opposed to the tsar could be recruited. Each *oprichnik* took a special oath that he would not have any contact with the *zemshchina*. According to Taube and Kruse, when swearing loyalty to their sovereign the *oprichniki* uttered the following words: 'I swear . . . not to eat and drink with the *zemskie* [the *zemshchina* men] and to have nothing to do with them.' Interesting details about the oath are provided in the memoirs of the German *oprichnik* Heinrich von Staden, who states that they swore not to speak to the *zemskie* – if their mother and father were in the *zemshchina*, they had to promise never to visit them.[3] The death penalty was imposed for breach of the oath. These foreign contemporaries might have exaggerated, but their accounts conveyed the essence of the phenomenon fairly accurately. The founders of the *oprichnina* aimed to emphasise in every way its 'separateness' from the *zemshchina*. Ivan Groznyi's ideological opponent, Kurbskii, missed no opportunity to engage in sarcastic wordplay with the term '*oprichnina*': he referred to the *oprichniki* as 'the men apart' (*kromeshniki*); and since the phrase '*t'ma kromeshnaya*' meant outer darkness, or hell, the *oprichniki* were the 'hellish host'. Under the tsar's decree, only those nobles admitted to the corps of *oprichniki* could remain in the districts which were part of the *oprichnina* territory. All other noblemen (the overwhelming majority) had to promptly leave their estates and move to the *zemshchina*, and their possessions were allocated to the *oprichniki*. These measures were intended to guarantee that the *oprichniki* served alone, separately from the *zemskie*. The *oprichniki* even had to look different to the *zemskie*; in particular, they had to wear black garments, on top of their ordinary clothing. Special 'distinguishing marks', a dog's head and a broom, were introduced for the *oprichniki*. Contemporary observers said the symbols meant that: 'they [the *oprichniki*] first bite like dogs, then sweep everything superfluous [that is, 'treason'] out of the country.'[4]

For a long time historians believed that those chosen as *oprichniki* were, as a rule, of lowly birth, and included even ordinary 'muzhiks' (peasants). To a certain extent this impression was created because of the statements of contemporary foreign observers who referred to the *oprichniki* as former slaves and 'beggarly clumsy muzhiks'. Detailed studies of the composition of the *oprichnina* court, carried out by V.B. Kobrin and other scholars, have, however, conclusively refuted this view.[5] In fact, the *oprichniki* frequently included members of very distinguished princely and boyar clans, such as the princes Odoevskii and Trubetskoi; and at a later stage the corps of *oprichniki* contained Shuiskii princes. It is true that, in general, members of the *oprichnina* court were of rather lower birth than those of the *zemshchina* court, and at the end of the *oprichnina* period men from lowborn provincial noble clans clearly made up most of its leadership. Nevertheless it seems that the main criterion for recruitment into the *oprichnina* was not so much the serviceman's social origin, but rather his personal qualities. The tsar willingly took into the *oprichnina* men with a 'tainted' past. For example, the corps of *oprichniki* later contained a whole group of nobles who had served the Staritskiis. It was thought that such men were likely to serve the tsar with particular devotion.

Members of the *oprichnina* were in a very privileged position compared with the *zemshchina* nobles. The imposition of an enormous tax on the *zemshchina* for the benefit of the *oprichnina* and the mass evictions of the *zemshchina* nobles from their lands enabled the *oprichnina* government to give the *oprichniki* more money and large service estates. In contrast to the *zemshchina* nobles, who were deprived of the right to have either service or hereditary estates in the *oprichnina* districts, the *oprichniki* lost only their service estates in *zemshchina* territory, while retaining their hereditary lands. Service in the *oprichnina* opened up for low-born nobles new opportunities for a successful career and to enhance the social standing of their clan. Sometimes *oprichniki* of humble birth, in defiance of the traditions of precedence, received higher service posts than more eminent *zemshchina* boyars and nobles. The latter, fearing the tsar's disfavour, did not dare openly defend the honour of their clan, and had to accept their loss of precedence.

Being completely dependent on state service, and obliged to the tsar for their career and material welfare, the *oprichniki* provided Ivan IV with a loyal and reliable base of support for implementing his political plans. Some historians have linked the creation of the *oprichnina* corps with the ideas of Ivan Peresvetov (the spokesman for the nobility mentioned earlier), and believe that he may have provided the ideological inspiration for the *oprichnina*. But in reality Peresvetov's call to the tsar to rule the country by relying on ordinary military servitors did not appeal to Ivan.[6] Unlike the monarchs of some other European countries, the tsar did not seek to rely on the nobility as a whole in his feud with the magnates. This was not just because the process of forming the nobility into a single estate was incomplete, in spite of the important steps taken in the reforms of the 1550s: Tsar Ivan did not want to strengthen the nobility (or any other estate for that matter), seeing this as threatening to limit his power.[7] The entire course of the *oprichnina* policy, and of its land policy in particular, led not to the strengthening but to the weakening of the nobility as a social estate. The significance of the introduction of the *oprichnina*, therefore, was not only the tsar's aspiration to free himself from the traditional tutelage of the boyars and the higher clergy. To an even greater extent, the *oprichnina* was directed against the estates as a whole. It represented an idiosyncratic reaction by the autocratic tsar against the development of estate-representative institutions, and was an attempt to halt any independent activity on the part of the estates and to push them in the direction of service to the state. In order to implement these aims the tsar chose to introduce a state of emergency and to divide the embryonic noble estate, one part of which was granted a special privileged status at the expense of the rights and privileges of the rest of the nobility.

With the introduction of the *oprichnina* the tsar was able to initiate treason trials at his own discretion, pass sentence himself and determine the level of punishment. Political cases, which had become one of the priorities of domestic policy, were removed from the traditional state institutions (the boyar duma and the chancelleries) and transferred to the jurisdiction of the tsar and his personal servitors, the *oprichniki*. In the words of the historian V.O. Klyuchevskii,

within the *oprichnina* there was established a higher police force to deal with cases of state treason; the corps of a thousand men appointed by the decree which introduced the institution became a corps of investigators of internal sedition and the guardians of the security of the tsar and the tsardom, while the tsar himself . . . became the supreme commander of this corps.[8]

Klyuchevskii drew attention to one of the most important functions of the *oprichnina* corps. It was from the ranks of the *oprichniki* that the tsar recruited the punitive apparatus for dealing with his political opponents. It was not just the duty but also the privilege of the *oprichniki* to take part in the investigation and prosecution of 'state criminals'. Imbued with extraordinary powers, the *oprichniki* frequently abused them; not only could they persecute 'enemies of the state' with impunity, but they could also settle scores with their enemies.

The role of the *oprichnina*, however, was not limited to that of a political police force. There was another, ideological side to it. In introducing the *oprichnina*, surrounding himself with devoted and loyal servitors, Ivan aimed to create a kind of ideal model of the social order, whose guiding principle was to be the complete subordination of his subjects to the power and will of the tsar. Ivan sincerely believed that only he, as an Orthodox sovereign placed on the throne by God Himself, had the right (by the grace of the Almighty) to guide the destiny of his realm. He regarded any insubordination to his royal will as a crime against God, deserving harsh punishment. For Ivan the ideal social order in many ways was that of a monastery, with all the inmates living according to the same rules, and subject to the will of a single leader. Ivan compared his power to that of a monastic Father-Superior (an abbot), who was not only the superintendant of his monks, but also their spiritual guide and their mentor both in worldly affairs and in matters of faith.

Of great interest in this regard are the accounts of Taube and Kruse, who describe the way in which life in the *oprichnina* resembled a monastic brotherhood. The head of this brotherhood – the abbot – was the tsar himself, its cellarer (the abbot's assistant) was Prince Afanasii Ivanovich Vyazemskii and the sacristan was the notorious Malyuta Skuratov. The members of the 'brotherhood' wore coarse monastic robes and carried long monastic staves. Early in the morning the tsar, holding a lantern, would climb the bell-tower, where he and the 'sacristan' would summon the 'brethren' to a church service. 'Brothers' who failed to attend prayers would have a penance imposed on them by the tsar-abbot. The service lasted from four till seven in the morning and then continued, after a short break, until ten. The tsar himself sang in the choir and prayed assiduously alongside his sons. From the church everyone went to the refectory. While the 'brothers' ate, the 'abbot' stood calmly beside them and read from edifying books. Food left over from the meal was distributed to beggars. After the evening meal, at nine, the tsar rested for a while, then at midnight he and the 'brothers' again went to the bell-tower and the church for the night-time service.

Of course, life in the *oprichnina* 'brotherhood' was not an exact replica of monastic life. The communal meals of the *oprichniki* were not distinguished by their asceticism: they were served with abundant food, a great quantity of mead, and rare imported wines. Under their coarse monastic habits the *oprichniki* wore expensive garments, lined with fur and embroidered with gold. Nor did they dispense with their weapons, the long knives which they were ready to wield on the tsar's command at any time and place. The establishment of the *oprichnina* monastery at Aleksandrova Sloboda cannot, however, be regarded as mere mockery by the tsar of the monastic way of life. There is considerable evidence that Ivan was deeply religious. He had a great love of church services and church singing, and was a devotee of monasteries. The manuscripts of liturgies and other religious books, copied out at Aleksandrova Sloboda on Ivan's orders and used by the 'tsar-abbot' and members of the *oprichnina* 'brotherhood' for church services and devotional reading, still survive to this day. But although Ivan may have been sincerely devoted to the monastic ideal, it was nonetheless regarded as blasphemous in medieval Russia for laymen to dress up as monks. The *oprichnina* 'brotherhood' resembled in some respects the parodies of church services and monastic practices which formed part of the comic culture of the age. It is not surprising, therefore, that the tsar's actions were condemned as sacrilegious by some Church leaders.[9]

In practice the tsar managed the affairs of the *oprichnina*, consulting only with a small group of his most trusted associates. The image of the *oprichniki* is usually identified with Malyuta Skuratov (Malyuta was a kind of nickname; his real name was Grigorii Luk'yanovich Skuratov-Bel'skii). Malyuta became a leader of the *oprichnina* at a comparatively late stage in its existence. In its first few years it was run by Aleksei Danilovich Basmanov-Pleshcheev and his son Fedor, their kinsman Zakharii Ivanovich Ochin-Pleshcheev, A.I. Vyazemskii (a fairly minor prince), and a few others. Officially the *oprichnina* duma was headed by the Kabardinian Prince Mikhail Temryukovich Cherkasskii, the brother of Ivan's second wife Mariya Temryukovna. There were rumours in Moscow, according to one foreign observer, that it was Mariya who had advised the tsar to set up the *oprichnina* bodyguard. (On the basis of this somewhat tenuous evidence, the Harvard scholar Donald Ostrowski has made the implausible suggestion that the institution of the *oprichnina* represented Ivan's invocation of a 'Tatar' principle in government: the creation of a 'steppe khanate within Muscovy in which the Church had no political power'.)[10] According to another source, a seventeenth-century chronicle, the *oprichnina* was established 'on the advice of evil men:

Vasilii Mikhailovich Yur'ev and Aleksei Basmanov'.[11] It is hard to verify such pieces of evidence, which in any case contradict one another. Nevertheless, some details and coincidences are worthy of note. Cherkasskii was in fact Yur'ev's son-in-law. The two boyars were close relatives of Ivan's first and second wives. The Basmanovs were kinsmen of the Zakhar'in-Yur'evs, as was the important *oprichnina* boyar Prince Vasilii Andreevich Sitskii. It should be remembered that the hostility of the Zakhar'ins towards Adashev and Sil'vestr played a significant part in the fall of the government of the 'Chosen Council' and the move towards a more repressive policy; and a group of relatives of Ivan's first two wives initially headed the *oprichnina*. But not everything here is entirely clear. It is strange that Vasilii Yur'ev, who supposedly gave the 'evil advice' to the tsar, is not listed among the *oprichniki* (and probably never served in the *oprichnina* at all), although his son Protasii was registered there. The tsar's close kinsman Nikita Romanovich Yur'ev, Tsaritsa Anastasiya's brother, remained in the *zemshchina*. This may be because the Zakhar'ins were closely linked by kinship ties with some of the 'suspect' *zemshchina* leaders. Nikita Yur'ev was married to the daughter of the boyar Prince Aleksandr Borisovich Gorbatyi-Suzdal'skii, who was one of the first to be disgraced when the *oprichnina* was set up. Vasilii Yur'ev was married to Anastasiya Dmitrievna Bel'skaya, the sister of Prince Ivan Dmitrievich Bel'skii, the leading boyar in the *zemshchina*. We cannot say exactly what role the Zakhar'in-Yur'evs played in the introduction of the *oprichnina*, whether Tsar Ivan involved them in his plans, or whether they gave him specific advice. But it is clear that this clan had considerable influence over the general course of events of the 1560s.

The *oprichniki* corps was not a homogeneous mass of servitors. It had its own élite, comprising the *oprichnina* duma and court. The structure of the court was similar to that of the pre-*oprichnina* court and the *zemshchina* court. According to the chronicle version of the *oprichnina* decree, the tsar 'set apart for himself' (took into the *oprichnina* court) boyars, *okol'nichie*, a steward, treasurers, secretaries 'and all types of chancellery officials', nobles and gentlemen, *stol'niki*, *stryapchie* and *zhil'tsy*. Admittedly, separate lists of court ranks in the *oprichnina* (distinct from the *zemshchina*) appear in the sources (the registers which record the service appointments of the upper ranks of the nobility) only at a comparatively late date, from the end of the 1560s. It seems that a separate boyar duma for the *oprichnina* was not formed immediately. Before 1566 only Aleksei Basmanov is clearly defined in the sources as an *oprichnina* boyar, and only after a further eighteen months did another two *oprichniki*, Zakharii Ochin-Pleshcheev and F.I. Umnoi-Kolychev, become boyars. As

S.B. Veselovskii pointed out, these boyars from the *oprichnina* were at the same time members of the national (*zemshchina*) boyar duma.[12] Nor did the *oprichnina* at first have its own system of chancelleries like that of the *zemshchina*, apart from the chancelleries which administered the royal household. The most important ones, such as the Ambassadorial Chancellery, the Chancellery of Landed Estates and the Military Chancellery, remained in the *zemshchina*. According to the *oprichnina* decree, the tsar had 'ordered that his Muscovite realm, military affairs, justice, governance and other affairs of state should be administered by his boyars who were instructed to be in the *zemshchina*', and all officials

he ordered to be in their chancelleries and to administer in the old way . . . and if any military news arrives, or any particularly significant affairs of state arise, then the boyars must come to the tsar, and the tsar and the boyars will take decisions on these matters.[13]

Thus all basic functions of the administrative, judicial and military governance of the country were retained by the old agencies of state power, which remained in the *zemshchina*. With the introduction of the *oprichnina*, however, the tsar's control over these traditional institutions was considerably strengthened. Moreover, the important activity of political investigation was removed from their area of responsibility. From this we may conclude that the *oprichnina* (at first, at least) was not a separate state isolated from the *zemshchina* (a 'state within a state'), but rather a kind of superstructure on the existing system of government. The main purpose of this political superstructure was to exert pressure on the old institutions of power to act in the way the tsar required. According to research by V.A. Kolobkov, a separate system of chancelleries, a boyar duma and a sovereign's court did not appear in the *oprichnina* until the beginning of 1568 at the earliest, when an ever-deepening split in society, and the tsar's ultimate loss of faith in the *zemshchina*, occurred as a result of the growth of the *oprichnina* repressions.[14]

The *oprichnina* decree gave the tsar an unlimited right to 'eradicate treason' and execute 'traitors' throughout his realm. The *oprichnina* was set up to guarantee the autocratic power of the tsar and to suppress any signs of opposition.

'A strange institution': problems of interpretation

As an emergency measure designed to crush opposition to the tsar's power, the *oprichnina* was a particularly dramatic episode in the history of political investigation in Russia. In studying the repressions during the time of the *oprichnina* we encounter a number of major problems, the biggest of which is the scarcity of surviving sources. Most of the original material relating to the judicial investigations of the 1560s and 1570s has not survived; only a few documents have been preserved, and even then only parts of them. What partly compensates for the loss is the inventory of the sixteenth-century royal archive, which gives an indication of the range of political cases detailed in it and a brief summary of their contents.[15]

A major source for details about the *oprichniki*'s political investigations, and the chronological sequence of the repressive measures in the *oprichnina* period, is the so-called Memorial List (*Sinodik opal'nykh*), compiled in 1582–3 on Ivan's instructions so prayers could be said for the souls of those who had perished. Work by R.G. Skrynnikov, who has made a special study of the list and reconstructed its text, has shown that the document was based on the original *oprichnina* archives.[16] However, because it was intended for commemoration in church, the information in it is brief – sometimes it records only the Christian names of victims. Debates continue among historians about how fully the list has recorded the names of those executed in the *oprichnina* years and the number of victims.[17] While important details about the political repressions of the period are provided by Russian chronicles, polemical works (especially the writings of Kurbskii) and the accounts of foreign contemporaries, authors are seldom unbiased in the way they present events. Often they provide differing or contradictory versions. It is also worth noting that most contemporary writers did not witness many of the events at court, and often resorted to repeating all sorts of gossip and rumours. An element of subjectivity is to be found, however, not only in the narrative sources, but also in the documents of the political investigations themselves, since it is seldom possible to reach firm conclusions about the extent of the accused's guilt on the basis of the surviving judicial documentation. Testimony provided in the course of the investigations was generally extracted by torture. The value of evidence obtained in such a way is minimal. Often the judges suggested to the accused the names of those they should implicate. The transcript of one of these interrogations, conducted in the presence of the tsar, survives. Ivan angrily asked those being tortured: 'Which of our boyars is a traitor: Vasilii Umnoi, Prince Boris Tulupov, Mstislavskii, Prince Fedor Trubetskoi, Prince Ivan Shuiskii, the Pronskiis, the Khovanskiis, the Khvorostinins, Nikita Romanov, Prince Boris Serebryanyi?'[18]

Thus the surviving sources permit us to paint the history of the political repressions of the *oprichnina* period only in outline. Often we can merely speculate about the real reasons for the instigation of particular political proceedings. The information we do possess provides conclusive evidence that, in the years of the *oprichnina*, political repression occurred on an unprecedented scale. The Memorial List shows that more than 3000 people were executed by the *oprichniki* with the sanction of the tsar. The scale of the repressive measures stretched the imagination not only of contemporaries but also that of later historians. As V.O. Klyuchevskii wryly remarked: 'This institution [the *oprichnina*] has always seemed strange, both to those who suffered from it, and to those who have studied it.'[19]

Who were the main victims? Did the *oprichnina* pursue a single, consistent political line in identifying and eliminating individuals or social groups as 'enemies of the state'? Historians still cannot agree on these questions. For a long time Russian historiography upheld S.M. Solov'ev's view of the *oprichnina* as a conflict between 'statist' and 'anti-statist' ('clan') tendencies. The latter was supposedly embodied by the appanage princes and the powerful boyars, especially those of princely origin. This interpretation was heavily influenced by comparisons with the history of western European countries, where important and locally powerful feudal lords persistently opposed the centralising policies pursued by the royal authorities. The concept of the *oprichnina* as a conflict between the power of the state, based on the ordinary nobility, on the one hand, and the mighty princely boyar aristocracy on the other, was most clearly and consistently developed in the works of S.F. Platonov.[20] The most important result of the *oprichnina*, in Platonov's opinion, was the destruction of the princes' and boyars' hereditary landholdings, which had provided the Russian aristocracy's political power-base. A modified version of Platonov's concept subsequently appeared in Soviet historiography. In the writings of S.V. Bakhrushin, I.I. Smirnov and other historians of the 1930s–1950s, the *oprichnina* was presented as a 'progressive' phenomenon, insofar as it strengthened the centralised state, destroying the power of the big boyar aristocracy, and preventing a return to the system of 'feudal fragmentation'. More recently, R.G. Skrynnikov has developed a view of the *oprichnina* as a conflict between the autocracy and the mighty princely aristocracy, which is similar in many ways to Platonov's. However, Skrynnikov believes that the *oprichnina* was not a consistent phenomenon throughout its existence, and that it assumed a distinctively anti-princely character only in its early stages.[21]

According to the traditional interpretation, the motor of political conflict in Russia in the sixteenth and seventeenth centuries, including the period of the *oprichnina*, was a campaign by the autocracy, supported by the nobility, against the recalcitrant boyar aristocracy. In recent decades this concept has been subjected to serious criticism in the works of A.A. Zimin, N.E. Nosov, V.B. Kobrin and other historians.[22] In particular, they questioned the view that the boyars as a whole were a reactionary force, opposed in every way to the centralisation of the country, and that the ordinary nobility were the main political base of support of the Russian monarchy. They also re-examined the notion that the boyars, including the princely boyar élite, comprised a mighty landed aristocracy, economically and politically capable of resisting the centralisation of monarchical power.[23] Historians recognised that the process of disintegration of hereditary princely boyar landownership had begun long before the *oprichnina*. By the middle of the sixteenth century the majority of the descendants of the appanage princes of north-eastern and south-western Rus', with the exception of the princes Vorotynskii and Odoevskii, had lost their special princely rights to their lands, and their 'principalities' had turned into ordinary *votchiny*. A particular feature of hereditary landownership in Russia was the absence of the principle of primogeniture – a mechanism which could prevent the disintegration of family estates. *Votchiny*, as a rule, were shared equally among the landowner's sons, which led to their sub-division and fragmentation, and eventually to the decline of entire clans. In the most fortunate position were those boyars and princes who managed to have a successful career at court and were rewarded by the sovereign with new hereditary estates. For many princes and boyars the new hereditary lands which they had purchased or been awarded were much more extensive than their old family estates. By the beginning of the *oprichnina* several princes had completely lost their ties with their ancestral homelands, and were based in service tenure and hereditary estates located in different parts of the country. Some members of the élite did not have any hereditary estates at all and held their lands only on a service-tenure basis. The expansion of service landholding, and the adoption in 1556 of the 'Code on Service' which equalised service from *pomest'ya* and *votchiny*, contributed to the formation of a single service class, all of whose members were obliged to perform military service to the sovereign. The princely and boyar élite served at court, but this did not mean that they comprised a special group of independent landed magnates similar to the aristocracies of some European countries. Rather, they simply constituted a component part of the military-service class, its highest stratum. Being heavily dependent on state service, the boyars as a whole could not – and did not even attempt to – oppose the centralising policy of the monarchy. Had they done so, many boyars would have lost many, if not most, of their estates, which they had received in return for state service.

In contrast to the traditional concept of the anti-boyar orientation of the *oprichnina*, A.A. Zimin and other historians considered that it was directed not against the princely boyar élite but rather against such 'outposts' of feudal fragmentation as the remnants of the appanages and of the 'freedoms' of Novgorod, and also against the independence and economic might of the Church. These claims were rightly criticised by R.G. Skrynnikov and others.[24] Let us examine Zimin's 'outposts' one by one.

When we consider the appanage princes, it is clear that Ivan Groznyi could have punished the Staritskiis without resorting to the *oprichnina*. Back in 1537, after the revolt of Andrei Ivanovich Staritskii, Elena Glinskaya's government had abolished the Staritskiis' appanage principality. But subsequently the appanage was restored and returned to Andrei Ivanovich's son, Prince Vladimir. A favourable opportunity for eliminating the Staritskii appanage had come on the eve of the *oprichnina*, in 1563, when Ivan received a denunciation of Vladimir (see Chapter 5). Having placed Staritskii in disgrace and disbanded his appanage court, the tsar did not, however, consider it necessary to abolish the appanage itself, and he allowed Vladimir 'to possess his *votchina* as before'. The liquidation of the Staritskiis' appanage occurred, as we shall see, only in 1569, that is, in the final stage of the *oprichnina*, and it was provoked not so much by Ivan's desire to do away with appanages as such, but rather by the logic of a specific political conflict, that is, by the tsar's fears that Vladimir would be used by the opposition as a weapon against him. But even if the opposition really did make an attempt to place Vladimir on the throne instead of Ivan, it is unlikely that the plotters aimed to return to a system of independent principalities. It was simply a question of replacing one individual on the throne with another. Ivan was not an active opponent of the remnants of the appanage system; in fact, he was more of a conservative on this issue. This is indicated, in particular, by the evidence of his Testament, in which the tsar expressed his intention to bequeath appanages to his sons and other members of his family (some of these appanages were as large as entire states). It is significant that although he punished Vladimir and his family in 1569 and abolished the Staritskiis' appanage, Ivan restored it for a time in the early 1570s, when he returned Vladimir's *votchina* to his son, Prince Vasilii Staritskii.

As far as Novgorod is concerned, its former 'freedom' had already been firmly ended by Ivan Groznyi's grandfather, Ivan III, who had abolished the city's elected assembly, the *veche*. At the end of the fifteenth century the old Novgorod boyars had been evicted from their hereditary estates, and their extensive lands had been settled by *pomeshchiki* originating from the central regions of the country, whose loyalty to the government in Moscow was not in any doubt.

Finally, was the *oprichnina* directed against the independence of the Church? Although in the years of the *oprichnina* some fairly significant and dramatic conflicts occurred between the secular and spiritual authorities, these clashes did not take the form of a conflict between Church and state for power and political predominance. The 'insubordinate' Church leaders spoke out in the 1560s and 1570s not against the existing order, nor against the autocratic monarchy in general, but only against the methods which Ivan Groznyi had adopted in order to consolidate the autocracy, and against the atrocities of the *oprichnina*. At least until the time of Patriarch Nikon (in the 1650s–1660s) the Russian Church never claimed political pre-eminence and remained dependent on the Muscovite sovereigns.

Thus we cannot see either the princely boyar aristocracy, or the remnants of the appanages, or 'mutinous' Novgorod, or the Church, as mighty anti-centralising forces which Ivan IV inevitably had to fight in the interests of preserving the unity and integrity of the state. The *oprichnina* cannot be explained and justified on these grounds.

Nor can we agree, however, with the views of V.O. Klyuchevskii and S.B. Veselovskii,[25] who did not see any great purpose in the *oprichnina*, and considered that in the last resort it simply amounted to the extermination of troublesome individuals, and did not change the social and political structure of the country as a whole. Klyuchevskii thought it strange that Tsar Ivan, who fought against the pretensions of the boyar aristocracy and who was supposedly employing terror 'exclusively against the boyars', 'attacked not only the boyars, and not even primarily the boyars'. The historian's perplexity stemmed from his assumption that the boyars were a force hostile to centralised power, and that the *oprichnina* was a means of resolving the developing conflict between the tsar and the boyar aristocracy. But such assumptions, as we have noted, are by no means indisputable.

The essence of the *oprichnina* conflict lay not in a contest between 'centralising' and 'anti-centralising' forces, but in a disagreement between the tsar and his former associates concerning the way in which centralisation should be implemented. The nub of this quarrel may be found in the famous correspondence between Ivan and Kurbskii. Tsar Ivan insisted on the unquestioning subordination of all his subjects – from the most eminent boyar to the humblest peasant – to the will of the autocratic monarch. Kurbskii thought that the tsar ought not to rule the country autocratically, without the advice of 'men who are wise . . . and brave, skilled in the art of war and in the governance of the state'. The tsar regarded as enemies of the state and of the Orthodox cause all those who could actually or potentially limit the power which he had been given by God. He considered that the princely boyar élite posed a particular threat to the consolidation of autocracy. In spite of the fact that, as we have noted, the Russian aristocracy was a service class and the boyars were heavily dependent on the power of the monarch, the boyars – and especially those of princely origin – retained great influence. The most eminent of the princes continued to own large family estates which were the remnants of their formerly independent principalities. They preserved their traditional ties to the nobility in these districts and exercised real power in the localities. At court they comprised their own highly cohesive 'corporations' – the Suzdal' princes, the Rostov princes, the Yaroslavl' princes and the Obolensk princes among them. These corporations were formed on the basis not only of the princes' common ancestry, but also of their possession of hereditary estates within their former principalities. When the princes lost their hereditary estates, they also lost their corporate links with their kinsmen, and merged into the ordinary provincial nobility. Although their ownership of hereditary estates did not mean that the princes were independent landed magnates and opponents of centralisation, it did imbue them with corporate solidarity and political influence at national level. Their eminent origins and long-standing ties to the court gave them great advantages in climbing the service ladder and obtaining the highest state and court positions, including the top duma ranks. The well-born princes considered membership of the boyar duma and occupancy of the most elevated state and court ranks to be their legitimate right. Conscious of their high birth, the eminent princes laid claim to the role of the tsar's closest counsellors. Such aristocratic pretensions on the part of the princely boyar élite could not fail to come into conflict with the autocratic aspirations of the first Russian tsar. It is revealing that the first blows struck by the *oprichnina*, as we shall see, were directed mainly against members of the princely élite and against their hereditary estates.

In the last analysis, however, it was not only the eminent princes who became victims of the repressive policy of the *oprichnina*. Other groups who suffered just as much were the untitled Moscow boyars, the nobility and the chancellery officials, who had long been a source of support for the centralising policies of the Muscovite rulers. Members of other estates – the clergy, the merchant élite and the ordinary townspeople – were also subjected to harsh persecution and repression. One of the main aims of the *oprichnina* was to subordinate all the estates to the state, to halt any independent activity on their part, and to push the entire social system in the direction of state service. Such a policy, which signified a serious infringement of the rights and freedoms which the various social groups had obtained as a result of the reforms of the mid-sixteenth century, could be implemented only by means of repression and social division. All forms of active and passive opposition to the *oprichnina* were harshly suppressed. As the measures intensified, discontentment with the *oprichnina* grew, and this in turn gave rise to new waves of repression. As a result, the mechanism which Ivan Groznyi had set in motion acquired a momentum of its own and began to spin out of its creator's control. At the end of the *oprichnina* it was the *oprichniki* themselves who became the victims of the tsar's anger.

Notes

1 *PSRL*, vol.13, pp.391–5; 'Poslanie Ioganna Taube i Elerta Kruze', trans. M. Roginskii, *Russkii istoricheskii zhurnal*, vol.8, 1922, pp.31–5.

2 *PSRL*, vol.13, pp.394–5.

3 Heinrich von Staden, *The Land and Government of Muscovy: a Sixteenth-Century Account*, trans. and ed. Thomas Esper, Stanford, CA: Stanford University Press, 1967, p.30.

4 'Poslanie Ioganna Taube i Elerta Kruze', p.38.

5 V.B. Kobrin, 'Sostav oprichnogo dvora Ivana Groznogo', *Arkheograficheskii ezhegodnik za 1959 god*, Moscow, 1960, pp.16–91.

6 R.G. Skrynnikov, *Oprichnyi terror*, Leningrad, 1969, p.237.

7 See Florya, *Ivan Groznyi*, pp.185–6.

8 V.O. Klyuchevskii, *Boyarskaya duma v drevnei Rusi*, 5th edn, Petersburg, 1919, p.330.

9 See, for example: Panchenko and Uspenskii, 'Ivan Groznyi i Petr Velikii', pp.57, 58; Likhachev, Panchenko and Ponyrko, *Smekh v drevnei Rusi*, pp.48–9.

10 Ostrowski, *Muscovy and the Mongols*, pp.192–3.

11 *PSRL*, vol.34, p.190.

12 Veselovskii, *Issledovaniya*, p.141.

13 *PSRL*, vol.13, p.395.

14 V.A. Kolobkov, 'Reforma oprichniny', *Istorik vo vremeni. Tret'i Ziminskie chteniya. Doklady i soobshcheniya nauchnoi konferentsii*, Moscow, 2000, pp.155–6.

15 *Opisi tsarskogo arkhiva XVI veka; Gosudarstvennyi arkhiv Rossii XVI stoletiya: Opyt rekonstruktsii*, parts 1–3, Moscow, 1978.

16 Skrynnikov, *Tsarstvo terrora*, pp.10–11, 529–45.

17 See Kobrin, *Ivan Groznyi*, pp.81–3.

18 *ChOIDR*, 1912, vol.2, section 3, p.29.

19 Klyuchevskii, *Boyarskaya duma*, p.327.

20 Platonov, *Ocherki po istorii smuty*, pp.92–141.

21 Skrynnikov, *Tsarstvo terrora*.

22 A.A. Zimin, *Oprichnina Ivana Groznogo*, Moscow, 1964, pp.340–41; Nosov, *Stanovlenie soslovno-predstavitel'nykh uchrezhdenii*, pp.386–420; Kobrin, *Vlast' i sobstvennost'*, pp.48–89, 199–219.

23 Kobrin, *Vlast' i sobstvennost'*, pp.48–89; Pavlov, *Gosudarev dvor*, pp.149–217.

24 Zimin, *Oprichnina Ivana Groznogo*, pp.212–305; Skrynnikov, *Tsarstvo terrora*, pp.508–18.

25 V.O. Klyuchevskii, *Sochineniya*, vol.2, Moscow, 1957, pp.184–5; Veselovskii, *Issledovaniya*, p.28.

Chapter 7

Repression and Resettlement

The first victims

The first executions of the *oprichnina* period began soon after Tsar Ivan returned from Aleksandrova Sloboda to Moscow. According to the official chronicle, in February 1565

the tsar imposed the death penalty for high treason on the boyar Prince Aleksandr Borisovich Gorbatyi and his son Petr, the *okol'nichii* Petr Petrovich Golovin, Prince Ivan Ivanovich Sukhovo-Kashin and Prince Dmitrii Andreevich Shevyrev. And the tsar ordered that the boyars Prince Ivan Kurakin and Prince Dmitrii Nemoi should be tonsured as monks.[1]

All of these men were leading members of aristocratic, primarily princely, clans, and their punishment shocked the Muscovites. A particularly heavy blow was inflicted on the Suzdal' princes. The execution of Aleksandr Borisovich Gorbatyi, an outstanding general and one of the heroes of the conquest of Kazan', along with his 17-year-old son, led to the extinction of that branch of the Suzdal' princely clan. Kurbskii wrote indignantly that Tsar Ivan destroyed people 'in entire clans'. It is certainly true that in the *oprichnina* and post-*oprichnina* periods of Ivan Groznyi's rule many branches of princely clans became extinct.

The actions of the first months of the *oprichnina* were not limited to the punishment of boyars. After its account of the execution and tonsure of many princes and boyars, the chronicle describes how the tsar's disfavour fell on a large group of princes and nobles who were deprived of their property and exiled along with their families to live in distant Kazan'. The significance of this is not entirely clear from the chronicle account, but additional light is cast on it by documentary sources, and especially by the data of the land registers (cadastres) of the Kazan' district. R.G. Skrynnikov, who was the first historian to carry out detailed research on the Kazan' cadastres, unearthed the names of about 180 princes and nobles who were exiled to Kazan' in 1565.[2] Among the exiles were many supporters of the government of the 1550s (including kinsfolk of Aleksei Adashev), and also relatives and acquaintances of men who had fled to Lithuania in the early 1560s. But the most important finding was that the majority of the exiles to Kazan' (about two-thirds of them), as R.G. Skrynnikov convincingly demonstrated, were men with princely titles, belonging predominantly to the special corporations of the Rostov, Yaroslavl', Starodub and Obolensk princes. Thus the men who were disgraced and exiled to the east were members of those princely families that had retained their corporate clan solidarity and continued to own hereditary family estates within their former principalities right up until the introduction of the *oprichnina*. It is highly unlikely that these princes (more than 100 of them) were exiled for any specific offences. It is more likely that their exile to the remote Kazan' region was a preventative measure, designed to weaken one of the most influential groups of servicemen and to prevent the possible unification of the princely boyar opposition over intensified repression of the élite.

The exile of the princes to Kazan' was accompanied by the confiscation of their family estates. In their stead they received lands in the Kazan' region, but this was far from a fair exchange. In the first place, the princes received their new lands not as hereditary estates, but on the basis of service tenure; and in the second place, their land allocations in Kazan' were very small, and inadequate compensation for the loss of their former estates. The resettlement had not only an economic impact but also a major political one. Traditionally, service at court was the privilege of landowners in the central 'towns' of Russia (the so-called Moscow region); the nobles of the outlying districts – including Novgorod and Pskov, the Seversk lands (in the south-west), and the Volga – had much weaker links with the court. The relocation of the princes from the central districts to Kazan' meant that in practice they were excluded from court membership and barred from participation in court life. And although the most eminent and famous of the exiles received senior appointments as governors in Kazan', Sviyazhsk and other towns in the Kazan' region, the great majority of those sent there were deprived of access to the highest military and administrative positions and were obliged to serve in minor posts. This weakened their precedence status, and damaged the honour of their clans.

The Kazan' exile was an act of great social and political significance: by imposing it, Ivan's government was attempting to undermine the political and economic might of the princely aristocracy. And in general the policy achieved its aims. It is noteworthy that in the post-*oprichnina* period we no longer find princely corporations specially designated in the court registers; the princely élite had been fully merged with the other court ranks.

Attempts to reach a compromise

The first half of 1566, in the view of most historians, saw a degree of relaxation of the repressions. In the spring, as a result of pleas from the *zemshchina* boyars, Ivan pardoned Mikhail Ivanovich Vorotynskii, the eminent boyar and service prince who had fallen into disfavour before the introduction of the *oprichnina*. He was allowed to return from exile, a considerable part of the hereditary principality of the Vorotynskii princes – the towns of Odoev, Chern' and Vorotynsk – was restored to him, and in addition he was given a considerable sum of money from the royal treasury to revive his neglected estates. The town of Peremyshl', however, which had long formed part of the Vorotynskiis' appanage lands, remained in the tsar's hands. In order to guarantee the prince's loyalty, a deed of surety was imposed on him.

An even more eloquent piece of testimony to the change of climate was the return of the exiles who had been forcibly resettled in Kazan'. In April 1566 the tsar issued a decree which granted an amnesty to those in disgrace. The princes began to return to service in Moscow and to their former family estates. Not all the exiles were pardoned, however. Some of the princes and nobles remained in the Kazan' region: the tsar's decree indicated that they would be returned from exile at a later date. Nonetheless, the amnesty represented a significant concession to the *zemshchina* on the part of the *oprichnina* authorities. The sources do not enable us to explain what precisely led to this concession. It is clear that the expulsions to Kazan', which affected the interests of dozens of leading aristocrats, had aroused widespread discontent among the magnates. It seems that the tsar himself did not initially intend to break completely with the *zemshchina*, who still retained control over the main administrative apparatus of the state. Moreover, the policy of mass resettlement of the princes in the Kazan' region had achieved its main aim – the power of the princely aristocracy had been significantly undermined. And although the administrative documents show that members of many branches of the princely clans remained in full possession of their hereditary estates even after 1566, princely landownership was seriously weakened as a result of the exile to Kazan'. One symptom of this was the marked increase in the number of hereditary estates donated to monasteries in the *oprichnina* years. Impoverished and uncertain about the future, members of the aristocracy willingly handed their lands over to monasteries, in the hope of obtaining eternal commemoration for themselves and their families, and also a possible place of refuge in the future within the walls of the monastic cloisters.

At the beginning of 1566 the tsar carried out another forced 'exchange' of lands with his cousin, Prince Vladimir Staritskii. As a result of this, Vladimir lost the core territory of his father's old appanage (the tsar acquired Staritsa, Aleksin, Vereya and various other lands) and obtained new lands in return – Dmitrov, Zvenigorod, Borovsk, Starodub and others. The swap meant that the Staritskiis finally lost their traditional links with local landowners. The majority of the boyars and nobles on the Staritskiis' appanage entered the service of Moscow, and some were taken into the *oprichnina*. Staritsa itself, which occupied an important strategic location, became one of the tsar's residences (and subsequently his main residence). Another development is worth noting. Soon after the exchange the tsar 'bestowed his favour' on Vladimir. His old palace in the Kremlin, which had been confiscated at the beginning of the *oprichnina*, was returned to him, and the tsar also granted him the site of the former palace of the boyar Prince Mstislavskii. This 'favour' was not just a gesture of reconciliation. It was evidently advantageous for the tsar to keep the appanage prince in the capital in order to control him. The aim of all this was undoubtedly to weaken the prince's power and influence, as he was potentially a dangerous rival of the tsar and a possible focus for political forces opposed to the *oprichnina*. Nonetheless, the anti-appanage measures of 1566 were characterised by the fact that they were implemented without any serious excesses, and without bloodshed. Characteristically, the tsar presented his concessions to the *zemshchina* and his relaxation of repression as bestowing his 'favour', and as a display of his great mercy. Ivan always wanted the widest possible support for his policies, and took care to present what he did in the most positive light.

To a certain extent the tsar's attempts to reach an understanding with the *zemshchina* were inspired by foreign policy considerations. The Livonian War, which had been going on for a number of years, would clearly be protracted. The struggle for the Baltic between Russia and Lithuania produced mixed success (the Russian armies had captured Polotsk, but then suffered a major defeat on the River Ula). In the mid-1560s the Lithuanians were experiencing serious problems (among them, the start of a war with Sweden) and they sent a mission to Russia to negotiate peace terms. The Lithuanian envoys proposed that a truce be concluded based on the status quo, and put forward a plan for dividing

Livonia between the two states. Ivan and his advisers (the negotiations were conducted by the boyar V.M. Zakhar'in-Yur'ev, who was at that time close to the tsar, and by the leading *oprichniki* A.I. Vyazemskii and Petr Zaitsev) interpreted the Lithuanians' proposals as a sign of weakness and demanded that they cede to Russia most of the Livonian lands, including the great port of Riga. The negotiations ended in deadlock.

On the threshold of a new war, the tsar decided to convene an Assembly of the Land – a gathering of the various estates of the realm. The Assembly which met in Moscow in June 1566 was one of the largest and most representative assemblies of the sixteenth century. Several hundred men took part in its sessions, including not only members of the clergy, boyars and nobles, but also merchants, who were involved for the first time in the work of an Assembly of the Land.

Some historians have been puzzled by the fact that such a large and representative Assembly should have been convened during the *oprichnina* period. Their uncertainty springs from the widespread view that Assemblies of the Land were the highest-level estate-representative institutions, similar to the parliaments of western Europe.[3] In more recent historiography this view has been increasingly questioned. The fullest critique can be found in the works of the German historian Hans-Joachim Torke. Explaining why Assemblies of the Land in sixteenth- and seventeenth-century Russia cannot be considered to be estate-representative institutions, Torke argued that Russia did not have politicised estates of the western type, and that the Russian estates were characterised by the absence of political rights and institutions which would have enabled them to obtain a degree of independence from the power of the ruler, influence the formation of government policy and impose some limitation on the power of the monarch.[4] The appearance of the Assemblies of the Land in the middle of the sixteenth century coincided with the development of the rights of the estates and their institutions of self-government, and there was a real possibility that Russia would evolve in the direction of an estate-representative monarchy: but the further development of 'parliamentarism' in Russia was very different to that in western Europe. The main reason for this was the interference of the state in the development of the estate system. As we have seen, Ivan Groznyi's *oprichnina* policy was designed to suppress the political independence of the estates and to consolidate autocracy – a very different type of state system to the estate-representative monarchies of western Europe.

In spite of its superficially representative character and its size, the Assembly of the Land of 1566 cannot be considered to be a truly estate-representative institution, in the sense of an organisation through which the various social groups could directly express their interests. Historians have noted that the Assembly was convened in haste, and that no direct elections of local representatives of the various estates took place. The only nobles who took part in Assembly sessions were those (mostly members of the sovereign's court) who were present in Moscow, performing their routine service in the capital. It is true that because of the territorial structure of the sovereign's court at that time (the nobles who served at court were also members of the provincial organisations of the nobility) the nobles who attended the Assembly could to some extent have represented the interests of their local corporations. But insofar as the participants in the Assembly had not been elected as delegates, they cannot be considered to have been true representatives of their localities or of their estates. Another important point is worth making about the representative character of the Assembly of 1566. Only members of the *zemshchina* took part in its sessions; apparently the *oprichniki's* approval of the tsar's foreign policy was taken for granted.

The evidence suggests that Ivan had not summoned the Assembly so he could consult the estates and take joint decisions with them. The prerogative of taking ultimate decisions undoubtedly belonged to the tsar and his immediate entourage of *oprichniki*. It is revealing that during the negotiations with the Lithuanian envoys no mention was made of the Assembly nor of the resolutions it adopted. In convening the Assembly of the Land, the tsar had no intention of extending the political rights of the estates. It seems more likely that he was seeking to pursue his own specific aims. Needing resources to fight the war, Ivan's government hoped to obtain the agreement of the leaders of the *zemshchina* for the introduction of new emergency taxes. With the assistance of the Assembly the tsar intended to shift all major military expenditure, the main burden of the Livonian War, on to the shoulders of the *zemshchina*. It is significant that many members of the merchant class were invited to the sessions: they comprised one fifth of Assembly members. In addition, it was important for the tsar to acquire information about how ready the nobility was for war, and about the mood of the army.

The tsar managed to win universal agreement for continuing the war in Livonia. The nobles declared that they were ready. The merchants' representatives spoke out even more decisively, saying they were willing to give for 'the sovereign's cause' not only their property but also their lives. In view of the merchants' vested interest in Russia's acquisition of the major commercial ports on the Baltic, their position is easy to understand.

Having obtained the Assembly's unanimous approval for his foreign policy, and having made some concessions to the *zemshchina*, the tsar must have hoped they would also accept his domestic policy and acknowledge the justice of introducing the *oprichnina*. But things turned out rather differently.

The rout of the *zemshchina* opposition

Historians generally agree that the first major and open criticism of the *oprichnina* by the *zemshchina* opposition occurred in connection with the Assembly of the Land of 1566. A large group of *zemshchina* nobles, delegates to the Assembly, pleaded with the tsar to abolish the *oprichnina*. According to one foreign observer, they said:

Most radiant tsar, our sovereign! Why do you order our innocent brothers to be killed? We all serve you faithfully and spill our blood for you. What kind of gratitude are you now showing us for our services? You have set your bodyguards [i.e. the *oprichniki*] on our necks, and they tear our brothers and kinsmen from us. They insult us, beat us, stab us, strangle and kill us.[5]

The appeal was followed by a written petition complete with signatures. This took Ivan completely by surprise. Unaccustomed to opposition from his subjects, he flew into a rage and responded to the *zemshchina*'s plea by renewing his policy of repression.

The tsar ordered the petitioners to be arrested and thrown into prison. About 300 nobles were seized; 50 of them were publicly flogged and some had their tongues cut out. Three noblemen who were acknowledged to be the ringleaders, Prince Vasilii Rybin-Pronskii, I.F. Karamyshev and K.S. Bundov, were executed. The treatment of the petitioners provoked widespread reaction, and the government even had to explain itself abroad. It told its envoys to Lithuania:

If they ask [in Lithuania] about Prince Vasilii Rybin and about Karamyshev, then they [i.e. the envoys] must say: 'The sovereign is merciful, but evildoers are executed everywhere. The sovereign discovered that these men had plotted evil against the state and, having become convinced of their guilt, he ordered them to be put to death.'

Thus, in spite of their loyal tone, the *zemshchina*'s pleas to the tsar for the abolition of the *oprichnina* were interpreted by the *oprichnina* authorities as an attack on the monarch's honour and on the security of the state.

The affair did not end with the execution of the three nobles and the punishment of their associates. This was only the prologue to widespread persecution of *zemshchina* leaders. Prince Rybin-Pronskii, Karamyshev and Bundov did not occupy important posts in the *zemshchina* administration and were unlikely to have been the real leaders of the protest. The tsar and his advisers realised they must have had the backing of more influential boyar groupings.

Their main suspicions fell on the boyar Ivan Petrovich Fedorov-Chelyadnin, one of the most powerful leaders of the *zemshchina* boyar duma. Fedorov held the high court rank of equerry (the head of the chancellery which was responsible for the tsar's stables), which allowed him to be both the formal and the actual leader of the *zemshchina* boyar duma. An eminent and wealthy boyar who owned extensive estates in various parts of the country, Fedorov, according to contemporaries, was renowned for his honesty and, unlike many other boyars and officials, he did not take bribes.

At first Ivan did not impose direct punishment on such an influential and authoritative boyar, and simply banished him from Moscow. The equerry was sent to the frontier town of Polotsk as governor (in practice, this was an honourable form of exile). However, as an experienced politician, Fedorov realised that the stormclouds were gathering over his head. It will be recalled that both Aleksei Adashev and Kurbskii had been sent to serve as governors in frontier towns when they were in disgrace. Fedorov, however, did not follow Kurbskii's example and defect, although he had the opportunity to flee to Lithuania. The authorities in Poland-Lithuania, eager to destabilise the internal political situation in Russia, tried to induce a number of eminent boyars to enter their king's service. A Lithuanian agent came to Polotsk with a letter from the king. But Fedorov was not tempted by the Poles, and even handed the spy over to the Russian authorities. The *oprichniki* were unable to find any evidence that Fedorov had committed treason. Nevertheless, with the growth of dissatisfaction and unrest in the *zemshchina*, the influential *zemskii* leader was an extremely dangerous figure in the eyes of the *oprichnina* authorities.

Dissatisfaction with the *oprichnina* was voiced not only by servicemen but also by leading clergymen. On 19 May 1566 Metropolitan Afanasii resigned as head of the Church and retired to a monastery. Before his elevation to the metropolitanate Afanasii had been the tsar's confessor and dean of the Blagoveshchenskii Cathedral in the Kremlin (before his tonsure as a monk he was known as Archpriest Andrei). Afanasii explained that he had decided to resign as metropolitan because of serious illness, but it is possible that the real reason was his disagreement with Ivan's *oprichnina* policy. At the Church Council in June 1566 held to elect a new metropolitan, the tsar proposed the candidature of German Polev, the Archbishop of Kazan'. Ivan was confident of German's loyalty – he belonged to a family with close connections to the Joseph-of-Volokolamsk Monastery, whose leaders had long supported the autocratic aspirations of the Muscovite rulers. But, contrary to expectations, Polev sharply disagreed with the *oprichnina* policy, reminding Ivan of the Last Judgment, when everyone, whether tsar or commoner, would have to answer for their actions before God. German Polev's behaviour sparked the tsar's anger. According to Kurbskii, Ivan told German: 'You have not yet become metropolitan, but you are already restricting my freedom!' Polev was expelled from the metropolitan's court and sent back to Kazan'. He was later executed by the *oprichniki*.

The tsar's next choice was Filipp Kolychev, the abbot of the Solovetskii Monastery, one of the most important monastic institutions in Russia. The reason for this choice is hard to fathom. Filipp was not the type to change his beliefs for short-term political advantage, and his background could not have provided the tsar with any grounds for confidence in his candidate's loyalty. The future prelate belonged to an old Moscow boyar clan, and specifically to a branch whose members had been closely linked with the Novgorod nobility and with the Staritskiis. At the age of 30, Filipp (whose secular name was Fedor Stepanovich Kolychev) was obliged to become a monk, fearing punishment for his involvement in Andrei Staritskii's 'revolt'. His piety and great organisational abilities led to his becoming abbot of the Solovetskii Monastery, which was situated in the far north on the island of Solovki in the White Sea. While Filipp Kolychev was abbot, an ambitious construction programme was implemented, involving both religious and secular projects. An entire network of canals was dug, linking the many lakes and enabling the efficient use of water-power for water-mills and other purposes; one of the largest brickworks in Russia was built; and many technical innovations were introduced which significantly lightened the burden of manual labour for the monastery workforce.

It is possible that the tsar was attracted by the Solovetskii abbot's outstanding abilities. It is probable that his appointment was influenced by the fact that Filipp's cousins Fedor and Vasilii Ivanovich Umnoi Kolychev, who at that time were close to the tsar, served in the *oprichnina*.

Filipp Kolychev was an opponent of the *oprichnina* and he made it a condition of his appointment that the tsar should abandon his harsh repressive measures. Nevertheless, he did not suffer the fate of German

Polev, and the tsar himself urged him to accept the role of metropolitan. The process of election of a new metropolitan was becoming a protracted one, and in the circumstances it seems that Ivan did not want to enter into open conflict with the powerful Church leadership over the enforced withdrawal of another candidate. Filipp, in his turn, yielded to the entreaties of the tsar and the bishops, agreed to accept the position of metropolitan and gave an undertaking that he would not interfere in the internal affairs of the *oprichnina*. On 25 July 1566 Filipp Kolychev was elevated to the post of Metropolitan of All Rus'. But the compromise reached between the tsar and the Church hierarchy turned out to be short-lived.

The events after the Assembly of 1566 showed that the most diverse groups of Russian society were deeply dissatisfied with the *oprichnina*. Tsar Ivan, for his part, made it clear to the *zemshchina* that he had no intention of compromising on the main issue, and was prepared at all costs to continue with the policy until he had completely eradicated 'treason' and consolidated the autocratic system.

Clear evidence of Ivan's growing distrust of the *zemshchina* is provided by the steps he took in 1566–7 to fortify the main centres of the *oprichnina*, to turn them into mighty strongholds which could protect the tsar and his family in the event of an armed uprising. At first, the special *oprichnina* court in the capital was situated within the Kremlin. However, the Kremlin was in the *zemshchina*, so the tsar decided to move his residence to the *oprichnina* sector of Moscow. Not far from the Kremlin, beyond the River Neglinnaya, between the Arbat and Nikitskaya Street, there rose a mighty castle, whose construction was completed at the beginning of 1567. The new *oprichnina* court was surrounded by high stone walls and had the appearance of a real fortress. Many bodyguards kept watch day and night. The walls and turrets of the castle were decorated with pictures of wild animals and birds which symbolised the awesome power and might of the *oprichnina*. The construction of this mighty fortress within Moscow made a great impression on the Muscovites and on the foreigners present in the capital. The government even provided a special explanation for foreign consumption: the tsar had supposedly built his new residence 'for his royal enjoyment [that is, rest and recreation]'. If foreigners suggested that the tsar had decided to separate himself from the *zemshchina*, Russian diplomats had to say that 'the tsar has no need to isolate himself from anyone'. The tsar decided to set up yet another fortified residence within the *oprichnina* at Vologda, an important strategic and commercial centre, through which the main routes from Moscow to the north passed. A strong stone fortress, equipped with powerful artillery, was built there. A large and majestic Uspenskii Cathedral, modelled on the Uspenskii Cathedral in the Moscow Kremlin, was built within the fortress. The construction of these stone fortifications and other military installations – in addition to Aleksandrova Sloboda – show that the tsar and the *oprichniki* were seriously afraid of internal unrest and were preparing to suppress a possible uprising by the opposition.

Growing dissatisfaction in various sectors of society made Ivan uncertain of the future and fearful for his own safety. He seriously considered becoming a monk, as he told the elders of the Kirillo-Belozerskii Monastery in strictest confidence. The strength of the tsar's fears is revealed by negotiations he initiated in the summer of 1567. Russia had developed strong and successful commercial and diplomatic ties with England. Economic relations between the two countries brought benefits to both sides. As early as the 1550s Ivan's government had granted the merchants of the English Muscovy Company the right to trade on Russian territory without paying taxes. After the Russian annexation of Astrakhan', the English merchants were attracted by the possibility of conducting trade through Russia (by the Volga river route) with Persia and other oriental lands. As a result of the English discovery of the northern sea route the Russians for their part acquired great new opportunities to establish direct commercial contacts with the more economically developed countries of western Europe. The English merchants brought to Russia important strategic commodities, especially non-ferrous metals, which were necessary for the production of armaments, and which had not yet been extracted in Russia. It is not surprising that it was with the English envoy Anthony Jenkinson that Tsar Ivan began to negotiate in the summer of 1567 about acquiring asylum in England in the event that he had to leave Russia. The tsar also requested Queen Elizabeth to send shipwrights and experienced sailors, apparently to enable him to get to England if the necessity arose.

The tsar's intentions were known in Russia. Ivan's open hostility towards the *zemshchina* could not fail to alarm its leaders. It is quite probable in the circumstances that the idea of removing the tsar and transferring the throne to his cousin Prince Vladimir Staritskii might have been discussed among *zemshchina* boyars. Two foreign observers – the Germans Heinrich von Staden and Albert Schlichting, who both served in the *oprichnina* – refer to a conspiracy of the *zemshchina* boyars in favour of Vladimir.[6] An unofficial Russian chronicle also mentions the 'inclination' of the opposition to promote Vladimir's candidature for the Russian throne. But according to a chronicle account there was no overt conspiracy, only discussions ('words'), for which the boyars who opposed the *oprichnina* paid a heavy price.[7] We cannot say with any certainty whether there was a real conspiracy or whether it was simply a case of careless talk. In any case, information about the mood of the *zemshchina* boyars reached the tsar's court. The *oprichnina* authorities took the news seriously. In the autumn of 1567 the tsar postponed his Livonian campaign, came quickly to Moscow and ordered the investigation of a *zemshchina* conspiracy. Fedorov was placed in disgrace and exiled to Kolomna. Nobles and officials among his supporters were arrested and executed, and many of the equerry's armed servants were exterminated. The *oprichniki* carried out several punitive raids against Fedorov's lands. Many of the inhabitants were slaughtered (some were put to the sword, while others were herded into their cottages and burned alive). According to Staden, women and girls were stripped naked 'and forced in that state to catch chickens in the fields'. Buildings were demolished, livestock was slaughtered and property destroyed.

In September 1568, when the investigation was finished, the *oprichnina* authorities punished the main 'conspirators'. Fedorov was executed along with the eminent boyars and princes M.I. Kolychev and his three sons, Prince A.I. Katyrev-Rostovskii, Prince F.I. Troekurov and M.M. Lykov and his nephew.

The 'conspiracy' of Fedorov and his supporters in 1567–8 was one of the most extensive political cases of the *oprichnina* period. According to the Memorial List several boyars and *okol'nichie* were executed. But the great majority of the victims were nobles, chancellery officials (secretaries and assistant secretaries) and the boyars' armed slaves. The list indicates that as many as 150 nobles and chancellery officials were put to death, along with about 300 boyars' servants.[8]

As a rule the accused were punished without due process of law. Only the most eminent of the 'conspirators' were brought to trial before the tsar and his boyars. We do not know exactly how the judicial process worked in relation to Fedorov. According to Schlichting's account, Fedorov was accused of wanting to seize the throne. When the disgraced boyar was brought to the palace, Ivan ordered him to dress in his royal attire and sit on the throne, holding the royal sceptre. Ivan then bowed and knelt before him, saying: 'Now you have what you sought and aspired to – to be Grand Prince of Muscovy and to occupy my place.' Then he added: 'Just as it is in my power to place you on this throne, so it is also in my power to remove you.' After that the tsar plunged a dagger into the boyar's chest, and the *oprichniki* who were present followed with knife blows of their own.[9] This is a very revealing episode. Not only does it illustrate Ivan's personal involvement in the cruel punishment of a 'traitor', but it also reflects the tsar's general love of play-acting – in this case, making Fedorov act out the crime of which he was accused. In the interpretation of B.A. Uspenskii, the incident demonstrates Ivan's belief that he was the only true, divinely appointed tsar, even when another man was seated on the throne. Fedorov was a false tsar, a tsar in outward appearance only, and Ivan's treatment of him exposed the hollowness of his alleged aspiration to occupy the throne.[10]

The intensification of the tsar's persecution of his subjects led Metropolitan Filipp to break his promise not to interfere in the affairs of the *oprichnina*, and he denounced the killings. According to Filipp's *vita*, the metropolitan's decision to protest was influenced by a collective appeal by members of all strata of society, from the magnates to the ordinary people, entreating him to intercede and defend them from the arbitrary actions of the *oprichniki*. In March 1568, during a sermon in the Uspenskii Cathedral, Filipp publicly expressed his view that it was necessary to put an end to the *oprichnina* and the pernicious division of the realm, and to halt the executions of innocent people. The main obligation of a ruler, the metropolitan told the tsar, was to implement universal justice and to punish only real criminals. Those who denounced innocent people, Filipp said, having the *oprichniki* in mind, deserved harsh punishment. The metropolitan reminded the tsar of God's judgment, when he would have to answer for the bloodshed and injury he had imposed on his subjects. Filipp continued to condemn the horrors of the *oprichnina* on many occasions, and this caused indignation among the tsar's associates. Filipp's position was made more difficult by the fact that other Church leaders, fearing the tsar's wrath, failed to support him. His protests were therefore regarded not as the opinion of the Church as a whole, but as the lone voice of an individual, albeit one who held the highest position in the Church. The metropolitan had many enemies among the clergy, notably Archbishop Pimen of Novgorod, and the tsar's confessor, Archpriest Evstafii of the Blagoveshchenskii Cathedral. The *oprichnina* authorities took advantage of this. In order to remove the awkward metropolitan, they decided to collect compromising material about him. In September 1568 a special commission was sent to the Solovetskii Monastery. It included Bishop Pafnutii of Suzdal' and Archimandrite Feodosii of the Spaso-Andronikov Monastery, as well as the *oprichniki* Prince Vasilii Ivanovich Temkin-Rostovskii and the state secretary Dmitrii Ivanovich Pivov. They arrived at Solovki accompanied by a detachment of *oprichnina* noblemen. With the help of bribes and threats the members of the commission forced some of the monks to provide the evidence they required about the 'debauched life' of Filipp Kolychev while he was abbot. The allegations against Filipp were so dubious that even the metropolitan's enemy, Bishop Pafnutii, refused to sign the document detailing the findings of the investigation. Nonetheless, when the commission returned from Solovki its findings were presented to the *oprichnina* authorities.

A Church Council was summoned for Filipp Kolychev's trial, and the boyar duma also took part. According to foreign observers, Tsar Ivan 'assembled all the spiritual and secular leaders and demanded that they dismiss the depraved metropolitan from his office . . .'[11] Archbishop Pimen of Novgorod made particularly vehement accusations against Filipp. False witnesses made their 'wordy speeches' against the metropolitan, and Filipp rejected all the accusations against him. However, on 4 November 1568, the intimidated and misinformed Church leaders passed a resolution in favour of removing the metropolitan. On 8 November, the feast of the Archangel Michael, Metropolitan Filipp was taking a service in the Uspenskii Cathedral. During the liturgy the *oprichniki* burst into the church, announced that the metropolitan had been dismissed, tore off his vestments and placed him under arrest. Filipp Kolychev was sent in disgrace to the Otroch Monastery in Tver', where he was incarcerated.

The political trials of 1566–8 provide evidence of widespread discontent in the *zemshchina* with the policy of the *oprichnina*, and reveal a deep rift within the ruling circles. It is significant that those who spoke out against the *oprichnina* at this time were primarily members of old Moscow untitled boyar families and of the higher strata of the nobility, that is, those social groups which had traditionally provided the bulwark of support for the Russian monarchy. The conflict between the *oprichnina* and the *zemshchina* had become irreconcilable. This is shown by the fact that, whereas at the beginning of the *oprichnina* Tsar Ivan had still found it possible to rely to an extent on the existing organs of state power (the *zemshchina* boyar duma and the chancelleries), by the end of the 1560s special *oprichnina* organs of power and political institutions were being formed alongside those of the *zemshchina*. V.A. Kolobkov, who has made a special study of the establishment and development of the administrative institutions of the *oprichnina*, concluded that the first reliable evidence of the existence of separate *oprichnina* chancelleries is found no earlier than 1568. With the rapidly deepening rift in society and the intensification of the repressions, the creation of separate organs of governance in the *oprichnina* indicated that a direct dictatorship had been established, in which the functions of control and suppression were permanently transferred to the *oprichnina* authorities.

The land resettlements

The widespread dissatisfaction in the *zemshchina* was caused not only by the direct repressions, but also by the policy of mass land resettlement which had been part of the *oprichnina* decree. According to the decree of 1565, all *zemshchina* nobles were liable to be expelled from the *oprichnina* districts and moved to *zemshchina* territory. The resettlement policy resulted from the need to ensure that the *oprichniki* carried out their military service separately from the *zemshchina* nobles. Unlike the exiles to Kazan', most of the nobility were forced to relocate not because they were in disgrace, but because they had not been considered worth admitting to the ranks of the *oprichniki*. In contemporary documents they were described as having been 'evicted with their entire town [i.e. district], and not in disfavour'.

Historians have expressed a range of views about the scale of the resettlements and how consistently the *oprichnina* decree was implemented. According to some scholars, such as S.F. Platonov, S.B. Veselovskii and R.G. Skrynnikov, the eviction of nobles during the *oprichnina* was on a massive scale; A.A. Zimin and V.B. Kobrin, by contrast, suggested the resettlement policy was either not fully carried out, or not implemented at all. However, a detailed study of sixteenth-century land censuses has confirmed that the former view is correct.[12] We can compare landholding patterns before and after the *oprichnina* on the basis of the cadastres from Vyaz'ma, Mozhaisk, Maloyaroslavets and part of Medyn' – areas which were included in the *oprichnina* from the outset. The analysis shows that significant changes took place in the second half of the sixteenth century. There was a turnover of more than 75 per cent in landholding families in these districts. A clear pattern emerged: those who remained were, as a rule, *oprichniki*, whereas the *zemshchina* nobles lost their lands in their home districts, and their estates (both *votchiny* and *pomest'ya*) were allocated to men from the *oprichnina*. This shows consistent implementation of the policy of land resettlement, and that the *zemshchina* nobles were expelled from the *oprichnina* districts virtually *en masse*. The evidence suggests that a similar situation can be found in other districts which were taken into the *oprichnina* in 1565, including Suzdal', Galich and Peremyshl'.

At first, *oprichnina* territory included only a few regions with noble estates. Land resettlement became more widespread and more catastrophic for the *zemshchina* nobles as the *oprichnina* grew to take in new areas. And whereas the *oprichnina* had originally included mainly frontier districts (Suzdal' was an exception) in which service-tenure landholding predominated, it subsequently came to incorporate many major central districts where a large number of hereditary estates remained.

The incorporation of new districts into the *oprichnina* resulted from the need to strengthen the 'sovereign's appanage' economically and militarily, and to increase the size of the *oprichnina* corps, as the conflict between the tsar and the *zemshchina* intensified. At the beginning of 1567 the *oprichnina* acquired the large district of Kostroma, from which all the landowners were evicted, apart from those recruited as *oprichniki*. The sources show that many Kostroma nobles were resettled in Vladimir, Smolensk, Novgorod and other *zemshchina* districts. At the end of the 1560s the *oprichnina* incorporated Staritsa (the former capital of the Staritskiis' appanage principality), Beloozero, Pereyaslavl', Rostov, Yaroslavl', Poshekhon'e and other districts. Subsequently, at the beginning of the 1570s, the *oprichnina* expanded again, to include some *pyatiny* (parts) of Novgorod district. In all these areas the land resettlement policy was put into practice. Resettlement affected not only *oprichnina* districts, but also those in the *zemshchina*. Forced migrants from the *oprichnina* districts received hereditary and service-tenure estates on *zemshchina* territory. Conversely, nobles recruited into the *oprichnina* lost their service lands in the *zemshchina* and had to move to *oprichnina* districts. However, the *oprichniki* did have the advantage over the *zemshchina* nobles in that they were able to retain their hereditary estates on *zemshchina* territory.

Over the entire period of the *oprichnina* the majority of Russian nobles may have been moved from their homelands, and many hundreds of service-tenure and hereditary estate owners suffered as a result of the resettlement policy. An indication of the scale of the migrations in the second half of the sixteenth century can be obtained by comparing the list of members of the sovereign's court in the middle of the century with that from the end of it. This shows that of the 153 men whose names and membership of district noble corporations in the 1550s can be found in sources from the end of the sixteenth century, 91 – i.e. the majority – appear in the court lists under different districts.

In terms of the scale of the land resettlement, the *oprichnina* was the most important act of its kind in Muscovite history, and in terms of the degree of consistency with which the resettlement policy was implemented it is comparable only with the expulsions of local boyars from Novgorod and some other regions in the reign of Ivan Groznyi's grandfather, Ivan III. But whereas in Ivan III's reign the forced migrants had mostly been landowners from newly annexed territories which had a different socio-political system from that of the Moscow principality, such as Novgorod, Pskov and Smolensk, in the years of the *oprichnina* the land resettlement affected virtually all Russian territory, apart from regions which lacked any kind of landholding by military servicemen.

It is hard to overestimate the social and political consequences of Ivan's resettlement policy. Its most serious consequence was to weaken the traditional land and service ties of the Russian nobility, including the links of the princely boyar élite with their districts and with the local gentry.

The resettlement of the nobles involved many problems and often led to their ruination and impoverishment. In theory they had the right to receive compensation in the *zemshchina* for lands they had lost in the *oprichnina*. But in practice this did not always happen. With its need for a levy of nobles capable of military service, Ivan's government did not of course intend to deprive the *zemshchina* nobles of their land and peasants. And indeed it did take some measures to help them settle in their new localities. Relocated nobles were given lands belonging to the state peasants. In Ryazan', as S.I. Smetanina's research has shown, the government ordered that some of the family lands of local hereditary estate owners should be confiscated and distributed to immigrants from other districts.[13] But in situations where resettlement was so intense, the government could not always fully compensate the landowners for the loss of their estates. Land often passed repeatedly from one owner to another, and fell into decline. Traditional farming methods were disrupted, and this had a dire effect on the peasants. The transfer of landed estates from *zemshchina* nobles to *oprichniki* usually led to increased exploitation of the peasantry.

The *oprichnina* caused particular harm to hereditary landownership. Although the government took measures to compensate *zemshchina* nobles for the loss of their service-tenure lands, it gave no firm guarantees of compensation for the confiscation of hereditary estates. Frequently the *zemshchina* nobles were obliged to 'seek out' hereditary lands for themselves in their new regions. Family estates abandoned by *zemshchina* nobles in *oprichnina* districts were usually transferred to *oprichniki* in the form of service lands. This policy of Ivan's in relation to service-tenure and hereditary estates is entirely understandable. He wanted not independent landowners, but obedient servants who held their land on condition of military service rather than as family property. Over the years of the *oprichnina* as a whole, the balance between hereditary and service lands, especially in the central regions of the country, shifted significantly in favour of service-tenure estates.

The *oprichnina* caused serious damage to hereditary boyar landowner-ship, and to the inherited estates of the princely families in particular. Detailed evidence to support this conclusion was first provided by S.F. Platonov, who considered that the destruction of the landholding of the princes and boyars was the main aim and outcome of the *oprichnina* policy.[14] Not all historians agreed. S.B. Veselovskii pointed out that only two regions of formerly independent princely rule had been included in the *oprichnina* – Suzdal' and Yaroslavl' – and of these, only Suzdal' was part of the original territory of the *oprichnina*.[15] A.A. Zimin questioned whether Yaroslavl' had ever been in the *oprichnina*, and concluded that all the main districts which contained the hereditary estates of the princely aristocracy had remained outside the *oprichnina*.[16] Platonov's view of the anti-princely complexion of the *oprichnina*, at least in its early days, was supported by R.G. Skrynnikov. Skrynnikov, however, considered that the main damage to the hereditary princely estates was caused by the events of 1565 and the Kazan' exile.[17] The exile of members of the princely aristocracy to Kazan' did indeed cause major problems, mainly economic, for hereditary princely landholding. But Ivan's government did not succeed in fully implementing its 1565 plans for the Kazan' exile. The episode was shortlived, and after a year the disgraced aristocrats were given an amnesty and began to return to their old estates.

The decisive blow against princely boyar landownership was struck with the resettlement of servicemen from the *oprichnina* districts in the *zemshchina*. Reliable evidence of the incorporation of the Yaroslavl' and Rostov districts into the *oprichnina* in 1569 has been discovered.[18] Starodub-Ryapolovskii was included in the post-*oprichnina* 'appanage', in 1580. If we bear in mind that Suzdal' district was in the *oprichnina* from the outset, then it appears that all the 'princely' districts of north-east Rus' (Suzdal', Yaroslavl', Rostov and Starodub-Ryapolovskii) formed part of the 'sovereign's appanage'. Analysis of the cadastres and official documents shows that most of the princes had lost their old family lands by the end of the sixteenth century. And the princes who retained hereditary estates in their homelands were mainly those who served in the *oprichnina*. The break-up of the boyars' family estates, the loss of their traditional links with the provinces, and the division of the service class into *oprichniki* and *zemskie*, significantly transformed the Russian aristocracy and led to a change in its mentality. As a result of the *oprichnina* the magnates became completely dependent on the monarchy.[19]

Merchants were also subject to forced resettlement during the *oprichnina*. After the incursion of the Crimean Tatars and the burning of

Moscow in 1571, which resulted in the destruction of the commercial district (*posad*) and the deaths of many of the city's inhabitants, the government transferred the wealthiest merchants from various provincial towns to Moscow on a large scale, in order to repopulate the capital and revive its trade. Although this was an emergency measure, it had very serious consequences for the fate of the Russian merchantry and of the urban population as a whole. B.N. Florya, who made a special study of this problem, has convincingly shown that as a result of the mass resettlement of merchants which continued throughout the 1570s and 1580s, the provincial trading quarters lost their most influential and wealthy élites, and the urban population was turned into a homogeneous taxpaying mass, who were required to pay dues and fulfil various kinds of obligations.[20] The position of the privileged merchants also changed significantly. Now they were concentrated exclusively in the capital, and instead of the privileges they had previously enjoyed they were compelled to serve in the financial institutions of the state apparatus. As a result of the policy the government pursued in the last third of the sixteenth century, a deep split emerged in the ranks of the embryonic 'third estate'. The merchant élite (the so-called 'guests' and the members of the guests' and clothiers' hundreds) were separated from most of the urban population. This seriously hampered the development of a single estate of townsmen, and impeded the growth of entrepreneurship and trade.

Important changes also took place in the *oprichnina* years in the position of the peasantry on the state and crown lands, many of which were allocated as service-tenure estates to private landowners, mostly *oprichniki*. The transfer of state peasants to personal dependency on noble overlords meant that their freedom to manage their own farms was severely restricted, and the obligations required of them were increased. The peasants' previous rights of *volost'* self-government were also abolished.

Thus the *oprichnina* affected the interests of all sectors of Russian society. The policy of forced migration brought huge discontentment with the *oprichnina* across the country. Ivan's executions and persecution of his political opponents were usually justified by the *oprichnina* authorities as necessary to stamp out treason and to eliminate abuses. But it was much more difficult to explain to the public the suffering (and sometimes also the deaths) of thousands of innocent people who were evicted from their homes and compelled to start a new life in distant parts.

The suppression of the *zemshchina* opposition in 1568 did not mark the end of the persecution. The following year it began again, on an even greater scale.

Notes

1 *PSRL*, vol.13, pp.395–6.

2 Skrynnikov, *Tsarstvo terrora*, pp.238–65.

3 See: M.N. Tikhomirov, 'Soslovno-predstavitel'nye uchrezhdeniya (zemskie sobory) Rossii v XVI v.', *Voprosy istorii*, 1958, no.5; Cherepnin, *Zemskie sobory*; Zimin, *Oprichnina Ivana Groznogo*, pp.156–211; Nosov, *Stanovlenie soslovno-predstavitel'nykh uchrezhdenii*; S.O. Shmidt, *Stanovlenie rossiiskogo samoderzhavstva: Issledovaniya sotsial'no-politicheskoi istorii vremen Ivan Groznogo*, Moscow, 1973, pp.120–261; N.I. Pavlenko, 'K istorii zemskikh soborov XVI v.', *Voprosy istorii*, 1968, no.5; R.G. Skrynnikov, *Nachalo oprichniny*, Leningrad, 1966, pp.308–52; V.I. Koretskii, 'Zemskii sobor 1575 g. i chastichnoe vozrozhdenie oprichniny', *Voprosy istorii*, 1967, no.5, pp.32–50.

4 H.J. Torke, *Die staatsbedingte Gesellschaft im Moskauer Reich: Zar und Zemlja in der altrussischen Herrschaftsverfassung, 1613–1689*, Leiden, 1974; Kh.Y. [H.J.] Torke, 'Tak nazyvaemye zemskie sobory v Rossii', *Voprosy istorii*, 1991, no.11, pp.3–10.

5 A. Shlikhting, *Novoe izvestie o Rossii vremeni Ivana Groznogo*, Leningrad, 1934, pp.38–9.

6 Staden, *The Land and Government of Muscovy*, pp.21–4; Shlikhting, *Novoe izvestie o Rossii*, p.22.

7 *PSRL*, vol.34, p.190.

8 Skrynnikov, *Tsarstvo terrora*, pp.530–31.

9 Shlikhting, *Novoe izvestie o Rossii*, p.22.

10 B.A. Uspenskij, 'Tsar and Pretender: Samozvančestvo or Royal Imposture in Russia as a Cultural-Historical Phenomenon', in Ju.M. Lotman and B.A. Uspenskij, *The Semiotics of Russian Culture*, ed. Ann Shukman, Ann Arbor: Michigan Slavic Contributions, 1984, pp.268–72.

11 'Poslanie Ioganna Taube i Elerta Kruze', p.43.

12 Pavlov, 'Zemel'nye pereseleniya v gody oprichniny'.

13 S.I. Smetanina, *Zemlevladenie Ryazanskogo kraya i oprichnaya zemel'naya politika*. Avtoreferat dissertatsii na soiskanie uchenoi stepeni kandidata istoricheskikh nauk, Moscow, 1982.

14 Platonov, *Ocherki po istorii smuty*, pp.92–105.

15 Veselovskii, *Issledovaniya*, pp.30–31.

16 Zimin, *Oprichnina Ivana Groznogo*, pp.316–19.

17 Skrynnikov, *Tsarstvo terrora*, pp.238–65.

18 Yu.V. Ankhimyuk, 'Zapisi letopisnogo kharaktera v rukopisnom sbornike Kirillo-Belozerskogo monastyrya – novyi istochnik po istorii oprichniny', *Arkhiv russkoi istorii*, no.2, Moscow, 1992, pp.121–9.

19 Pavlov, *Gosudarev dvor*, pp.151–60.

20 B.N. Florya, 'Privilegirovannoe kupechestvo i gorodskaya obshchina v Russkom gosudarstve', *Istoriya SSSR*, 1977, no.5, pp.145–60.

Chapter 8

The Culmination of the Terror

The devastation of Novgorod

In the autumn of 1569 Tsar Ivan heard about a plot against him by the Novgorodians. It supposedly involved the entire social élite of the city – the head of the Church and his court, the chancellery administration of the city, and the upper classes (the nobles and merchants). The accusations against the Novgorodians were contradictory: on the one hand, that they wanted to place Prince Vladimir Staritskii on the throne and, on the other, that they planned to surrender Novgorod to the Polish king. The sources do not enable us to say with any degree of certainty whether there was any real foundation to the accusations. Nor is it easy to determine just where the boundary lay between 'treason' and the tsar's suspicious nature. All we know is that Ivan took the affair seriously, fully believed the report of the plot and began to prepare to ruthlessly punish the Novgorod 'traitors'.

To understand the causes of the tsar's rift with the élites of Novgorod society, we need to consider the broader political situation in the country at the end of the 1560s and the beginning of the 1570s. The investigation into the Novgorod 'treason' and the punitive expedition by the tsar and the *oprichniki* against the 'rebellious' city was a continuation of Ivan's policy of suppressing opposition to his autocratic power and to the existence of the *oprichnina*. The political trials of the second half of the 1560s provide evidence of the extent of dissatisfaction with the *oprichnina* in the *zemshchina*, and of the depth of the division in the ruling élite. In spite of his harsh suppression of opposition in Moscow, the tsar was evidently afraid that new signs of unrest would appear.

Ivan was seriously alarmed by the situation in the north-western region. At the beginning of 1569 a detachment of Lithuanian troops approached the fortress of Izborsk. The Russian defector T.I. Pukhov Teterin, dressed as an *oprichnik*, ordered the guard to open the gates, and the Lithuanians captured the fortress. After the city was retaken by the Russians, the *oprichniki* held an enquiry into the 'Izborsk treason', and several members of the chancellery administration of Izborsk and some nearby fortresses were executed. Meanwhile, the authorities expelled from Novgorod and Pskov townspeople suspected of disloyalty. About 2,000–3,000 people, including women and children, were banished.[1]

The tsar was particularly afraid of the growing mood of opposition in Novgorod, which was the most important political and economic centre in the north-west, and the second largest city in Russia. In spite of the fact that Ivan III had put an end to its independence, Novgorod still retained its political significance in the sixteenth century, and its administrative and military organisation had certain distinctive features. In particular, the governors of Novgorod had the right to conduct relations independently with Sweden. The Novgorod servicemen were the largest noble organisation in Russia at this time. They carried the main weight of the Livonian War on their shoulders, but were deprived of political rights by comparison with the nobles of other towns which had been taken into the *oprichnina*. Because of the peculiarities of their organisation and structure the Novgorod nobility had weak links with the court in Moscow. At the same time they had longstanding connections with the Staritskii appanage princes – back in 1537 some of the Novgorod nobles had taken part in the 'rebellion' of Andrei Staritskii. Among the Novgorod nobles and officials there were many men who had links not only with the Staritskiis' court, but also with the disgraced Moscow boyars. It is not surprising that all of this aroused the tsar's suspicions of the 'disloyalty' of the Novgorodians, and led him to believe all kinds of denunciations.

The tsar's fears multiplied when envoys brought him news that the Swedish king Eric XIV had been overthrown by his brothers, with the backing of discontented nobles and townspeople. His fear of a coup d'état similar to that in Sweden, and his concern that his opponents might unite around Vladimir Staritskii, just as the Swedish opposition had united around their princes, led the tsar to act decisively and inflict a pre-emptive strike.

This new twist in the policy of repression was also influenced by the changes which took place in the leadership of the *oprichnina* court at the end of the 1560s. Leading positions in the *oprichnina* came to be held by new men of lower birth (such as Malyuta Skuratov and Vasilii Gryaznoi). It was they who played the main role in implementing the attack on Novgorod.

The tsar decided to strike his first blow against the Staritskiis. A case was fabricated to the effect that Prince Vladimir was planning to 'spoil' (that is, poison) the tsar and his family. One of the tsar's cooks claimed that Vladimir had persuaded him to kill the tsar and had given him poison and 50 roubles to carry out the deed. At the end of September 1569, Vladimir was ordered immediately to the tsar's residence. En route he was surrounded by a detachment of *oprichniki* headed by Malyuta Skuratov Bel'skii and Vasilii Grigor'evich Gryaznoi. After a 'trial', the *oprichniki* inflicted their punishment on the Staritskiis, forcing Prince Vladimir to take poison, along with his wife and nine-year-old daughter. Meanwhile, Vladimir's mother, Princess Evfrosin'ya, was killed by the *oprichniki* in the Goritskii Monastery.

In the course of the investigation of the Staritskii affair additional information was 'obtained' about the 'treason' in Novgorod, and thereafter preparations for the campaign began. The tsar assembled all available *oprichnina* forces to take part in the expedition. By this time the *oprichnina* corps had significantly increased in size as a result of the inclusion of nobles from districts newly incorporated into the *oprichnina*. Foreign observers estimated the size of the *oprichnina* force at 15,000 men, although this seems to be an exaggeration.[2] At the end of November the *oprichniki* set off. En route to Novgorod they laid waste the towns of Klin, Tver' and Torzhok and their surrounding districts. In the Otroch Monastery in Tver', according to legend, Malyuta Skuratov strangled the former metropolitan, Filipp Kolychev, who refused to bless the expedition.

On 2 January the vanguard of the *oprichniki* reached Novgorod. They sealed up the property of the monasteries, churches and the houses of wealthy individuals, and carried out arrests. On the evening of 6 January Tsar Ivan himself arrived in Novgorod, and set up his camp at Gorodishche, on the outskirts of the city. On the 8th, which was a Sunday, the tsar set off to attend a service in the cathedral of St Sophia. On the bridge over the River Volkhov he was given a ceremonial welcome by Archbishop Pimen and the clergy. But the tsar refused to accept a blessing from the prelate, accusing him and the people of Novgorod of treason and alleging that 'in their evil thoughts' they were planning to 'betray' Novgorod to the Polish king. After the service Pimen invited the tsar to dine in the archiepiscopal palace. During the meal Ivan ordered the *oprichniki* to arrest the archbishop and his servants. A wave of arrests spread through the city. So began the tragedy of the sack of Novgorod, which was to last for six weeks.

On Monday 9 January the trials began in the tsar's camp at Gorodishche. The investigation involved appalling methods of torture, with which the *oprichnina* judges extracted the evidence they required from the accused. The victims were set alight with a mixture of inflammable substances, tied to sledges and taken to the Volkhov, where they were thrust alive beneath the ice. It was not only adult men who were put to death in this way, but also their wives and children.[3] The main victims of the repressions were the boyars and nobles of the archbishop of Novgorod. Some of them were executed at Gorodishche, and the rest were taken to Moscow for trial. Archbishop Pimen, who was considered to be the ringleader of the Novgorod 'traitors', was subjected to humiliation and mockery. Not long before, Pimen, seeking to curry favour with the tsar, had been one of the main accusers of Metropolitan Filipp. Now he himself had become the object of the tsar's anger. The archbishop's white cowl was stripped from him, he was dressed in the costume of a *skomorokh* (a kind of popular entertainer) and 'married' to a mare. Pimen was tied to the back of the horse, and was sent under convoy to Moscow in the guise of a minstrel, strumming on a lyre and blowing on a set of bagpipes which the tsar had given him. As B.N. Florya has observed, such treatment of eminent churchmen convicted of treason was not new – the Byzantine emperors had dealt in this way with patriarchs who were implicated in conspiracies against them.[4] But Ivan's public humiliation of Archbishop Pimen also fitted into a broader pattern of mockery and humiliation of his most eminent victims, such as Prince M.P. Repnin and I.P. Fedorov; in this case, the archbishop was identified with his cultural opposite, a *skomorokh*.[5] Harsh punishment was also inflicted on Novgorod land-owners and officials who were suspected of links with the Staritskiis and with the disgraced Moscow boyars. The main accused were V.D. Danilov, G.I. Voronoi-Volynskii and V.A. Buturlin, members of prominent and influential boyar families. During the Novgorod trials those executed included the chief Novgorod secretary A.V. Bessonov, the Novgorod secretaries A.M. Babkin and I. Matveev, the chief Pskov secretary Yu. Sidorov and several dozen assistant secretaries. Leading members of the Novgorod merchant class – the Syrkovs, Tarakanovs and others – were also disgraced and persecuted.

When they were in Novgorod the *oprichniki* did more than set about eradicating 'treason'. One of the aims of the expedition was to fill the coffers of the *oprichnina* at the expense of the wealthy Novgorod monasteries and merchants. The property of all the city's monasteries and churches was confiscated. A heavy fine was imposed on the Novgorod clergy, and the abbots of the monasteries and deans of the cathedrals that did not pay the required sums were publicly beaten. As a result, the *oprichnina* treasury acquired the huge wealth accumulated by the Church in Novgorod over many centuries. The marvellous Vasilii doors, made by Novgorod craftsmen in the fourteenth century and removed from the city by Ivan, may be seen to this day in the Uspenskii Cathedral in the town of Aleksandrov (the former capital of the *oprichnina*). The trading quarter of Novgorod was also raided. The *oprichniki* pillaged not only the commercial premises and warehouses but also the homes of the townspeople. Anyone who tried to oppose the violence was killed on the spot. The money and goods confiscated from the citizens went into the coffers of the *oprichnina* and sometimes ended up in the hands of individual *oprichniki*. The German *oprichnik* Heinrich von Staden wrote boastfully in his memoirs that when he set off on the Novgorod expedition he had only one horse, but when he returned he had 49, 22 of which were harnessed to sledges full of all kinds of goods. The looting was not limited to Novgorod itself, but also affected its suburbs and the entire Novgorod region. Detachments of *oprichniki* raided Ladoga, Oreshek, Ivangorod, Korela and their surrounding districts.

The *oprichniki* devastated Novgorod. Thousands of people in the wealthy mercantile city perished. Historians disagree on the number of victims. Figures as high as 20,000–30,000 dead have been cited, but this is an exaggeration, since the entire population of Novgorod at that time did not exceed 30,000. R.G. Skrynnikov, on the basis of the Memorial List which he reconstructed, estimates the number of deaths at 2,000–3,000.[6] V.B. Kobrin, however, has suggested that the list does not fully convey the number of those executed and reflects the activity of only one of the various punishment detachments, that of Malyuta Skuratov. In Kobrin's opinion, the number of victims was as high as 10,000–15,000.[7]

To consolidate his position in Novgorod and its hinterland Ivan Groznyi incorporated part of the territory into the *oprichnina*. The *oprichnina* sector included the trading side of Novgorod, whose administration was headed by *oprichnina* governors and secretaries. The Sophia side of the city (where the Novgorod kremlin and the cathedral of St Sophia were situated) was administered by *zemshchina* officials. The *oprichnina* also included two out of the five Novgorod *pyatiny* – Bezhetsk and Obonezhsk, which became important bases for the allocation of land grants to the *oprichniki*. Several hundred Novgorod nobles were recruited into the *oprichnina*. At the same time, all the *zemshchina* nobles were expelled from these new *oprichnina* territories. They were resettled either in other *zemshchina* districts of Novgorod or in other parts of the country. The introduction of *oprichnina* arrangements in Novgorod led to increased state regulation of various aspects of the social and economic life of the city.

Having punished the Novgorodians, the *oprichnina* army headed for Pskov. But here the repressions were not so extreme, and primarily affected the local clergy. Among the victims were the leaders of the Pskovo-Pecherskii Monastery – the abbot, Kornilii, and the cellarer Vassian Muromets. The latter was friendly with Kurbskii and had corresponded with him. In Pskov the *oprichniki* confiscated valuables from the monasteries and cathedrals. Several dozen nobles and officials were executed. But in general Pskov suffered much less than Novgorod. Here there were no mass executions, murders and pillage. According to legend, the town was saved from complete devastation by the local *yurodivyi* (holy fool) Nikola, who prophesied that great misfortune would befall Ivan Groznyi if he destroyed Pskov. Frightened by the prophecy, the tsar departed from the town, leaving it in peace. It is highly probable that this episode did indeed take place, as it is described in a range of sources of both Russian and foreign provenance.[8] *Yurodstvo* (folly in Christ) was the highest form of Christian asceticism. When someone decided to assume this role as a way of serving God, he completely renounced all social ties and abandoned his home; he adopted the appearance of a madman (as a result of which he was often subjected to abuse by the crowd) in order to expose the madness of this world; in fair weather and foul, he always wore rags and went barefoot, carrying heavy iron chains. Russians paid great attention to the predictions of *yurodivye*, believing they had been divinely endowed with the gift of prophecy and that they spoke with the voice of God. In particular, Russian holy fools (rather like their functional equivalents, the court jesters of the West) were supposed to be able to denounce powerful men, including tsars, with impunity. Ivan, as a profoundly religious person, is likely to have shared these attitudes towards *yurodivye*. Thus it is not improbable that Ivan Groznyi, who would not accept advice and censure even from his most highly placed subjects, might have heeded the denunciatory words and threats of the 'mad' beggar. There were, however, other reasons for Ivan's relatively mild treatment of Pskov: the Pskovans had, for example, been persecuted at the time of the 'Izborsk treason', before the campaign against Novgorod began.

The executions in Moscow

On leaving Pskov, Tsar Ivan returned to Aleksandrova Sloboda, where the investigation of the Novgorod 'treason' continued. Several hundred disgraced nobles were brought from Novgorod with members of their families. In the torture-chambers of the *oprichnina* the 'traitors' arrested in Novgorod were subjected to harsh questioning, in which Tsar Ivan himself took part. As the *oprichnina* interrogators and torturers worked on their victims, an extensive dossier was compiled.

The actual indictment in the Novgorod 'treason' trial of 1570, like other judicial documents of the *oprichnina*, has not survived, but a detailed description of it is preserved in the inventory of the archive of the Ambassadorial Chancellery which was compiled after the Moscow fire of 1626. This source provides a fairly clear indication of the identities of the individuals implicated in the affair, the nature of the accusations against them, the ways in which the investigation was conducted, and the forms of punishment inflicted on those found guilty. The document states:

> The list of articles of the investigation of the case of treason . . . against Archbishop Pimen of Novgorod and the Novgorod secretaries and assistant secretaries, and the merchants, and the prelate's [archbishop's] officials, nobles and assistant secretaries: that they had dealings in Moscow with the boyars Aleksei Basmanov and his son Fedor; the treasurer Nikita Funikov; the Keeper of the State Seal, Ivan Mikhailovich Viskovatyi; Semen Vasil'evich Yakovlya; the secretaries Vasilii Stepanov and Andrei Vasil'ev; and Prince Afanasii Vyazemskii, about the surrender of Great Novgorod and Pskov, which they and Archbishop Pimen wanted to hand over to the Lithuanian king; and with malice aforethought they planned to kill Tsar and Grand Prince Ivan Vasil'evich of All Rus', and to place Prince Vladimir Andreevich [Staritskii] on the throne. And during the investigation many people testified under torture to the treason of Archbishop Pimen of Novgorod and his accomplices and admitted their own guilt. And in connection with this case many people were put to death in various ways, and others were sent to prison . . . [9]

As we can see, Ivan Groznyi and his entourage had organised large-scale judicial proceedings in Moscow. The investigation was carried out with horrific forms of torture, as a result of which the *oprichniki* not only obtained from the accused confessions of their own 'guilt', but also forced them to provide the evidence they desired against individuals who had incurred the tsar's displeasure.

In the course of the investigation the *oprichniki* acquired information about the supposed existence of an extensive and far-reaching conspiracy, involving not only the Novgorodians, but also members of the higher echelons of the Moscow *zemshchina* bureaucracy, as well as a number of prominent *oprichniki*. As the investigation developed, the main 'conspirators' turned out to be not the Novgorodians but individuals who had recently formed part of the tsar's immediate entourage and had acted as his advisers for many years. The main figures accused of 'treason' included the eminent statesman Ivan Mikhailovich Viskovatyi, who was

Keeper of the State Seal and secretary of the Ambassadorial Chancellery; the treasurer, Nikita Afanas'evich Funikov; and some other leading figures in the *zemshchina* administration. These men came from ordinary noble families and had made successful careers at court thanks to their outstanding personal qualities and the patronage of the tsar. Were they capable of betraying their sovereign in favour of Russia's enemy, Lithuania? Evidence casts serious doubt on the truth of such accusations. The Polish archives contain a very interesting letter from the Vice-Chancellor of the Grand Duchy of Lithuania, Ostafii Volovich, to the Lithuanian magnate Mikołaj Krzysztof Radziwiłł. In response to a question from Radziwiłł about the reasons why Viskovatyi was in disgrace, and whether he had really betrayed his sovereign in favour of Lithuania as well as the Turks and Tatars, Volovich wrote: 'I don't know about these Muslims [i.e. the Tatars and Turks], but he [Viskovatyi] was not well-disposed towards our Master's state [Poland-Lithuania] and His Royal Majesty's envoys always found him intractable'.[10]

It is hard to believe that the Basmanovs, Prince Afanasii Vyazemskii and other prominent *oprichniki* could have turned traitor. These men occupied their high offices of state solely as a result of the tsar's patronage and their service in the *oprichnina*. We cannot conclusively judge whether the disgraced Novgorodians really had contacts with leading figures in the *oprichnina*, or what form such contacts might have assumed. The charge that Vyazemskii and the Basmanovs were involved in the Novgorod conspiracy was brought on the basis of 'confessions' extracted under torture, which can hardly serve as evidence of the true state of affairs. According to Schlichting, the tsar received a denunciation against Vyazemskii which claimed that he had tried to warn the Novgorodians of the punitive expedition against them. There is nothing in other sources, however, to confirm this information; and Schlichting himself states that the denunciation was unfounded.

Why did Tsar Ivan repudiate his closest advisers, who had headed the state administration for so many years? Even in this milieu doubts had begun to emerge about the wisdom of continuing the policy of total repression. According to Schlichting, Viskovatyi tried to persuade the tsar to stop the executions and 'to think about who might fight for him, or even live with him, if he executed so many brave men'. The incessant terror did not appear to be justified by any valid political considerations, and it seems that some of the *oprichniki* themselves had become alarmed and dissatisfied by the mass executions and punishments which the tsar was inflicting on his subjects. It is certainly clear that at the end of the 1560s and beginning of the 1570s a deep division had taken place not just between the *oprichnina* and the *zemshchina*, but within the *oprichnina* court itself. All the evidence suggests that the tsar had lost confidence in his former associates even before the start of the Novgorod expedition. It is significant that A.D. Basmanov, a prominent general and one of the founders of the *oprichnina*, was not allowed to take part in the Novgorod campaign of 1570.

By the beginning of the 1570s the leadership of the *oprichnina* had been changed. The new men who came to the fore were of lowly birth. Unlike the former leaders of the *oprichnina* court, these men, coming as they did from the provincial nobility, had no longstanding links with the *zemshchina* magnates, and secretly hated the aristocracy. In view of the deepening divisions in society and the increasing harshness of the repressions, Ivan Groznyi may have hoped that such men would provide him with a loyal base of support in his campaign against 'sedition' and his suppression of the growing opposition to the *oprichnina* regime. The most prominent figures in this new cohort, Malyuta Skuratov and Vasilii Gryaznoi, had demonstrated their loyalty to the tsar by killing many 'traitors to the sovereign'. These men headed the political investigation apparatus and in practice were in charge of the *oprichnina* in its final stage. The leader of this new group, the notorious Skuratov was to become a symbol of the *oprichnina* in Russian folklore. Because he enjoyed the tsar's favour, Skuratov acquired a high position at court. By the spring of 1570 he had been given the rank of conciliar courtier (*dumnyi dvoryanin*). Although this was a relatively modest duma rank (because of his humble origin he could not hope to obtain rapid promotion to the highest duma ranks of boyar or *okol'nichii*), his real power and influence were enormous. The marriages of his daughters testify to this. One of them was married to Boris Godunov (the future tsar, the brother-in-law of Tsarevich Fedor); another to the eminent prince Ivan Mikhailovich Glinskii, a relative of the tsar; and a third to a member of the princely family of Suzdal', Prince Dmitrii Ivanovich Shuiskii (the brother of future tsar Vasilii Shuiskii). Around Skuratov there formed a fairly large and cohesive circle of like-minded men who, like Skuratov, came from the ranks of the provincial nobility and hoped, thanks to the *oprichnina*, to reach the highest echelons of power. In Skuratov's wake his many relatives began to find advancement at the *oprichnina* court. His nephew Bogdan Yakovlevich Bel'skii had a particularly successful career in the *oprichnina* and post-*oprichnina* years: he became a conciliar courtier and arms-bearer (*oruzhnichii*), and subsequently an *okol'nichii* and later even a boyar. As a result of his power and influence, Skuratov built up strong support in the chancellery secretariat. His relatives and supporters included the influential and energetic secretaries, the brothers Andrei and Vasilii Yakovlevich Shchelkalov, as well as the Klobukovs, the Sukins and other prominent members of the Moscow bureaucracy.

But to establish themselves firmly in power, the new cohort of *oprichniki* and officials had to remove the royal advisers who had headed the administration for so many years. In the intense political struggle which developed for power and primacy at court, the denunciation and slander of political opponents played an important part. This was one of the main reasons for the dismissal and disgrace of the old leaders of the Ambassadorial and other major chancelleries, including Viskovatyi and Funikov, and also of the previous leaders of the *oprichnina* – the Basmanovs, Vyazemskii and Cherkasskii. The fate of the members of the tsar's old entourage was sealed by the fact that Ivan Groznyi sided with the new group of *oprichniki* and chancellery officials, whom he hoped to mould into a firm base of political support for himself.

It seems more than just coincidence that so many prominent members of the Moscow *zemshchina* bureaucracy were accused of involvement in the Novgorod-Moscow treason trial alongside the leaders of the *oprichnina* court. Not only had these two groups worked together in government for many years, but they were also linked by close personal and family relationships.[11] The *zemshchina* treasurer, Nikita Afanas'evich Funikov, was married to the sister of the *oprichnik* Prince Afanasii Vyazemskii. Another prominent *oprichnik*, Fedor Alekseevich Basmanov, was married to the daughter of Prince Vasilii Andreevich Sitskii and his wife Anna Romanovna, née Zakhar'ina-Yur'eva, who was the sister of Tsaritsa Anastasiya. As a result of this marriage, the Basmanovs were related to another of the accused, Semen Vasil'evich Yakovlev-Zakhar'in, and to the Zakhar'in clan as a whole. It is worth noting that Ivan Mikhailovich Viskovatyi and Nikita Funikov owed their careers largely to the support and patronage of the Zakhar'ins. The Zakhar'in clan, the kinsmen of Tsar Ivan's first wife, had had enormous influence on the course of political events in the 1550s and 1560s. The Zakhar'ins' hostility towards Adashev and Sil'vestr had contributed to the dismissal of the latter and hence to the tsar's abandonment of the reform policy of the 1550s. Members of the Zakhar'in clan had also played a role in the introduction of the *oprichnina*. As we have seen, one of the chronicles states that the *oprichnina* was instituted on the advice of the 'evil men', Vasilii Mikhailovich Zakhar'in-Yur'ev and Aleksei Danilovich Basmanov; while other sources claim that the tsar was advised to introduce the *oprichnina* by his second wife, Mariya Temryukovna. The kinsmen of Ivan's first and second wives were linked by marriage ties. Tsaritsa Mariya

Temryukovna's brother, Prince Mikhail Temryukovich Cherkasskii, was married to a daughter of Vasilii Mikhailovich Zakhar'in-Yur'ev. It is significant that many members of the Zakhar'in clan, as well as Prince Mikhail Cherkasskii, fell victim to repression soon after the Novgorod-Moscow 'treason case' ended. According to some sources, after the Novgorod expedition there were sharp disagreements between the tsar and his elder son. The tsarevich may have championed the interests of his mother's kinsmen, the Zakhar'in boyars, who were seriously worried about the intensification of the repressions and their extension to the old Moscow boyar aristocracy and the upper echelons of the bureaucracy – the milieu with which they were closely linked.[12]

Thus at the beginning of the 1570s Ivan Groznyi's suspicions were aroused by all those who had until recently comprised his closest entourage, had headed the government and had determined the course of domestic and foreign policy. Because he was so convinced that his policy of consolidating autocratic power in Russia was right, he regarded the 'wavering' of the former government leaders, and their critical attitude towards his actions, as overt treason. The tsar was particularly angered by the fact that this 'treasonous' stance had been adopted by those closest to him, people he had trusted for many years and on whose loyalty he had counted.

In the summer of 1570 the punishment of the 'conspirators' began. In the second half of July the *oprichnina* authorities got a Church Council to condemn Archbishop Pimen and strip him of his archiepiscopal status. The disgraced prelate was sent to the Venevskii Monastery, where he died shortly afterwards. After Pimen's dismissal the tsar ordered the execution of his 'accomplices', the Novgorod nobles and officials, and also the most prominent heads of the Moscow chancelleries. The executions took place in Moscow on 25 July 1570 on a square in Kitai-gorod, which was popularly known as Pagan Meadow. About 300 condemned men were brought out on to the square; 134 of them were pardoned and released in return for deeds of surety (many of them were subsequently imprisoned or exiled to various towns), while the remainder were executed. Horrible deaths awaited the Keeper of the Seal, Viskovatyi, and the treasurer Funikov. The executioners soaked Funikov alternately with boiling and freezing water. Viskovatyi was tied to a post and all the *oprichniki* had to stab him with their daggers. The *oprichnik* who struck the final, fatal, blow was immediately accused of shortening his torment out of pity and sympathy towards the 'traitor'. Some of the others were also subjected to cruel and horrific forms of execution: their arms, legs and other parts of their bodies were cut off before they were beheaded.

The dreadful spectacle of these mass executions made a strong impression on the people of Moscow. According to Schlichting, the tsar asked the citizens whether he was right to execute traitors, and the people obediently endorsed his actions. But Ivan's bid for popular approval did not succeed in gaining him universal support. The tragic events of 1570 were recalled in the 'Tale of the merchant Khariton Beloulin', which was composed in the Moscow trading quarter. It told how before the very eyes of the terrified Muscovites 300 blocks and axes were set up in the centre of Moscow, with 300 executioners, one to each block. The tsar himself rode into the square, dressed in black and mounted on a black horse. He ordered the execution of 100 princes, 100 boyars and 100 merchants. One of the merchants, Khariton Beloulin, who was very tall and strong, pushed the executioners aside and cried out to the tsar, 'Why are you spilling innocent blood?' Beloulin continued to denounce the tsar even after he was beheaded, so the story went – his corpse stood upright and began to shake, knocking the executioners down. The tsar was terrified and retreated to his palace, ordering the remaining victims to be freed.[13]

News of the Moscow executions and of the atrocities committed by the *oprichniki* spread throughout Europe in the form of 'fly-sheets' (pamphlets).[14] In one German engraving Tsar Ivan is depicted as a mythical monster, sitting on a throne in the middle of a square which is littered with the corpses of his victims.

The Moscow executions bore a superficial resemblance to the public implementation of sentences imposed after due process of law, but the cruel and bizarre forms of punishment imposed on the 'traitors' were closer to the brutal and arbitrary killings and tortures which were routinely carried out by the *oprichniki*. Sources such as Kurbskii's 'History' and the accounts of foreign eye-witnesses describe deaths by impaling and dismemberment. Victims were sometimes baited with dogs or bears; more frequently they were strangled, stabbed, beheaded, drowned or burned alive, and their womenfolk were raped or indecently assaulted. No doubt in individual cases the sources exaggerate for sensational effect, in order to add weight to their denunciation of Ivan's tyranny; but the general picture they paint is consistent, a common theme being the horrific attacks by the *oprichniki* on the bodily integrity of their victims. The tsar himself is often said to have participated in the atrocities, or to have personally observed them; and Ivan's reputation as a blood-thirsty villain is based largely on these dreadful episodes.

The brutal methods involved in Ivan's executions and punishments were regarded by most contemporaries as evidence of the tsar's personal sadism and even as symptoms of madness; and, as we noted in the Introduction, many subsequent historians have also interpreted them in this way. Some recent scholars have, however, tried to explain them in terms of the religious concepts of the sixteenth century, and also of aspects of Russian popular culture.

S.B. Veselovskii in his study of the Memorial List noted that in many cases the tsar's victims were killed suddenly, and their bodies were often dismembered and left unburied. This meant that they were unable to receive the last rites of the Church, so that the tsar, in his self-appointed role as the agent of divine justice, not only punished their earthly bodies, but also deprived them of the opportunity to save their immortal souls. Other scholars have drawn attention to the fact that some of the more gruesome punishments inflicted by the *oprichniki* correspond to the torments of hell described in the Apocrypha and in the vision of the Last Judgment contained in the Book of Revelation. Like some of the victims of the *oprichniki*, sinners in hell were devoured by wild animals, or roasted alive. The alternation of heat and cold – as when the tsar's victims in Novgorod were set alight before being thrust under the ice, and when Funikov was tortured with boiling and freezing water – echoes medieval notions of hell as a place of great extremes of temperature. The concept of the *oprichnina* as the Last Judgment is consistent with Ivan's view of himself as God's representative on earth, with a right and a duty to punish sinners. A.M. Panchenko and B.A. Uspenskii have argued that the God whom Ivan served was the Old-Testament 'God of Sabaoth', God the Father in his most patriarchal and punitive mode. The warrior-hero of Ivan's youth, the Archangel Michael, may also have acted as a model in this respect, since Michael too, in his role as the 'dread Angel-General', was associated with the idea of divine punishment. Certainly, much of the symbolism of Ivan's punitive actions in the *oprichnina* period reflects the ideas about autocratic power which are expressed in his correspondence with Kurbskii and other writings; while the peculiarly 'hellish' features may be related to contemporary apocalyptic notions of the imminent end of the world. A.L. Yurganov has suggested that Ivan's choice of such forms of torment stems from the tsar's belief that the Second Coming of Christ, which had failed to materialise in 1492 or 1562 (7000 and 7070 years after the Creation respectively), would occur instead in 1569 (7077). The growth of evil and lawlessness in Russia, especially after 1562, indicated to Ivan that the 'last days' were indeed approaching and that it was his sacred duty to punish the wicked ahead of the Last Judgment.[15]

Other scholars stress the influence of popular culture on the often grotesque aspects of Ivan's terror. S.K. Rosovetskii has noted that several anecdotes which contemporary observers recount about Ivan are variants of tales about the fifteenth-century Wallachian prince, Vlad Tepes (better known as 'Vlad the Impaler', or Dracula). They reflect the tsar's assimilation to the folklore stereotype of a wickedly clever tyrant whose ingeniously devised tortures and executions contain an element of black humour. One example of this is a story told by Kurbskii about the landowner Nikita Kazarinov, who had sought to avoid the attentions of the *oprichniki* by becoming a monk ('he accepted the great angelic habit'). When Kazarinov was brought to Aleksandrova Sloboda, the tsar made him sit on a barrel of gunpowder and blew him up, saying, 'He is an angel: he ought to fly up to heaven!' (Dracula had supposedly impaled monks on a tall stake in order to help them to reach heaven more quickly). Such tales are not necessarily apocryphal: Rosovetskii suggests that Ivan deliberately aimed to create his own image as a Dracula-type figure through such behaviour, and that this device helped to form his subsequent folklore reputation as a champion of the people's interests. The tsar's harsh treatment of 'traitors' may have met with a degree of popular approval: some of the forms of Ivan's terror against the boyars, as Rosovetskii notes, are similar to those employed by the participants in Russian popular uprisings of the seventeenth century; and it may be worth recalling, too, the brutal way in which Prince Yurii Glinskii and his retainers were killed by the Moscow crowd in June 1547.[16]

The darkly comic elements in some of the tsar's cruel punishments may have helped to make them more acceptable to the ordinary Russian people. Developing ideas first put forward by Mikhail Bakhtin, some cultural historians have drawn attention to 'carnivalesque' features of Ivan's behaviour, such as his 'dethronement' of I.P. Fedorov in 1568, and his ritualised mockery of Archbishop Pimen of Novgorod in 1570. By utilising the idioms of comic folk culture in order to humiliate his highborn victims, the tsar may have consciously or unconsciously sought to gain public support for his eradication of treason. Certainly the bizarrely cruel forms of his actions made a strong and not entirely unfavourable impression on the Russian folk memory, especially when they were directed against unpopular figures such as boyars and officials. Folksongs about the tsar recalled, apparently with approval, how he boiled 'traitor-boyars' alive in cauldrons (a theme which may have been based on the torturing to death of Funikov in 1570), impaled them on stakes, and sewed them into bearskins and threw them into rivers. Even one of the most horrific of the Moscow executions of 1570 – the butchering of Viskovatyi on trumped-up charges of treason – was later recalled as a wittily appropriate form of execution for a corrupt official who had taken a goose stuffed with money as a bribe: cutting him up like a bird which was being prepared for the oven.[17]

These various scholarly approaches to the symbolic forms of the *oprichnina* terror are not necessarily mutually exclusive. There was no insurmountable gulf between 'high' and 'popular' culture in sixteenth-century Russia, and the tsar himself was familiar with both: we know, for example, that he employed minstrels as court entertainers. The symbolism of Ivan's behaviour was complex and multi-layered, containing elements drawn both from the Christian and from the semi-pagan folk traditions.

After the Moscow executions, harsh punishments were imposed on *oprichniki* accused of treason to the tsar. Admittedly Ivan, afraid of discrediting the *oprichnina* in the eyes of the Moscow crowd, did not choose to subject his servants to public execution. He preferred to dispose of his erstwhile henchmen secretly and without fuss. The tsar's former favourite Vyazemskii was arrested and savagely beaten, before being sent to the town of Gorodets on the Volga, where he was left to die in prison, fettered in iron chains. Aleksei Basmanov and his son Fedor were exiled to Beloozero, where they both died in disgrace. If Kurbskii's account is to be believed, Fedor Basmanov killed his father with his own hand, on the tsar's orders, but this did not save him from disgrace, and he died in prison.[18]

The punishment of the Basmanovs and Vyazemskii marked only the start of the 'eradication of treason' among the *oprichniki*. After the Basmanovs' disgrace their kinsmen the Pleshcheevs also fell into disfavour. A number of prominent *oprichniki* died in disgrace in the early 1570s, including Prince Mikhail Cherkasskii; the boyar and steward Lev Andreevich Saltykov; the boyar Prince Vasilii Ivanovich Temkin-Rostovskii, who had been involved in the removal of Metropolitan Filipp; the conciliar courtiers Ivan Fedorovich Vorontsov and Petr Vasil'evich Zaitsev; and the *kravchii* Fedor Ignat'evich Saltykov. The clan of the Zakhar'in boyars was decimated. The boyar Semen Vasil'evich Yakovlev, mentioned in the Novgorod investigation together with other 'traitor-Novgorodians', was killed by the *oprichniki* along with his son Nikita. The offspring of one of the initiators of the *oprichnina*, Vasilii Mikhailovich Yur'ev, were harshly punished: the tsar ordered the deaths of his daughter and grandson, and did not permit them to have a Christian burial. The *oprichnina* boyar Vasilii Petrovich Yakovlev-Zakhar'in, who served Tsarevich Ivan Ivanovich as his steward, was executed, as was his brother, the *zemshchina* boyar Ivan Petrovich Khiron Yakovlev. The Zakhar'ins' kinsman, the boyar Ivan Vasil'evich Bol'shoi Sheremetev, was forced to become a monk in order to avoid the tsar's disfavour.

The events of 1569–70 marked the culmination of the *oprichnina* terror. This period was characterised not only by the extraordinary and unprecedented scale of the executions and disgraces, but also by the fact that for the first time the persecution affected the *oprichniki* themselves. And although the old cohort of *oprichniki* who had lost the tsar's confidence were replaced by the new men headed by Malyuta Skuratov, who managed to demonstrate their devotion to the tsar, Ivan Groznyi's attitude towards the *oprichniki* had changed. The tsar began to lose his previous trust in his *oprichnina* bodyguard as his main and only base of support. All of this spoke of a deep crisis in the tsar's *oprichnina* policy.

The abolition of the *oprichnina*

At the end of the 1560s and beginning of the 1570s Russia found itself in a difficult situation. The political crisis coincided with an economic one. A bad harvest in 1569 and outbreaks of disease aggravated the desperate condition of the population. The Livonian War, which was now entering its second decade, had exhausted the country's material resources. And the population suffered not only from the *oprichnina* policy itself, but also from the arbitrary actions of the *oprichniki*. When he issued the *oprichnina* decree, the tsar had promised the people that with the establishment of autocracy and the eradication of 'treason', law and order would be guaranteed in Russia. But in practice things often turned out very differently. Taking advantage of their exceptional powers and privileges, what the *oprichniki* got up to was often illegal, including robbery. In his account of the events of this period, Heinrich von Staden describes his 'deeds' of pillage and violence with amazing cynicism. Staden informs us, evidently on the basis of his own experience, that if an *oprichnik* lived next to someone from the *zemshchina*, he could take his neighbour's land and property without any fear of being brought to account. Things reached such a pass that all sorts of social riff-raff dressed up as *oprichniki* and robbed others with impunity, taking advantage of the universal fear of the *oprichnina*. It was difficult and even dangerous to seek redress against the *oprichniki*. Complaints against them often failed to reach the tsar, and piled up in the *oprichnina* chancelleries. It was only after Ivan's death that the *zemskie* tried to obtain redress for the 'injuries' inflicted on them by the tsar's servants. But until then, as is evident from the wording of their subsequent petitions, they 'kept quiet' and 'dared not' complain, because the *oprichniki* 'had then had freedom to do whatever they wanted'.

Of course the tsar himself did not encourage outright banditry, and took some steps against it, particularly after his removal of the leading *oprichniki* at the beginning of the 1570s. For example, the *oprichnina* boyar Prince Vasilii Temkin-Rostovskii was brought to trial after he incurred the tsar's displeasure. He was charged with refusing to repay a large sum of money he had borrowed from an official, and with killing his creditor's son to intimidate him. The court confiscated Temkin's estate. But such measures were unable to halt the illegal acts of the *oprichniki*, since the root of the phenomenon lay in the very nature of the *oprichnina* policy, involving as it did the division of the realm and of the service class, and the granting of various kinds of privileges to the *oprichniki*, including the right to implement their own form of justice. The outrages committed by the *oprichniki* fuelled popular dissatisfaction with the tsar's policy. In the end the *oprichniki* themselves became demoralised with the violence and pillaging. A graphic picture of the state of the morale of the *oprichnina* leadership is provided by Staden, who visited the tsar's Moscow residence in the early 1570s. When he entered the *oprichnina* court, he tells us, he found that nothing was being done: everyone was depressed and scared, and concerned only with himself. The tsar had every reason to be dissatisfied with his *oprichniki*. The *oprichnina* corps had grown rapidly with the incorporation of new territory into the *oprichnina*, and its members had become weighed down with the goods they had stolen during the punitive expeditions. As a result, they lost their ability to carry out effectively their main function of protecting the life and lands of their sovereign. This was graphically illustrated by subsequent events connected with the Crimean khan's attack on Moscow.

At the end of the 1560s Russia's international position became more difficult. At Lublin in 1569 Poland and Lithuania formed a union which led to the combination of their military forces against Russia. The coup in Sweden which overthrew Ivan's ally, King Eric XIV, had destroyed all hope of a coalition of their two states against Poland and Lithuania. Russia now faced the danger of conflict in the Baltic against two enemies simultaneously: the united Polish-Lithuanian Commonwealth and Sweden. Admittedly, in the summer of 1570 the tsar's diplomats managed to negotiate a three-year truce with Lithuania, which was unprepared for war with Russia and wanted peace. Taking advantage of this respite, the Russian government attempted to strengthen its position on the Baltic. The Muscovite diplomats put forward a bold and imaginative plan for the creation of a vassal Livonian kingdom under Russian control. It was to be headed by Duke Magnus, the brother of the Danish king, Frederick

II. In the summer of 1570 Magnus came to Moscow and took an oath of allegiance to the tsar, in which he agreed to provide the Russian army with a specified quantity of cavalry and infantry. In return he would receive the Livonian crown and the support of Russian troops. The new state was promised considerable autonomy: the estates were to retain their traditional rights; the population would preserve its religious freedom; and Russian officials and tax-collectors were not to be allowed to enter its territory. The tsar's agreement with Magnus was reinforced with ties of kinship: the Danish prince was betrothed to the tsar's cousin Evfim'ya, the daughter of the executed appanage prince Vladimir Staritskii. Using as his emissaries Johann Taube and Elert Kruse, the Livonian noblemen serving in the *oprichnina*, the tsar negotiated with the Livonians about their transfer to Russian control. Some Livonian nobles were persuaded to support the tsar, but the inhabitants of Tallin, the most important city in northern Livonia, refused to recognise Magnus as their ruler. The army of the 'King of Livonia', accompanied by a large Muscovite force, was sent against the 'rebellious' city. Tallin was subjected to a fierce artillery bombardment, but without a fleet it was very difficult to take the well fortified sea-port. Russia hoped for naval support from her ally Denmark, but the Danish vessels failed to arrive. Soon peace was concluded between Denmark and Sweden. The tsar's plans for the rapid and painless conquest of the Baltic had ended in failure.

As large Russian armies were concentrating on Livonia, Ivan faced a threat from the south. Taking advantage of Russia's weakness, Turkey and the Crimean khanate began to move against her. Their aim was to force Russia out of the Volga region. If they had succeeded, they would have wiped out Ivan's gains of the 1550s, the annexation of Kazan' and Astrakhan'. In 1569 Turkey sent a large army to Azov which subsequently headed for Astrakhan' with the Crimean Tatars. However, the campaign failed in its aim of capturing Astrakhan'. In the spring of 1571 the Crimean khan Devlet-Girei launched a raid on Moscow in which all the military forces of the Crimean Horde took part. The *zemshchina* regiments were stationed on the River Oka to confront the Tatars. To strengthen the Russian defences, an *oprichnina* army headed by the tsar himself went to assist them. What happened next was unexpected. With the assistance of some Russian traitors (led by Kudeyar Tishenkov, a nobleman from Belev) the Tatars managed to cross the Oka at an undefended point and outflanked the Russian army from the west. This meant that the first Russian troops the Tatars encountered were the *oprichnina* army. The appearance of the Crimeans close to the tsar's headquarters took Ivan and his generals completely by surprise. The tsar was unwilling to join battle with numerically superior forces, and he rapidly retreated northwards with his main army. By-passing Moscow, he went to Aleksandrova Sloboda, and then to Yaroslavl', entrusting the defence of the capital to the *zemshchina* regiments. Kurbskii was quick to accuse Ivan of cowardice. But evidence suggests that the *oprichnina* army sent against the Tatars was relatively small, and the tsar did not want to risk his personal bodyguards, who were his main political base of support. He did not have great faith in the military prowess of his *oprichnina* troops, who were more used to 'fighting' the population of their own country. But the sources suggest the main problem was Ivan's fear of treason on the part of the *oprichniki*.

The *zemshchina* generals managed to withdraw their troops to Moscow and organise the defence of the capital. Encountering strong resistance from the Russian forces, the khan decided to avoid an open battle. He took advantage of the fact that the Moscow trading quarter was not defended by stone walls, and ordered its wooden buildings to be set alight. Moscow was gripped by a terrible fire, in which virtually the entire city was destroyed and much of the capital's population perished. Many people were burned alive; and those who sought refuge in the stone-built houses and cellars died from smoke and suffocation. The commander-in-chief of the *zemshchina* army, the leading boyar Prince Ivan Dmitrievich Bel'skii, was killed by the effects of smoke. On the day after the fire the Tatars withdrew from Moscow.

On 15 June Tsar Ivan arrived in Moscow. He blamed the *zemshchina* boyars and generals for what had happened. During the investigation the *zemshchina* boyar Prince Ivan Fedorovich Mstislavskii 'admitted' he had led the Tatars to Moscow. But in spite of such a serious admission – the death penalty was usually imposed for such treason – the tsar not only spared Mstislavskii's life, but also let him remain in the duma, although he took some of the prince's lands away from him. It seems the tsar did not believe the accusations against Mstislavskii. By publicly blaming the leading *zemshchina* boyar, he probably hoped to divert responsibility for the military defeat from himself. He was profoundly shocked by the sight of his capital burnt to the ground. The tsar also suffered great stress during his negotiations with the Crimean envoys. The khan was convinced that Russia would take a long time to recover from the blow, and thought that he could easily bring her to her knees and impose his will on her. The khan's envoys behaved arrogantly, as if they were dealing with a defeated power. In order to prevent a new Tatar raid the Russian government was prepared to make concessions and, in particular, to surrender Astrakhan' to the khan. But the Tatar envoys demanded that

Kazan' also be handed over. This was unacceptable to the Russians, and the negotiations were deadlocked.

The tsar prepared to repel Tatar aggression by assembling all available military forces on the southern frontier. In view of the danger which threatened the country, the rivalry between the *oprichnina* and the *zemshchina* was temporarily forgotten. Ivan's government took the important decision to combine the *zemshchina* and *oprichnina* forces and place them under a unified command.

In the summer of 1572 a huge Crimean army headed by Devlet-Girei again invaded Russia. The decisive battle took place at the end of July and beginning of August near the village of Molodi, 45 kilometres from Moscow. The combined army of the *zemshchina* and the *oprichnina* under the *zemshchina* boyar Prince Mikhail Ivanovich Vorotynskii inflicted a crushing defeat on Devlet-Girei. One of the *oprichnina* generals, Prince Dmitrii Ivanovich Khvorostinin, also distinguished himself in the course of the battle, when at a crucial moment he organised the defensive use of a *gulyai-gorod* – a mobile wooden fortress on wheels, containing *strel'tsy*, artillery and detachments of foreign mercenaries. The victory was a total one. The khan's sons were killed in the battle, as were many prominent Tatar generals. By routing the Crimean Horde in open warfare, the Russian army inflicted a shattering blow to the military might of the Crimea. The threat of Tatar-Turkish expansion at Russia's expense was eliminated for many years to come.

The victory at Molodi clearly showed that it was only by uniting her armed forces that Russia could sustain her independence when threatened by a foreign power. Even Tsar Ivan himself was coming to realise this.

In the autumn of 1572 Ivan abolished the *oprichnina* just as suddenly as he had introduced it. Even the use of the word '*oprichnina*', according to Staden, was prohibited on pain of punishment. Ivan's decision to do away with the *oprichnina*, it seems, was not an impulsive one, but the result of long reflection on the future of the Russian state and on the fate of the *oprichnina* itself. Such reflection was prompted by the development of a serious internal political crisis and by the threat of foreign conquest. Shortly before the invasion by the Crimean khan in 1572, when Tsar Ivan was in Novgorod waiting with trepidation for the arrival of news from the southern frontier, he set about composing a new version of his will. In it he included a short but significant phrase about the *oprichnina*: 'As far as the *oprichnina* which I have established is concerned, my sons Ivan and Fedor are free to decide this issue as they choose, but the model [of state administration in the form of the *oprichnina*] is already available and ready prepared.'[19] Ivan leaves it entirely up to his sons to decide whether to retain or abolish the *oprichnina* after his death, and the statement reveals a certain degree of indifference on the tsar's part about the fate of his beloved project.

Historians still cannot agree whether Ivan really decided to put an end to his pet scheme, or whether the abolition of the *oprichnina* was just another manoeuvre to appease public opinion. Some scholars suggest that the *oprichnina* continued to exist (admittedly under different names – 'court' or 'appanage') after 1572, and right up until Ivan's death.[20] The proponents of this view cite the fact that even after 1572 Ivan's government carried out widespread repressions and divided the servicemen and the country into the *zemshchina* and the 'sovereign's appanage'. But two separate issues need to be distinguished here: the issue of the abolition of the *oprichnina* in the form in which it had been instituted in 1565; and the issue of the application of *oprichnina*-style measures in government policy after 1572.

That the *oprichnina* was abolished in 1572 is indisputable. It is directly and unambiguously attested to in Staden's memoirs and in the accounts of other contemporaries. But particularly valuable evidence is provided by impartial official documents which show that from 1572 the *oprichnina* and *zemshchina* territory were reunited, as was the state apparatus. Thus, for example, between March 1572 and March 1573 the division of the Novgorod administration and of the territory of Novgorod itself into an *oprichnina* (trading side) and a *zemshchina* (Sophia side) sector was ended. After 1572 the *oprichnina* and *zemshchina* regiments were merged. Some of the disgraced courtiers were pardoned. *Zemshchina* nobles who had been expelled from *oprichnina* districts were able to return to their old estates. For example, the Taratin nobles got back their confiscated hereditary lands in the *oprichnina* district of Pereyaslavl'.

The abolition of the *oprichnina* raised the hopes of the Russian people that long-awaited peace and justice would be restored. But, as subsequent events were to demonstrate, these hopes were not to be fulfilled. The country did not (and, indeed, could not) return to the old pre-*oprichnina* ways.

Notes

1 Skrynnikov, *Tsarstvo terrora*, p.361.

2 Staden, *The Land and Government of Muscovy*, p.25; 'Poslanie Ioganna Taube i Elerta Kruze', p.48. According to R.G. Skrynnikov, the entire *oprichnina* army comprised no more than 6,000–7,000 men, including nobles, *strel'tsy* and military slaves: R.G. Skrynnikov, *Tragediya Novgoroda*, Moscow, 1994, p.81.

3   *Novgorodskie letopisi*, St Petersburg, 1879, p.342.

4   Florya, *Ivan Groznyi*, pp.238–9.

5   Uspenskij, 'Tsar and Pretender', p.282.

6   Skrynnikov, *Tragediya Novgoroda*, pp.102–5.

7   Kobrin, *Ivan Groznyi*, pp.81–3.

8   For various versions, see Perrie, *The Image of Ivan the Terrible in Russian Folklore*, pp.77–9.

9   *Opis' arkhiva Posol'skogo prikaza 1626 goda*, Moscow, 1977, pp.257–8.

10 Gralya, *Ivan Mikhailov Viskovatyi*, p.369; Florya, *Ivan Groznyi*, p.248.

11 For further details, see Gralya, *Ivan Mikhailov Viskovatyi*, pp.373–4.

12 Skrynnikov, *Tsarstvo terrora*, pp.431–3.

13 See D.N. Al'shits, 'Drevnerusskaya povest' pro tsarya Ivana Vasil'evicha i kuptsa Kharitona Beloulina', *TODRL*, vol.17, 1961, pp.255–71.

14 Andreas Kappeler, *Ivan Groznyj im Spiegel des ausländischen Druckschriften seiner Zeit. Ein Beitrag zur Geschichte des westlichen Russlandbildes*, Frankfurt am Main, 1972.

15 Veselovskii, *Issledovaniya*, pp.325–36; Panchenko and Uspenskii, 'Ivan Groznyi i Petr Velikii', pp.66–78; Yurganov, 'Oprichnina i strashnyi sud', pp.52–75. See also Hunt, 'Ivan IV's Personal Mythology of Kingship'.

16 S.K. Rosovetskii, 'Ustnaya proza XVI-XVII vv. ob Ivane Groznom – pravitele', *Russkii fol'klor*, vol.20, 1981, pp.71–95.

17 Mikhail Bakhtin, *Rabelais and his World*, trans. Helene Iswolsky, Cambridge, MA: M.I.T. Press, 1968, pp.270–71; Perrie, *The Image of Ivan the Terrible in Russian Folklore*.

18 *Kurbsky's History*, pp.288–9.

19 *Dukhovnye i dogovornye gramoty velikikh i udel'nykh knyazei XIV-XVI vv.*, Moscow and Leningrad, 1950, p.444.

20 For a robust statement of this position, see D.N. Al'shits, *Nachalo samoderzhaviya v Rossii: Gosudarstvo Ivana Groznogo*, Leningrad, 1988, pp.233–4.

Chapter 9

After the *Oprichnina*

The 'grand princely rule' of Simeon Bekbulatovich

After the abolition of the *oprichnina*, Tsar Ivan reigned for almost twelve more years: that is, for considerably longer than the *oprichnina* had lasted. The final period of Ivan's reign (1572–1584) is perhaps the most obscure and puzzling. The main question which the historian has to face is this: did Ivan Groznyi really decide in 1572 to put an end to the *oprichnina*, or was the termination of his pet project only another stratagem on the tsar's part, designed to mollify public opinion? As shown in the previous chapter, the abolition of the *oprichnina* was fact, not illusion. Major changes took place in national life after 1572: the state and the nobility were no longer divided into *oprichnina* and *zemshchina* sectors; the forcible resettlements ceased, as did the mass executions and disgraces. In the post-*oprichnina* period of Ivan's reign we do not find any further large-scale repressions such as the dreadful events of 1570, in Novgorod and then in Moscow. After 1572 some of those who had been disgraced were pardoned and returned to their old estates. A decree was issued about the restoration to *zemshchina* nobles of landholdings confiscated from them during the *oprichnina* period. Heinrich von Staden's memoirs provide evidence of this, as do contemporary documents. Of course, it was very difficult in practice to implement this policy, which involved the large-scale expropriation of lands from their new *oprichniki* owners, and the allocation of other lands to the latter in their stead. In the context of the general devastation of the economy it was essentially unrealistic even to attempt this. As a consequence only a small proportion of the *zemshchina* nobles received their old estates back.[1] Nevertheless, the very fact that some hereditary estates were returned to their former owners was a major indicator of the changes under way.

It may have seemed that after 1572 the country was beginning to return to the good old days which had existed before the introduction of the *oprichnina*. But there is considerable evidence that Ivan Groznyi had no intention of restoring the old order or of renouncing his general policy of repression. In the spring of 1573, only a few months after the abolition of the *oprichnina*, a major political trial was held in which the defendants were the prominent and high-born boyars Prince Mikhail Ivanovich Vorotynskii (the victor over the Tatars at the battle of Molodi), Prince Nikita Ivanovich Odoevskii and Mikhail Yakovlevich Morozov. They were all charged with treason and put to death in April 1573. It is not entirely clear why they had fallen into disfavour. According to Kurbskii, Vorotynskii was accused on the basis of a denunciation by one of his servants who claimed that he had tried to 'bewitch' the tsar. Ivan Groznyi personally took part in interrogating Vorotynskii. Horrific means of torture were applied, from which the prince subsequently died. The disgraces and executions of 1573 marked the start of a new wave of repressions. But what is noteworthy is not just the repressions, but the methods of conducting political investigations, which had not changed in any way since the days of the *oprichnina*. As in the *oprichnina* period, the tsar imposed punishment without trial and without due process of law, and was guided primarily by his own political preoccupations. The investigations were carried out with appalling methods of torture, and all sorts of far-fetched denunciations were brought into play. We have already referred to the revealing account of an interrogation in which, while the victims were undergoing torture, the tsar angrily demanded to be told which of the boyars had betrayed him, whereupon he prompted the witnesses to provide the testimony he desired against named individuals.[2] This interrogation was one the tsar conducted in January 1574 of Russian prisoners who had returned from the Crimea; and the account clearly demonstrates the methods by which investigations were carried out in both the *oprichnina* and post-*oprichnina* periods. Thus we cannot speak of any return after 1572 to the norms of legality which had existed in the conduct of political investigations before the introduction of the *oprichnina*. The Englishman Jerome Horsey, who first went to Russia in 1573, witnessed tortures and executions that were just as cruel and bizarre as those described by Schlichting, Staden, and Taube and Kruse in the previous decade.

Further evidence that Tsar Ivan retained his former ways of ruling is provided by the fact that the political leadership remained in the hands of more or less the same circle of royal favourites and henchmen who had held power before the abolition of the *oprichnina*. The key positions in government were filled even after 1572 by the group of low-born conciliar courtiers, headed by Malyuta Skuratov, who had run the country at the end of the *oprichnina* period. These men had come to power by squeezing out members of the old aristocracy, and so they had a vested interest in the continuation of the *oprichnina* policy. Ivan's relationships with his low-born favourites are well illustrated by his correspondence with Vasilii Gryaznoi,[3] who was held captive by the Crimean Tatars in 1573. In his letter to Tsar Ivan, Gryaznoi wrote: 'How can I not mention my [lowly] origin? If it were not for your royal graciousness, I could not have become such a [great] man. You, sire, like God, rank [i.e. exalt] both great and small.' Ivan in his turn constantly reminded Gryaznoi of his humble origin; he claimed that he had promoted low-born men like him because of the treason of the old princes and boyars, in the expectation that his new servants would be unquestioningly loyal to him. So we can see that Ivan's views on the nature of the relationship between the sovereign and his subjects had changed little since the *oprichnina* period. Even after 1572 the listing of *zemshchina* nobles and of members of the tsar's special court continued to be done on separate documents. The historian D.N. Al'shits discovered a list of boyars and nobles from 1573, which, as he and A.L. Stanislavskii have demonstrated, contains only the names of members of Ivan Groznyi's special court, and does not include *zemshchina* men.[4] Historians have also noted that the 'court' of 1573 was very similar to the *oprichnina* court of the late 1560s and early 1570s. It is difficult to judge whether the existence of separate lists of *zemshchina* men and 'court' men (members of the tsar's personal entourage) meant that these two groups were really differentiated from a service point of view, or whether the distinction was purely a technical one, as S.B. Veselovskii believed (the compilation of a single new consolidated list of members of the sovereign's court after the abolition of the *oprichnina* would have taken some time). But one thing is undoubtedly clear: Ivan was in no hurry to part with his old *oprichnina* cronies.

In the middle of the 1570s there was a new wave of persecution. After Malyuta Skuratov was killed beneath the walls of the Livonian fortress of Paida in January 1573, the government was headed by the tsar's favourites Vasilii Ivanovich Umnoi-Kolychev and Prince Boris Davydovich Tulupov, who were both former *oprichniki*. The new government, however, did not last long. As a result of court intrigues, the Bel'skiis (Malyuta's kinsmen), the Godunovs and the Nagois managed to have Kolychev and Tulupov removed from power. In August 1575 Kolychev and Tulupov were executed, along with some of their relatives and supporters, accused of conspiring against the tsar. It is difficult to tell whether there was any basis for the accusations against them. As in other such cases, the tsar was totally confident that what he was doing was correct. The executions of Kolychev and Tulupov began a new spiral of repression. Among those disgraced was Ivan Groznyi's personal physician, Eleazar Bomelius. As well as treating the tsar's illnesses, this 'evil sorcerer', as he was popularly known, prepared potions to poison courtiers who had fallen out of favour, made astrological predictions for the tsar and engaged in court intrigues. Eventually, having accumulated a considerable fortune as a result of his dirty deeds, Bomelius decided to flee abroad, but he was detained and brought to Moscow, where he was tortured to death. Another victim at this time was Archbishop Leonid of Novgorod. According to Jerome Horsey, Leonid was accused of practising sorcery and keeping witches, and of other crimes. He was condemned to death, but the sentence was commuted to imprisonment, and the disgraced archbishop soon died in captivity. One chronicler claims that the tsar had Leonid sewn into a bearskin and set dogs on him.[5] Abbot Evfimii of the Chudov Monastery and Abbot Iosif of the Simonov Monastery were also persecuted. All of these victims, including the clergymen, had recently belonged to the tsar's closest circle of confidants. In October 1575 Protasii Vasil'evich Yur'ev-Zakharin was executed; he was a close associate of Tsarevich Ivan Ivanovich, and a nephew of Tsaritsa Anastasiya Romanovna.

Ivan again began to suspect that his subjects were preparing a wide-ranging conspiracy against him, and that the core of the 'plotters' were members of his immediate entourage. He was so unsure of the stability of his position, and so fearful for his personal safety, that in 1574 he again returned to the question of obtaining asylum in England, an issue which he raised in discussions with the English envoy Daniel Sylvester.

Faced with a serious political crisis, Tsar Ivan again announced his abdication. In the autumn of 1575 he placed the baptised Tatar khan Simeon Bekbulatovich on the throne in his stead. According to a chron-icler, Ivan played the role of one of Simeon's boyars.[6] The text has survived of a very strange 'petition' from Ivan Groznyi to Simeon Bekbulatovich, dated 30 October 1575. In this document, 'Ivanets Vasil'ev with his little children' (as was customary in real petitions, Ivan referred to himself and his sons in diminutive forms and without titles) humbly begged 'the sovereign and grand prince Simeon Bekbulatovich' to 'have mercy' and allow him 'to sort out his people', that is, to choose new servants for himself and to dismiss the unsuitable ones.[7] In sending a demeaning 'petition' to Simeon, Ivan was blatantly play-acting and dissimulating (in this respect, the petition was entirely consistent with the style of some of his other literary compositions, and with aspects of his 'comic' mode of behaviour).[8] It was clear to all that he remained the real master of affairs, and Bekbulatovich was merely a figurehead. It is revealing that

Bekbulatovich bore the title not of tsar, but only of 'Grand Prince of All Rus''. Tsar Ivan himself, in a conversation with Daniel Sylvester, stressed that Bekbulatovich had not been crowned or elected to the tsardom, but placed on the throne at Ivan's wish, and that Ivan retained for himself the sceptre and other symbols of supreme power, as well as all the royal treasure.

Contemporaries and historians have put forward various explanations of this strange and unusual political act. It has been suggested that Ivan may have temporarily transferred the crown in order to facilitate his own election to the Polish throne during an interregnum in Poland.[9] Alternatively, he may have wanted to shift on to Bekbulatovich the responsibility for unpopular financial measures concerning the abolition of tax concessions for monasteries.[10] One Russian seventeenth-century chronicle reports a rumour that Tsar Ivan placed Bekbulatovich on the throne because he was afraid of the predictions of sorcerers who had prophesied that that year would witness 'the death of the Muscovite tsar'.[11] None of these suggestions, however, has found unanimous support amongst historians.

One issue which has particularly exercised some scholars is the significance of Bekbulatovich's Tatar identity. He was a Chingisid, a descendant of Genghis Khan, and was the great-grandson of Akhmat, the last khan of the Great Horde; his father, Khan Bekbulat, had entered Russian service in the 1560s. Bekbulat married a sister of Tsar Ivan's second wife, Mariya Temryukovna, so that Simeon Bekbulatovich was the tsar's nephew by marriage. Around 1570 Ivan appointed him as khan of the Kasimov khanate, which had been part of the Muscovite state since the mid-fifteenth century (Simeon Bekbulatovich was a distant relative of Shigalei, the former khan of both Kasimov and Kazan'). In 1573 he was baptised (his former name was Sain Bulat), and in 1575 he married Anastasiya, the daughter of I.F. Mstislavskii, who was related to the Russian royal family.[12] Thus it may have been Bekbulatovich's close kinship with the dynasty that led Ivan to appoint him as 'grand prince'. Omeljan Pritsak and Donald Ostrowski, however, attach greater importance to Bekbulatovich's Chingisid origin. They have noted that non-Chingisid steppe rulers such as Tamerlane set up Chingisid puppet khans in order to imbue their own rule with Chingisid charisma. Pritsak suggests that Ivan too was attempting to benefit from this charisma, to strengthen his position at a time when the new wave of executions indicated that he faced further resistance from his opponents. Ostrowski also believes that Ivan was consciously imitating the actions of non-Chingisid rulers; he states that Ivan's abdication in favour of Bekbulatovich 'can best be understood in terms of the secular authority's residual Mongol orientation'.[13]

A rather different and perhaps more persuasive approach to the symbolism of the Bekbulatovich affair has been taken by B.A. Uspenskii, who compares the episode not only with Ivan's mock abdication in 1564, but also with his enthronement, dethronement and killing of I.P. Fedorov in 1568. By putting false tsars on the throne in his place, Uspenskii argues, Ivan was emphasising that he himself was the true, God-given ruler, even if he discarded the formal, external attributes of monarchy. In setting up Bekbulatovich as a 'pretender on the throne', Ivan was demonstrating that the Tatar khans who had formerly ruled Russia had themselves been false tsars, who had now given way to the true tsars, the grand princes of Moscow. Thus in the Bekbulatovich episode Ivan was making a point both about the end of illegitimate Tatar rule and about the divinely ordained nature of his own power.[14] For Uspenskii, therefore – in contrast to Ostrowski, who sees it as a Mongol tactic – the Bekbulatovich episode was entirely consistent with Ivan's neo-Byzantine concept of the sacred and charismatic nature of the power of the tsar.

Speculation will no doubt continue about the symbolism of this curious affair. One thing is clear, however: Simeon Bekbulatovich's 'grand princely rule' was not just a masquerade, as V.O. Klyuchevskii, S.F. Platonov and other historians believed.[15] Studies have shown convincingly that the political regime established after the elevation of the Tatar khan to the throne was similar in many respects to the former *oprichnina*.[16] As in the years of the *oprichnina*, the territory of Russia and the service class were again divided into two sectors: the *zemshchina* and the 'sovereign's appanage' or 'court'. The 'court' (this term came to signify both the special geographical area of the country and also the special institution: that is, in practice, a new *oprichnina*) contained a number of towns and districts, including both some former *oprichnina* territories (including Staritsa, Rzhev, Vologda, Poshekhon'e, Rostov and Dvina) and some lands which had not previously formed part of the *oprichnina* (Pskov, Dmitrov and others). Staritsa, which was the centre of the extensive 'appanage' (the new *oprichnina*), became Ivan's main residence.

The tsar also recruited new personnel into his special 'court'. As a preliminary measure he carried out a 'purge'. Not long before Simeon Bekbulatovich was 'enthroned', as we have seen, several of the tsar's former favourites fell into disgrace and were executed. By no means all of the former *oprichniki* were enlisted into service in the special 'court'. Nevertheless, as S.P. Mordovina and A.L. Stanislavskii showed in their detailed study of the subject, most members of Ivan's special 'court' after 1575 were either men who had served in the *oprichnina*, or their relatives.[17] The 'court' of the mid-1570s was the successor of the *oprichnina* court not only in the genealogical sense. Like the corps of *oprichniki*, it fulfilled the role of Ivan Groznyi's personal bodyguard, and as a special privileged group it was counterposed to the remaining mass of *zemshchina* nobles. The overwhelming majority of members of the special 'court' were scions of low-born provincial noble clans. Of more than a hundred 'courtiers' whose names are known to us, only a few men – the princes Shuiskii and Trubetskoi – belonged to prominent princely or boyar families. Nominally the boyar duma of the 'court' was headed by the prominent Gediminid prince, Fedor Mikhailovich Trubetskoi. The special court also included his kinsmen Princes Nikita and Timofei Romanovich Trubetskoi and Andrei Vasil'evich Trubetskoi, all of whom had previously served in the *oprichnina*. The 'court' also contained members of the most eminent clan of Ryurikid princes – the Shuiskiis (the princes Ivan Petrovich Shuiskii, the future tsar Vasilii Ivanovich Shuiskii and his brothers, and Vasilii Fedorovich Skopin). Thanks to their service in the *oprichnina* and the 'court' the princes Trubetskoi managed to retain their family estates in Trubchevsk, and the Shuiskiis not only regained their hereditary lands in Suzdal' which had been confiscated when the Suzdal' district was taken into the *oprichnina*, but they also acquired the properties of their kinsman Prince Aleksandr Borisovich Gorbatyi-Suzdal'skii, who had been executed by Ivan in 1565. The old Moscow untitled boyar clans were represented in the 'court' only by the Godunovs, the most prominent of whom were the former *oprichnina* chamberlain (*postel'nichii*) Dmitrii Ivanovich Godunov, who later became a boyar, and his nephew Boris Fedorovich Godunov, who had joined the royal family as a result of the marriage of his sister Irina to Tsarevich Fedor Ivanovich. The advancement of the Godunovs and the Shuiskiis at Ivan's court was facilitated by the marriages of Boris Godunov and Prince Dmitrii Ivanovich Shuiskii (the brother of Vasilii Shuiskii) to the daughters of Malyuta Skuratov. Another of Skuratov's daughters became the wife of the prominent prince Ivan Mikhailovich Glinskii, a kinsman of the tsar's mother, Elena Glinskaya. It is possible that Glinskii also belonged to the 'court' entourage of Ivan IV; but he was mentally feeble and played no discernible part at court.

Neither the Shuiskiis nor the Trubetskois, nor even the Godunovs, however, played the decisive role in the 'court' government. The sources indicate that the greatest influence at court in the 1570s was enjoyed by a group of low-born conciliar courtiers – Bogdan Yakovlevich Bel'skii (who later obtained the important court rank of arms-bearer); the Keeper of the Seal, Roman Vasil'evich Alfer'ev, and Mikhail Andreevich Beznin (both of whom belonged to the Nashchokin clan); and the Nagois and others, who were the real initiators of the internal and external policy of the 'court'.[18] The leader of this group was Malyuta Skuratov's nephew Bogdan Bel'skii. Like his notorious kinsman, Bel'skii was cruel and determined, with a tendency to impulsive actions. The conciliar courtiers also comprised most of the 'court' duma, which in 1575–6 included only two boyars, an *okol'nichii*, a *kravchii* and eight conciliar courtiers. The descendants of low-born nobles comprised the overwhelming majority of the *stol'niki*, *stryapchie*, and *zhil'tsy* in the 'court'. The situation in the *zemshchina* was very different. Here members of the princely and boyar aristocracy clearly predominated both in the duma and in the Moscow ranks.

The 'court' contained not only its own separate security corps, but also its special administrative organs, the chancelleries. The separate Military Chancellery of the 'court' organised the tsar's personal servants. Special chancelleries – the 'Grand Income' and the *Chetverti* – dealt with the financial affairs of the 'court'.

Like the *oprichnina* in its day, the special 'court' of Ivan IV occupied a privileged position in comparison with the *zemshchina*. Thus in 1576, when the tsar set off with his 'court' regiments to defend the southern frontier against the Crimean Tatars, he demanded from Simeon Bekbulatovich as head of the *zemshchina* the large sum of 40,000 roubles in order to pay the wages of his troops. This was in spite of the fact that in order to cover the material costs of his 'appanage' Ivan had incorporated many wealthy northern districts into the territory of the 'court'.

Large-scale land resettlement, like that of the *oprichnina* years, began again. *Zemshchina* nobles were deported from districts which had been taken into the 'sovereign's appanage', and their estates were reallocated to 'court' servicemen. For example, the nobles of the Obonezhsk *pyatina* of Novgorod district who were registered in the 'court' were transferred to the 'court' district of Porkhov, and the lands which they vacated in the Obonezhsk *pyatina* were allocated as service estates to *zemshchina* nobles exiled from the 'court' districts of Rzhev and Zubtsov.[19] The land reallocation in the post-*oprichnina* period, however, appears to have been on a smaller scale than that of the *oprichnina*, and it did not always involve wholesale deportation of *zemshchina* nobles.[20] Historians have noted that the lands which Ivan sought to bring into the 'sovereign's appanage' were mostly located to the west of Moscow, and the great majority of the 'courtiers' received estates in western and north-western districts of Russia (including Vyaz'ma, Rzhev, Kozel'sk, Staritsa and Porkhov).[21] The fact that the tsar chose to relocate his most loyal servants in these particular areas was evidently linked with his preparations for the final decisive phase of the Livonian War.

Like the *oprichnina* years, the post-*oprichnina* period was characterised by a policy of state terror. In November 1575, soon after Ivan's 'abdication' in favour of Simeon Bekbulatovich, a number of executions took place in Moscow. The names of the victims can be found in the Memorial List: they included Prince Petr Kurakin, Iona and Dmitrii Buturlin, Nikita and Vasilii Borisov, Druzhina Volodimerov, Prince Danila Drutskii and Iosif Il'in. Of these, only Prince Kurakin belonged to the *zemshchina* aristocracy; all the other boyars and noblemen were former *oprichniki*. The scale of the repression carried out under the post-*oprichnina* government was, however, much smaller than that of the *oprichnina* period. The punitive policies of the mid-1570s were directed not so much against members of the *zemshchina* as against former *oprichniki*. Nevertheless, it is clear from the evidence that the political regime which Ivan Groznyi created in 1575 was essentially a restoration of the former *oprichnina* system.

The Tatar khan occupied the Russian throne for only about a year. In the autumn of 1576 he was removed from his position and was given the town of Tver' as an appanage. But we should not accept S.F. Platonov's view that Ivan's action in placing Bekbulatovich on the throne was merely 'some kind of game or whim', 'the meaning of which is obscure and its political significance minimal'.[22] Even after 1575–6, and indeed right up until Ivan's death, both the territory and the nobility of Russia continued to be divided into a 'court' (*oprichnina*) half and a *zemshchina* half; the territory of the 'sovereign's appanage' was further extended; and Tsar Ivan continued his favourite *oprichnina* policy of 'divide and rule'. Thus we have every reason to speak of the *oprichnina* and post-*oprichnina* governments together as a single period.

The end of the Livonian War

The start of the 1570s witnessed a lull in military activities. After the rout of the Crimean Horde at Molodi, there was a temporary cessation of Tatar attacks on Russia's southern frontiers. On 19 July 1572 the Polish King Sigismund II died. He was the last member of the house of Jagiełło, and his death made the election of a new king a particularly contentious issue for the ruling circles of Poland-Lithuania.[23] Tsar Ivan openly displayed his interest in personally replacing King Sigismund. If he headed both of the greatest powers of eastern Europe simultaneously, the Russian tsar could establish his position on the Baltic without bloodshed, and organise the joint defence of the frontiers of the two states against Tatar raids and Turkish expansion. In addition, he could strengthen Russian influence in the Belorussian and Ukrainian lands, which would enable him to fulfil the Muscovite rulers' age-old dream of uniting all the lands of Kievan Rus' under their sovereignty. In spite of the religious and political differences between the two states, and in spite of the fact that Ivan's methods of dealing with his subjects were well known in Poland-Lithuania and in Europe as a whole, his candidacy found a considerable degree of support both among the Orthodox population of the Grand Duchy of Lithuania and among the lesser Polish nobility. The latter were unhappy with the political dominance of the big magnates, which had resulted in losses of land by the petty nobles. As early as September 1572, when the Polish envoy Fedor Vorypai came to Moscow to report the death of Sigismund II, Tsar Ivan launched his election campaign. In his address to the Polish emissary the tsar promised that if he were elected to the Polish throne he would not only preserve the 'rights and freedoms' of the Polish and Lithuanian nobility, but would also increase them; he spoke much about the advantages which the union of two Christian states under a single monarch would bring; and he promised to cede to Poland-Lithuania the recently captured fortress of Polotsk, and other lands.

The Lithuanian magnates initiated their own negotiations with the tsar concerning the future of the Polish throne. But they wanted to have as their king not Ivan IV, but his younger son Fedor. The Lithuanian ambassador Mikhail Garaburda approached the tsar with this proposal in December 1572. Ivan welcomed the initiative of the Lithuanian nobility. But he firmly rejected the idea of having Tsarevich Fedor elected to the Polish-Lithuanian throne, realising that his weak-willed and sickly son might easily become a plaything in the magnates' hands, and he insisted on his own candidature. The negotiations produced no significant results.

In line with his views about the dignity of a tsar, Ivan decided not to send his representatives to the electoral conference in Poland-Lithuania; he preferred to wait for the Poles and Lithuanians to approach him with an offer of the crown. Ivan's decision to play a waiting game more or less guaranteed the failure of his candidacy at the election. The main contest at the electoral conference in Warsaw was played out between representatives of the Habsburg and Valois dynasties. In the end the supporters of the French prince Henri of Anjou emerged victorious. Henri came to Poland and on 24 February 1574 he was solemnly crowned King of Poland-Lithuania. Henri of Anjou had the backing of France, which was then an ally of Turkey, and his election was a major setback for Ivan IV. It was clear that Poland-Lithuania was dominated by elements that favoured confrontation with Russia, and that it was therefore necessary to prepare for war.

But Henri remained on the Polish throne for only a short time. In June 1574, on hearing of the death of his brother, Charles IX, he secretly fled to Paris in order to claim the French crown. In the new interregnum which followed, the tsar again displayed his interest in being elected to the Polish-Lithuanian throne (it was during this second interregnum that his mock abdication in favour of Simeon Bekbulatovich occurred). Yet again, however, Ivan procrastinated, preferring to wait for the electors to invite him to occupy the Polish throne, so that he could dictate his own terms. Ivan's passivity partly arose from the fact that his informants told him that the only other serious candidate for the Polish throne was the Habsburg emperor Maximilian II, whose election would have suited him nicely. The tsar reckoned that in return for Russian support against the Ottoman Turks the Habsburgs would be prepared to make concessions to Russian interests on the Baltic. This would facilitate a successful resolution of Russia's foreign-policy problems in the west and in the south simultaneously. And it must be admitted that the tsar's expectations were well founded. In negotiations with the Imperial envoy the Muscovite side declared their support for the Austrian candidate for the Polish throne and their willingness to participate in an anti-Ottoman alliance. In the agreements which were concluded, tempting new prospects were opened up for Russia to establish her influence in the Belorussian and Ukrainian lands (at the suggestion of the Austrian side the allies even discussed a plan for dividing Poland-Lithuania into spheres of influence: Poland was to come under the control of the Emperor, while the lands of the Grand Duchy of Lithuania would be the tsar's domain). The Habsburgs promised to support the tsar's ambition to expand into Livonia at the expense of the Swedish king.

But the allies' plans were not destined to succeed. In the tense electoral contest the Habsburgs' opponents prevailed, and they elected the Transylvanian prince Stephen Bathory as King of Poland-Lithuania. His coronation took place on 1 May 1576. Bathory's election marked a major defeat for Russian diplomacy. The advocates of war against Russia had triumphed again.

During the contest for the vacant Polish throne, military hostilities between Russia and Poland-Lithuania had been temporarily halted. Nonetheless, Ivan's government continued to conduct an aggressive policy in Livonia. The tsar undertook measures to bind himself closer to his ally and vassal, the 'Livonian king' Magnus, who was backed by Denmark. In April 1573 Magnus married Prince Vladimir Andreevich Staritskii's daughter Mariya (his previous fiancée, her elder sister Evfim'ya, had died) and so the Danish prince became related to the Russian royal house. At this time, too, Vladimir Staritskii's son Vasilii was granted his father's former appanage estate, the town of Dmitrov. In the spring of 1574 Russian troops began a major offensive against Swedish possessions in Livonia. As a result of this campaign a number of towns were occupied, and only Revel' (Tallin) and its surrounding district remained in Swedish hands. When he received the news of Bathory's election Tsar Ivan began to prepare a large-scale attack on Poland's Livonian possessions. The tsar decided to head the army himself, and it marched from Pskov on 13 July 1577. The smaller Livonian fortresses and castles surrendered without much resistance. By the autumn of 1577 nearly all of Livonia to the north of the Western Dvina, with the exception of Riga and Tallin, was under the sway of the Russian tsar.

Ivan celebrated his victory, considering it to be a sign of God's benevolence towards him. From the town of Wolmar the tsar dispatched letters to King Stephen, to the Lithuanian hetman Jan Chodkiewicz, to the 'traitor' Kurbskii and others. In Ivan's eyes it was highly symbolic that it was from Wolmar that Kurbskii had sent him his first letter after his flight to Lithuania. Now that he had gained a foothold in Livonia, the tsar did not miss the opportunity to let the fugitive prince know whose side God was on. In his message to Stephen Bathory the tsar informed the king that Livonia had come under Russian control and proposed that he recognise the existing situation.

However, Ivan greatly exaggerated the significance of his victories. The main bulwarks of Swedish and Polish dominance in Livonia – Tallin and Riga – remained beyond his grasp. The triumphal march of the Russian troops turned out to have a negative side. Poland-Lithuania allied with Sweden against Russia. In October 1578 Polish-Lithuanian and Swedish forces defeated Russian troops outside the town of Wenden. The Crimean khanate also allied itself with Poland and Sweden in the war against Russia. As a result Russia faced the danger of having to fight on several fronts simultaneously. The Russians had gradually come to find themselves internationally isolated. In the course of his march on Livonia in 1577 the tsar's interests had come into conflict with those of the 'Livonian king' Magnus. Having occupied most of the territory of Livonia, Tsar Ivan no longer required Magnus's services. He issued a severe reprimand to his vassal for his unauthorised seizure of some Livonian towns, and informed him that all the towns he had occupied without the tsar's permission would be taken from him, and his 'kingdom' would exist only within boundaries which he, Ivan, would decide.

The inhabitants of the towns which had voluntarily surrendered to Magnus were subjected to harsh reprisals. These events led to a complete break-down of relations between the tsar and Magnus, who at the beginning of 1578 openly betrayed Ivan and went over to the side of the Polish king. The rift with Magnus led to the cooling of relations with Denmark, Russia's traditional ally on the Baltic. The tsar had hoped that the Habsburgs, having been defeated in the contest for the Polish throne, would engage in military conflict with Bathory, but his expectations were not fulfilled. Rudolph II, who acceded to the Austrian throne after the death of his father Maximilian II, established peaceful relations with the Polish king.

Ivan grossly underestimated his main opponent and was convinced that his position in Poland was unstable. The decisive and energetic Bathory, however, quickly became master of the situation in his new kingdom and consolidated his position on the Polish-Lithuanian throne. By the summer of 1579 he had managed to muster a large army for a campaign against Russia; in addition to Polish and Lithuanian troops, it included mercenaries hired in Hungary and Germany. As the main target of his military operations in 1579 he chose Polotsk, which occupied an important strategic position on the main routes between Russia and the Grand Duchy of Lithuania. By capturing this fortress Bathory hoped to inflict on his opponent not just a serious military blow, but also a moral defeat. We have already noted what great significance Ivan Groznyi had attached to the capture of Polotsk in 1563. The Russian commanders knew about Bathory's military preparations. But the information they received did not permit them to appreciate the full danger of the situation and take appropriate measures to repel the attack. The advance on Polotsk of the king's large army, well armed and well prepared, came as a surprise to the Russian generals. After a four-week siege the Poles managed to burn down the wooden walls of the Polotsk citadel and on 31 August 1579 they occupied the town. At Sokol, soon after this, Bathory's army routed Russian troops which the tsar had sent to assist besieged Polotsk. Russia had suffered its first serious defeat in the Livonian War. After his capture of Sokol and several other fortresses, Bathory sent the tsar a letter in which he triumphantly informed Ivan of his victories over him. It was also Kurbskii's turn to gloat. In his reply to Ivan's letter from Wolmar, the prince wrote mockingly that the 'fugitive' was now Tsar Ivan himself, and he again took up the theme of denouncing the tsar's 'bloodthirsty' dynasty and morally justifying his own flight from Russia.

The news of the military defeats had a dispiriting effect on the tsar. As usual, he laid the main blame for the failures on his boyars and commanders. Historians, however, from Karamzin onwards, have traditionally considered the cause of the disaster to have been the inactivity and cowardice of Tsar Ivan himself, who had been with the main body of the Russian army at Pskov, but had not chosen to march to relieve the besieged fortress of Polotsk. This view was developed by V.V. Novodvorskii, the author of a major specialist study of the final phase of the Livonian War. Novodvorskii suggested that Ivan had a 300,000-strong army at his disposal, and could well have stopped Bathory's advance, but had not taken advantage of the opportunity.[24] It is not correct, however, to assume that Ivan had such a large army ready to advance. Russia needed to hold very considerable forces in reserve, in order to defend her southern frontiers against raids by the Crimean Tatars, and also for deployment on the Volga to suppress the incessant uprisings of the indigenous peoples. In addition, a large part of the army had to garrison the Livonian towns and deter the incipient incursion of Swedish troops. In particular, it was necessary to send reinforcements for the defence of Narva, a vitally significant port for Russia on the Baltic. According to R.G. Skrynnikov's calculations, the Russian army stationed at Pskov with the tsar numbered not much more than 30,000 and was numerically considerably inferior to Bathory's army of almost 42,000 men.[25]

Heartened by his victory, Bathory began to prepare for a new campaign against Russia, which took place in the summer of 1580. The main objective was Velikie Luki, an important Russian fortress, situated on the border with Lithuania. The Russian commanders did not have accurate intelligence about the direction from which the enemy's main blow was likely to come, nor did they have a sufficiently large army to counter Bathory's troops in open battle. Documents discovered in the Polish archives enable us to clarify the Russian plans for military action in the event of a new campaign by Bathory. The 1580 campaign archive of the Russian commander Prince Vasilii Dmitrievich Khilkov shows that the decision was made not to send the main Russian forces against the king's army, but to hold them well back in reserve.[26] Military action was to be limited to a 'small war' (attacks on individual enemy detachments). The main effort was to be devoted to the defence of the fortresses.[27] This tactic, as it turned out, was pretty ineffective in the context of warfare against a regular army equipped with powerful siege artillery. Bathory's army of 48,000 men crossed the Russian border unopposed and laid siege to Velikie Luki on 27 August 1580. The garrison of the fortress offered stubborn resistance. The intensive artillery fire, however, set light to the wooden walls, and this sealed the town's fate. Soon the king's troops routed detachments commanded by Vasilii Khilkov at Toropets and seized the fortresses of Nevel', Ozerishche and Zavoloch'e. Occupation of the Velikie Luki district provided Bathory with a convenient bridgehead for further action against Russia. The Russians' difficulties were compounded when Sweden started military operations. The troops of the Swedish general Pontus Delagardie invaded Karelia and seized the town of Korela, which was the main centre of the Russian possessions in that region. In the spring of 1580 the Crimean Tatars renewed their attacks on the southern frontiers.

With such grave danger hanging over the country, Ivan's government began to make every effort to obtain peace. The tsar's envoys informed King Stephen that Russia was prepared to cede to him virtually all her possessions in Livonia with the exception of Narva. But Bathory demanded Narva was handed over too, and also the payment of an enormous indemnity of 400,000 Polish zloties, which was completely unacceptable to the Russians. It was clear that the Polish king planned to continue the war to a victorious end. In these circumstances Tsar Ivan took a step unprecedented in the history of Muscovite Russia, and turned to the Pope with a request for him to act as a peace mediator between Russia and Poland-Lithuania. Hitherto the tsar had repeatedly stressed his hostility to 'Latinism', so this decision provides further clear evidence that the tsar was capable of allowing his actions to be governed not only by his emotions but also by sober political calculation. The tsar justified his appeal to the head of the Catholic world by evoking the need for Christian nations to unite against Turkish expansionism, and he asked the Pope to exert his pastoral influence on the Polish king, whom he blamed for the 'spilling of Christian blood'. The appeal aroused great interest in the Vatican, which did not want to miss the opportunity to attempt to convert Russia to Catholicism. The Pope sent Antonio Possevino, one of his best diplomats, to Kraków and Moscow to act as a mediator (and also with missionary aims).

Alongside these diplomatic negotiations, Ivan's government began to organise defensive measures in preparation for a new attack by the enemy. The main objective of Bathory's third military campaign against Russia was Pskov. The capture of this town would have enabled the king to establish control over north-western Russia. At the end of July 1581 Bathory's army, comprising 47,000 soldiers, invaded Russian territory. Its core comprised German and Hungarian mercenaries. This time the Russian commanders managed to anticipate the enemy's plans, and reinforcements and artillery were rushed to Pskov. The tsar entrusted the defence of the town to the boyar Prince Ivan Petrovich Shuiskii, one of his finest commanders. The Russian troops stationed in Pskov were outnumbered by more than three to one. But on this occasion Bathory's army faced not a fortress with wooden walls, but a mighty stone citadel. Pskov was one of the most strongly fortified towns not only in Russia, but in Europe as a whole. It was surrounded by three rows of massive stone walls, whose total length was nine kilometres. The walls were crowned with forty towers, the largest of which – the Pokrovskaya – was forty metres high and ninety metres in circumference; the walls were six metres thick at their base.

At the beginning of September Bathory's army began its siege of Pskov. On 7 September they launched a mighty artillery bombardment. They broke through the south wall between the Pokrovskaya and Svinusskaya towers, and began an assault on the citadel. But in the nick of time the Pskovans managed to construct an additional wooden fortification inside the exterior wall, and to position cannon on it. When the enemy troops tried to break through to the inner citadel, they were surprised to encounter artillery fire. The Russian cannon destroyed the battlements of the towers, killing the attackers who had occupied them. As a result, the assault was repulsed with great losses for the enemy. Subsequent attempts to take Pskov by storm also ended in failure, and consequently the invaders had to resort to a protracted siege of the town. Bathory's plans for a speedy military campaign were thwarted. At the beginning of October the first frosts set in. Bathory's troops were not prepared for a winter campaign, and the Polish-Lithuanian encampment began to suffer from an acute shortage of provisions and military supplies. The Pskovan soldiers inflicted huge losses on the besieging forces, with numerous sorties. The losses, the cold and the lack of food demoralised the king's troops. On 1 December 1581 Bathory left his camp outside Pskov and handed over command of the siege to Hetman Jan Zamoyski. But no further serious attempts were made to take the town. It was clear that the Pskov campaign had failed.

The military failure and the exhaustion of the human and material resources of Poland-Lithuania during the eastern campaigns, together with the growing danger of domestic opposition, forced Bathory to seek peace with Russia. The peace negotiations under the mediation of Antonio Possevino resulted in the signing of a ten-year armistice at Yam Zapol'skii. According to its terms, Russia renounced all her possessions in Livonia (the question of Narva was left open) and Poland-Lithuania returned the Russian towns it had captured, but Polotsk reverted back to Lithuania. It seemed to many contemporaries that Tsar Ivan had been far too quick to make peace and had made unnecessary concessions to Bathory. For example, the author of the Pskov chronicle wrote that the tsar had been 'deceived' by Lithuania, which had sent him 'the priest Anthony from the

Pope of Rome' to tell him that Pskov had fallen, and that the tsar had given the king 'fifteen Livonian towns in exchange for Pskov'.[28] But in concluding the peace agreement with Poland-Lithuania, Ivan's government was influenced by quite specific and hard-headed considerations. While the Polish army was marching on Pskov, the Swedes had significantly escalated their military activities in Livonia. On 4 September 1581 they took Narva by storm, and followed this success with the capture of the Russian towns of Ivangorod, Yam and Kopor'e. The Russians faced the prospect of being completely cut off from access to the Baltic Sea. In these new circumstances the Russian government decided to make peace with Bathory at the price of conceding the Livonian towns and fortresses, and to turn its armoury against the Swedes in order to win back the Russian towns and Narva, which was such a significant port for Russia on the Baltic.

As soon as he received news of the signing of the peace treaty with Poland-Lithuania, Tsar Ivan ordered his generals to launch an assault on Narva. Prince Dmitrii Ivanovich Khvorostinin (the former *oprichnik* and hero of the battle of Molodi in 1572) managed to defeat some Swedish detachments. But no large-scale military action against Sweden ensued. A major uprising against Russian domination broke out among the indigenous peoples of the Volga basin, requiring the dispatch of significant forces to the region. In addition, the capture of Narva by Russian troops might have provoked a new military conflict with Poland-Lithuania, which had claims of its own to the Baltic port. In these circumstances Ivan's government was obliged to enter into peace negotiations with Sweden, which resulted in the signing of a three-year armistice on the River Plyusa in August 1583. By the terms of the treaty Sweden obtained all the Russian towns she had seized – Ivangorod, Yam, Kopor'e and Korela, as well as Narva. Russia retained only a small strip of land on the Gulf of Finland around the mouth of the River Neva.

The Livonian War had lasted for 25 years and it ended with a heavy defeat for Russia. The Russians not only lost all the territory they had conquered, but they were also obliged to surrender some lands which they had long regarded as their own. The military defeat exacerbated what was already a difficult internal situation.

The Russian failures on the Baltic were counterbalanced to some extent by a major success in the east: the beginning of Russia's annexation of Siberia. In the middle of the sixteenth century the Siberian khan Ediger had declared himself to be a vassal of the Russian tsar. But his successor, Khan Kuchum, renounced his vassalage relationship with the Muscovite sovereign and refused to pay him tribute. Taking advantage of

Russia's difficulties at home and abroad, Kuchum began to launch raids against Russian possessions, with the aim of driving the Russians out of the Urals. The bastion of Russian domination of the western approaches to the Urals was provided by the extensive lands of the Stroganovs, a wealthy dynasty of merchants and manufacturers. In order to protect their possessions (which were, in effect, the eastern frontiers of Russia) they had acquired the right to maintain their own armed detachments and to construct fortified settlements. To combat Khan Kuchum, whose raids were devastating their possessions, the Stroganovs hired a band of 'free' cossacks headed by the *ataman* (chieftain) Ermak Timofeevich, and sent him off to conquer the town of Kashlyk, the capital of the Siberian khanate. Ermak's Siberian campaign began on 1 September 1581 (or 1582, according to R.G. Skrynnikov).[29] Ermak's men travelled along the Siberian rivers on their lightweight boats, until they reached Kuchum's capital. Being equipped with guns and artillery, the cossacks were able to defeat the numerically superior Tatar forces, who were armed mainly with bows and spears, and to occupy Kashlyk. Kuchum fled into the steppe. The local inhabitants recognised Ermak's authority, and rendered him tribute. But his small band of cossacks had sustained heavy losses in battle, and they were not able to retain power in Siberia for long. Khan Kuchum launched a surprise attack on the cossack camp and killed most of the band. Ermak himself, according to legend, drowned in the River Irtysh, being unable to swim because of the weight of his suit of armour, which he had received as a gift from the tsar. However, Ermak's expedition marked the beginning of the Russian annexation of Siberia. Campaigns against Siberia were continued soon after Ermak's demise and the death of Ivan Groznyi. By the end of the sixteenth century Siberia had become an integral part of Russia.

The last years of Ivan's reign

The final years of Ivan Groznyi's reign witnessed a major social and political crisis in Russia. The country suffered from its division into two parts: the *zemshchina* on the one hand, and the *oprichnina* or 'sovereign's appanage' on the other. This division of the land and of the nobility lasted for nineteen years altogether: the seven years of the *oprichnina*, and the twelve years of the post-*oprichnina* period (the division of the realm into the *zemshchina* and the 'court', which was, in essence, the continuation of the *oprichnina*, did not come to an end after Simeon Bekbulatovich was removed from the throne). And although there were fewer episodes of mass terror in the post-*oprichnina* period than there had been in the *oprichnina* years, Ivan's long-running policy of dividing the nobility led to profound conflicts within that class, and created an atmosphere of political tension and mutual distrust. The tsar and his entourage lived in constant fear of boyar treason. One of the symptoms of this was the fact that during the war against Bathory, Ivan attached his own emissaries from the 'court' to all the *zemshchina* commanders. In practice this often created confusion in the line of command of the armed forces, and had a detrimental effect on the conduct of military operations.

Tsar Ivan's closest entourage in the second half of the 1570s and early 1580s was still dominated by a group of conciliar courtiers. They headed a whole cohort of low-born servicemen who had been promoted to the highest Moscow ranks of the nobility because of their service in the 'court'. It was these low-born 'court nobles', together with their leaders among the conciliar courtiers, who determined the social and political complexion of Ivan Groznyi's special 'court'. Being all too aware of the lowliness of their origin compared to that of the *zemshchina* aristocracy, these new members of the tsar's retinue formed a separate close-knit clique. Often they joined the 'court' in entire family groupings interlinked by ties of kinship.[30] The leader of this group, and the tsar's most trusted confidant right up until the end of his reign, was Bogdan Yakovlevich Bel'skii, who invariably participated in all the most important negotiations with foreign envoys. It was only because of their personal meritorious service and the tsar's favourable disposition towards them that the low born 'courtiers' had managed to make such brilliant careers and come to stand at the helm of state. Men of this type had a vested interest in the maintenance of the status quo and in the continuation of the 'court' (*oprichnina*) policy. They provided Tsar Ivan with a loyal base of support, and he tried in every way to use them as a counterweight to the *zemshchina* aristocracy. Ivan not only brought these new men into the centre of power, but showed them favour in precedence cases. For example, the 'court' conciliar courtier Roman Vasil'evich Alfer'ev-Nashchokin managed to win a precedence dispute against Prince Vasilii Vasil'evich Mosal'skii. Subsequently, the outcome of this case was reviewed, and it was recognised that in comparison to the Mosal'skiis the Alfer'evs were 'people of no pedigree'. Ivan also displayed blatant favouritism towards members of the aristocracy who served in his special 'court'. For example, in the military campaign register 'court' prince Timofei Romanovich Trubetskoi was listed above the *zemshchina* prince Ivan Ivanovich Golitsyn. Golitsyn, whose family had entered the service of the Moscow court before the Trubetskois and was considered to be more eminent, did not dare to insist on his seniority over Tsar Ivan's protégé. Thus a precedent was created, and as a result Ivan Golitsyn's descendants had to receive lower-status appointments than Trubetskoi's heirs; severe damage was done to the honour of the Golitsyn clan. In 1578 the 'court' noble Boris Godunov succeeded in winning a precedence dispute with the *zemshchina* noble Prince Ivan Sitskii. Although at that date Godunov did not play a key role in Ivan's government, he was slowly but surely moving up towards the pinnacle of power. In 1577 he received the important court rank of *kravchii* (responsible for the tsar's food), and in 1580 he was awarded the highest duma rank of boyar. For Boris Godunov, who did not belong to the most eminent category of the aristocracy, who had not reached a venerable age (he was still under thirty), and who had not yet provided any major administrative or military service, this promotion was undoubtedly a great honour. The privileges obtained by the members of the special 'court', and the fact that the majority of them were scions of non-aristocratic noble clans into the bargain, inevitably provoked dissatisfaction among senior *zemshchina* figures.

The territorial division of the country, which continued even after the removal of Simeon Bekbulatovich from the throne, had a disastrous effect on Russia. The basic core of towns and districts which comprised Ivan Groznyi's appanage was determined at the time of Bekbulatovich's 'rule'. Subsequently the territory of the 'court' was expanded by the inclusion of new districts. In 1580, for example, Starodub Ryapolovskii, the hereditary possession of the Starodub princes, was added to the 'court' domain. This district still contained the extensive family estates of local princes such as the Pozharskiis and the Romodanovskiis. Unlike other districts of hereditary princely landholding in north-eastern Rus' (Suzdal', Rostov, and Yaroslavl'), it had not previously formed part of the *oprichnina* or of the 'court'. When Starodub was taken into the 'court', the Starodub princes had to leave their family properties, and their lands were allocated as service estates to 'court' nobles. On this occasion the government gave the Starodub princes money from the treasury rather than lands in other districts as compensation for the loss of their hereditary possessions. The territorial division of the country was also accompanied by large-scale deportations of ordinary servicemen from their estates, which had a devastating effect on the fortunes of many dozens of noble families. But it was not only and not even primarily the servicemen who suffered from the land reallocation policies of the *oprichnina* and post-*oprichnina* periods. The main victims were the peasant population of the nobles' hereditary and service estates. The frequent turnover of landownership meant that the nobles ceased to be interested in the long-term economic development of their estates and were concerned only to extract the greatest possible income from them.

The Russian economy was severely damaged by incessant increases in taxation in order to pay for the Livonian War, by the military operations themselves, by the repressions and by the policy of forcible land resettlements. The main stay of the economy – the agricultural sector – suffered most of all. The problems were compounded by natural disasters which afflicted Russia in the late 1560s and early 1570s: disease epidemics and crop failures. As a result of all these factors, the economic life of the country was plunged into crisis, which had a number of symptoms: a reduction in the sown area, which reached catastrophic proportions; the decline of the rural and urban population; the impoverishment of the peasants and townspeople; and a sharp increase in the number of deserted landholdings. The western and north-western regions of the country, which were closest to the theatre of military operations, found themselves in a particularly dire situation. The Novgorod land-tax registers (cadastres) present a terrible picture of economic devastation. For example, at the beginning of the 1580s in the Derevsk *pyatina* of Novgorod district, 98 per cent of the arable land was uncultivated, and the population was only 7.1 per cent of its level in the first half of the century.[31] Other regions also suffered severe decline. According to a survey of 1580, more than 70 per cent of the land of Bekbulatovich's estate in Tver' was uncultivated.[32]

Many noble estates were so badly neglected that their owners were no longer able to perform military service. There was a sharp increase in the number of impoverished and ruined landowners who were not only unable to equip themselves for military service, but could not even feed their families. This had a devastating effect on the size and military capability of the Russian army, whose main nucleus at that time comprised cavalry units made up of nobles with service estates. The frequent military campaigns took them away from their farming activities. Exhausted and impoverished by war, they lost much of their willingness to fight. Increasing numbers of nobles failed to turn up for military service, or deserted from their regiments in order to return to their villages. There were even occasions when frontline offensives had to be cancelled because significant numbers of nobles had failed to put in an appearance at the service muster point. These nobles, who were known as 'naysayers' (*netchiki*, from the word *net*, which means 'no'), were hunted down, beaten, and sent back to their regiments under guard, often shackled in chains. Even harsh measures such as these, however, failed to bring about a reduction in the number of 'naysayers'.

One of the main concerns of Ivan Groznyi's government was the intro-duction of measures which would provide economic support for these impoverished servicemen by supplying them with land and a workforce. The measures included limiting the growth of monastery landownership at the expense of servicemen's holdings. In the *oprichnina* and post-*oprichnina* periods – in conditions of political instability, when a land-owner could at any moment lose his estate, or even his life – there was a sharp increase in the number of estates which servicemen bequeathed to monasteries 'for the remembrance of their souls'.[33] This led to the further impoverishment of the nobility. The interests of the state were damaged too – 'the taking of land out of service' (the transfer of the landholdings of military servicemen to another type of property-owner) undermined the material basis of the nobles' fighting capacity. On 15 January 1580, as a result of pressure from the secular authorities, a Church Council passed a law which forbade the donation of hereditary noble estates to monas-teries; in addition, monasteries were not to be permitted to buy lands from laymen or to accept them as security for loans. The law did, how-ever, make a major concession to the monasteries: they were allowed to retain those hereditary estates which they had acquired before 15 Janu-ary 1580. But this last provision did not apply to lands which the monas-teries had obtained from princes: these estates could be expropriated from the monasteries by the treasury. Most of the lands confiscated by the treasury were to be reallocated to servicemen.

As a result of the military defeats the government was obliged to resort to emergency taxation. Additional taxes were imposed on 'all the land', but the government attempted to collect especially large sums from the state lands in the north of Russia, which had suffered least from the war and from the *oprichnina* resettlements. The merchants were also targetted. Tsar Ivan extracted enormous amounts of money (1000 roubles in 1581, and 500 in 1582) from the English merchants of the Muscovy Company. There was a major innovation in fiscal policy in the early 1580s: levies were widely imposed on properties which had previ-ously enjoyed tax concessions known as '*tarkhany*'. The treasury collected large sums from important and privileged landowners such as the Kirillo-Belozerskii and Joseph-of-Volokolamsk Monasteries. The decision to impose taxes on the '*tarkhanshchiki*' was to be followed by the legal aboli-tion of the '*tarkhany*' at an assembly of 20 July 1584, at the beginning of the reign of Tsar Fedor Ivanovich. In the long run the limitation and eventual abolition of the tax privileges of large landowners led to a more equitable distribution of state taxes and impositions, and this was in the interests of the majority of servicemen, townspeople and peasants.

In order to obtain a fuller picture of the payment capabilities of the tax-liable population, the government began in 1581 to undertake a land survey. The survey started with the most severely devastated regions, such as the Novgorod district.

An important issue for the nobility was the provision of a labour force for their estates. In the crisis years a considerable proportion of the peasant population had died from starvation or disease; many peasants were ruined and abandoned their homesteads in an attempt to escape the exorbitant demands imposed on them by their landlords and by the state. A real battle for peasants ensued. Large and influential landowners often lured peasants away from the estates of their smaller neighbours; sometimes they simply abducted them by force. Previously the transfer of peasants had been governed by strict rules: they could leave their landlords at the end of the agricultural year, the week before and the week after the autumnal St George's Day (26 November) if they had paid their rent and an additional sum known as the '*pozhiloe*'. In the crisis years, which had witnessed the widespread flight and forcible abduction of peasants, this traditional system, established by the Law Codes of 1497 and 1550, essentially ceased to operate. It was the petty landholders who suffered most from the new situation. In the interests of this group, which constituted the backbone of the military service class, Ivan's government introduced in 1581 the so-called 'forbidden years', in which peasants were prohibited from leaving their landlords even on St George's Day. The 'forbidden years' were brought in as a temporary measure (to help noble landholding to overcome its crisis), and they were not implemented everywhere, but only in regions, such as the Novgorod district, which had suffered most from the crisis. But in the view of most historians they laid the basis of the system of serfdom in Russia, which was to last for more than 250 years.

The measures taken by the 'court' government were designed for the long term. They were unable to provide an immediate solution to the profound crises which affected the Russian economy in general and noble landownership in particular.

Economic and political problems were compounded by a dynastic crisis resulting from the death in 1581 of the tsar's elder son and heir, Tsarevich Ivan Ivanovich. Ivan Groznyi's domestic life had turned out to be very complicated. His second wife, Mariya Temryukovna, had died in September 1569; the marriage had lasted for eight years, and Mariya had borne him a son, Vasilii, who had died in infancy. After Mariya's death, Ivan sought a new wife by means of a 'bride-show' – the summoning of hundreds of eligible young women to Aleksandrova Sloboda to be inspected by the tsar. Ivan's choice was Marfa Vasil'evna Sobakina, the daughter of a nobleman from Kolomna, and he married her on 28 October 1571. Soon the tsaritsa fell ill, and died on 13 November, apparently before the relationship had been consummated. In order to obtain permission to enter a fourth marriage (Church law permitted only three), the tsar convened a special Church Council, at which he managed to get his way – admittedly, at the price of having to repent and perform penance in church. The tsar's new wife was Anna Alekseevna Koltovskaya, whom he married in the spring of 1572. But it seemed that God himself refused to bless Ivan's marriages which were conducted in defiance of the Church's established rules. At the beginning of September 1572 the tsar divorced Koltovskaya and sent her to a convent. His next – fifth – wife was Anna Grigor'evna Vasil'chikova, but she did not live long, dying at the end of 1576 or the beginning of 1577. At the end of the 1570s Ivan took as his wife Vasilisa Melent'eva, the widow of the state secretary Melentii Ivanov. Finally, in September 1580 the tsar married for the seventh time: his new bride, Mariya Fedorovna Nagaya, the niece of his favourite, Afanasii Fedorovich Nagoi, was to give him another son, Dmitrii.

The precise status of Ivan's last marriages is uncertain, and the exact details of some of them are unclear. The tsar's frequent remarriages, and his choice of brides, appear to have been influenced by court politics as much as by Ivan's personal preferences: we know that some of these later wives were protégées of his current favourites. In addition to those with whom he went through a form of wedding ceremony, Ivan evidently had sexual relations with many other women (and at least one man, if the gossip about Fedor Basmanov had any basis). When accused by Kurbskii of unchastity, the tsar tacitly admitted the charge by stating that 'we are all human'. Many foreign observers allege that Ivan joined in the depraved sexual abuse of women; Horsey claims that the tsar boasted of a 'thousand virgins he had deflowered and thousands of children of his begetting destroyed'.[34] No doubt Horsey – or Ivan – greatly exaggerated; but it seems clear that in his last years, in particular, the tsar's personal life was disordered.

On 19 November 1581 the heir to the throne, Tsarevich Ivan Ivanovich, died suddenly. Historians have generally agreed that the tsarevich was killed by his father, who struck him with his staff during a quarrel. Russian and foreign contemporaries claimed Tsar Ivan murdered his son. But they offer contradictory explanations for this 'murder'. The author of the Pskov chronicle recorded that the tsar stabbed his son with the sharp tip of his staff because the tsarevich had demanded that he send troops to relieve the siege of Pskov. A similar version, with a number of additional details, can be found in the writings of several foreigners (the Polish chronicler Reinhold Heidenstein, and Paul Oderborn): the tsarevich supposedly told his father that he intended to command the Russian troops in their march on Pskov, which made the tsar angry and resentful. A different explanation is provided by Jerome Horsey, who states that the tsar fell out with his son and struck him the fatal blow because he had ordered an official to give a nobleman some horses without the tsar's permission. Horsey also reports that Ivan Groznyi was jealous of the tsarevich and worried about his popularity with the people. The majority of historians, however, prefer the version contained in the account of Russia written by the papal nuncio, Antonio Possevino. According to Possevino, the tsar came across the tsarevich's wife dressed only in her underwear. He considered this indecent, and in spite of the fact that his daughter-in-law was pregnant, he began to hit her with his staff. When the tsarevich tried to defend his wife, the tsar struck him the fateful blow on the head, as a result of which he died soon afterwards. It is doubtful how well informed Possevino was, and the same is true of the others who have written about the death of Tsarevich Ivan. All of their accounts were based only on rumours. As S.B. Veselovskii rightly observed, 'the varied and contradictory nature of the reports about the death of the tsarevich can be explained by the simple fact that the incident occurred in the innermost chambers of the palace, which were accessible only to a few members of the tsar's immediate entourage'.[35] An official document has also survived which casts some light on the events of these tragic days: a letter written by Tsar Ivan from Aleksandrova to the leaders of the *zemshchina* boyar duma, in which he says he is unable to come to Moscow because of the grave illness of his son.[36]

It is difficult to come to any firm conclusions about the true cause of the death of Tsarevich Ivan Ivanovich. What is much more important, however, is the fact that his death raised the issue of the fate of the dynasty itself. The situation at court also became much more complicated. The succession to the throne, according to tradition, had to pass to the ruler's next eldest son – Tsarevich Fedor. The problem was that Fedor was sickly. On 19 October 1582 the tsar acquired another son, Dmitrii; but he was still only an infant at the time of his father's death. The two tsareviches had different mothers (see Figure 9.1). Fedor Ivanovich, the son of Ivan Groznyi's first wife, Anastasiya Romanovna, was the close kinsman of the Romanov (Zakharin-Yur'ev) boyars, and his wife, Irina, was the sister of Boris Godunov. Tsarevich Dmitrii's mother, Mariya Nagaya (Groznyi's seventh wife), belonged to the Nagoi clan, who

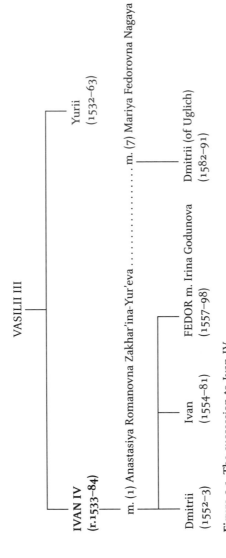

Figure 9.1 The succession to Ivan IV
Note: Reigning grand princes and tsars are indicated in capitals

were very influential in the last years of Ivan's reign. This inevitably created rivalry among the various groupings at court and intensified the country's serious political crisis.

The death of his elder son and heir was a blow to Tsar Ivan. According to Horsey, 'the emperor tore his hair and beard like a mad man, lamenting and mourning for the loss of his son'. In remembrance of the soul of Tsarevich Ivan he made huge donations to monasteries. The tsar continued to grieve for his son right up until the day of his own death. On 6 January 1583, for example, at the monastery of the Trinity and St Sergius, he ritually abased himself by repeatedly bowing to the ground, while he bitterly 'wept and sobbed' for Tsarevich Ivan.

It was probably as a result of the impact of the death of his son and heir that the tsar took what was for him an unprecedented step: he posthumously 'pardoned' all the victims he had executed. In 1582, on Ivan Groznyi's orders, the secretaries compiled detailed lists of those who had been put to death in various years of his reign. In the full Memorial List the victims numbered more than 3,000 people; it provided the names of only a third of these, the rest being unnamed. Copies of the lists were distributed to various monasteries, along with enormous sums of money for the remembrance of the souls of those who had been executed. Altogether the monasteries received tens of thousands of roubles as payment for prayers for the souls of Ivan's victims. These generous endowments were provided at a time when the country was suffering from an acute financial crisis, so it is obvious that the tsar's action was not just a demagogic gesture, and that he attached great significance to it. But Ivan's behaviour can hardly be regarded as evidence of his profound remorse for the terror he had implemented, nor of his recognition that the *oprichnina* policy of repression had been a mistake. The best way of acknowledging his error would have been to abolish the division of the land and the nobility, but there is no evidence that Ivan had any intention of doing this. In organising such extensive commemoration of his victims, Ivan Groznyi's main concern was the salvation of his own soul. When he punished those who offended him he also made sure they were deprived of a Christian burial and of commemorative prayers; in so doing, as B.N. Florya has observed, he encroached on a sphere of activity that properly belonged to God, as the 'only true arbiter' of the fate of human souls.[37] By making these generous donations to the monasteries in memory of his victims, Tsar Ivan, who had recently suffered so many misfortunes, hoped to expiate his grievous sin of pride and to regain God's favour.

Ivan Groznyi also planned, apparently, to alleviate the tense political situation within Russia and reduce his conflicts with the *zemshchina*.

This is indicated by a special decree, 'On false witness and false claims', which was issued in March 1582.[38] This legislation was designed to eradicate the practice of false denunciations, which had been common in the preceding years. Anyone found guilty of making false accusations was now liable to harsh punishment. The text of the decree stated that those who accused someone of an attempt on the life of the tsar, or of sedition (treason) or 'mutiny' (rebellion or uprising), but could not provide proof of the accusation, would themselves be subject to the death penalty. Undoubtedly this decree indicated a certain relaxation of the policy of repression. But it hardly marked a full return to the system of legality which had operated before the introduction of the *oprichnina*. Unlike earlier legislation (in particular, the Law Codes of 1497 and 1550), the decree of 1582 clearly and specifically identified the most heinous political crimes as those which were directed against the life of the sovereign. Thereby the idea became firmly inculcated into Russian political consciousness that political crimes were crimes directed primarily against the person of the ruler, and this was one of the most important results of Ivan Groznyi's long battle to consolidate autocratic power.

In his search for a way out of the difficult internal and external political situation that he faced, Tsar Ivan again looked towards England, which was the only state with which Russia retained relations of friendship and alliance. He hoped to obtain armaments and direct military assistance from England, and – although still married to Mariya Nagaya – planned to cement his English alliance by marrying Mary Hastings, a relative of Queen Elizabeth. By taking as his wife a member of the English royal family (rather than the daughter of one of his own 'servile' subjects, as he had done previously) the tsar hoped to raise the international and domestic prestige of the Russian monarchy, and also to guarantee himself a safe haven in England in the event of a rebellion by his subjects. In the spring of 1582 he sent his envoy Fedor Andreevich Pisemskii to England, with instructions to propose a political and military alliance to the queen, and to inform her of the tsar's intention to marry Mary Hastings. In the autumn of 1583 the queen's envoy Jerome Bowes travelled to Moscow. The negotiations, however, proved difficult. The English were interested in trade with Russia, and insisted on obtaining monopoly rights. But England had no desire to be drawn into Russia's military conflict with Poland-Lithuania and Sweden. For this reason the queen was unwilling to be allied to the tsar by marriage ties. Elizabeth justified her refusal to consent to the marriage by claiming that Mary Hastings was ill. The tsar agreed to grant the English the monopoly right to trade with Russia and to exclude the Dutch and the French. To this end the boyar

Nikita Romanovich Yur'ev and the secretary Andrei Shchelkalov, whom the tsar considered to be too reluctant to make concessions, were dismissed from the negotiations with Bowes, and the tsar's close confidant Bogdan Bel'skii was appointed in their stead. Ivan Groznyi suggested that the queen should find him another of her relatives as a bride in place of Mary Hastings (there is no independent evidence to confirm Horsey's claim that Ivan considered proposing marriage to Elizabeth herself). The tsar was evidently anxious to see a successful outcome to the negotiations. But his plan to conclude a military alliance with England against Poland and Sweden was unrealistic.

Ivan Groznyi was physically and emotionally exhausted by military failure, by the death of his son and heir, and by his constant anxiety for the future of his state and his dynasty. Various sources indicate that the tsar was gravely ill in the last years of his life. According to Paul Oderborn, Ivan often collapsed and lost consciousness. Shortly before his death the tsar wrote to the monks of the Kirillo-Belozerskii Monastery requesting them to pray fervently to God to 'grant him remission of his sins and deliverance from his grievous mortal illness'. On examining Ivan's remains the anthropologist M.M. Gerasimov discovered salt deposits (osteophytes) in the tsar's spine which would have hampered his mobility and caused him severe pain; in addition, his bones contained a large amount of mercury, indicating that this had been heavily used to treat him for illness.[39]

Tsar Ivan died on 18 March 1584. The most detailed and vivid account of his death is contained in the memoirs of Jerome Horsey.[40] According to Horsey, not long before his death the tsar ordered magicians to be brought to him to tell his fortune. The tsar's favourite, Bogdan Bel'skii, was entrusted with the task of visiting the magicians and reporting the results of their divinations. When Ivan learned that the soothsayers were foretelling his death for 18 March, he 'fell in rage' and threatened to have them burned if their predictions were not fulfilled. That day the tsar felt quite well and spent a long time in the bath (Russian documentary sources confirm this part of Horsey's account) and after bathing he sat down to play chess with Rodion Birkin, one of his courtiers. The tsar's closest confidants – Bogdan Bel'skii, Boris Godunov and others – stood nearby. Suddenly the tsar 'faints and falls backward'. A great commotion ensued. They sent for alcohol, and also for his confessor and physicians. 'In the mean[time],' Horsey continues, 'he was strangled and stark dead' – clearly hinting that Ivan Groznyi suffered a violent death. Some later writers (the author of the Novgorod chronicle, the secretary Ivan Timofeev, the Dutchman Isaac Massa and others) report that Ivan

Groznyi was poisoned by Bogdan Bel'skii and Boris Godunov. These sources reflect widespread contemporary rumours that Tsar Ivan did not have a natural death. Some historians also accept the version that he was murdered by Bel'skii and Godunov.[41] But it is unlikely that Ivan's death would have been in the interests of Godunov and especially Bel'skii, who owed their careers to the tsar's patronage and their service at his 'court'.

The consequences of the *oprichnina* and post-*oprichnina* regimes

When Ivan died he bequeathed to his successors a ruined country with a mass of unresolved problems. At the beginning of the reign of his weak-willed heir Fedor Ivanovich, an acute power-struggle broke out within the ruling boyar élite. The losers were the faction headed by Bogdan Bel'skii: the most committed and determined advocates of continuing the former policy of the 'court' (*oprichnina*). In the second half of the 1580s all traces of the previous division of the country and the nobility were eradicated. Not only did Ivan Groznyi's former 'court' nobles fail to retain their privileges, but most also lost their previous high ranks and appointments, giving way to members of the princely and boyar aristocracy who began to occupy the most important positions by virtue of their pedigrees.[42] On the face of it, this seems to indicate that Ivan Groznyi's *oprichnina* and post-*oprichnina* policy had come to nothing.

There is evidence, however, which points to rather a different conclusion: that the prolonged and intensive struggle which Ivan Groznyi had waged by means of the *oprichnina* in his attempt to consolidate the autocratic system did not fail to leave its mark on Russian history, and that it had very significant consequences.

As a result of the land resettlement policies, the majority of Russian nobles were moved away from their long-established places of residence. The traditional bonds which linked the nobility had been based on landholding and service; these ties were virtually destroyed, weakening the position of the local associations of servicemen vis-à-vis the monarchy. The *oprichnina* badly damaged the family estates of the princely and boyar aristocracy, and it particularly harmed the hereditary landownership of the princes. The destruction of the boyars' hereditary landholding, and the loss of their previous links with the local nobility, led to a significant transformation of the Russian aristocracy, and made it completely dependent on the monarchy. The disruption of the older links based on landholding also brought about major changes in the very structure of the ruling élite. The sovereign's court had previously had a territorial structure, with the most aristocratic and eminent nobles not only serving at court but at the same time heading their local associations of the nobility. By the beginning of the 1570s this had ceased to be the case, and the court had become organised on a new and more hierarchical basis. The privileged élite of the nobility, the Moscow ranks (the *stol'niki*, the *stryapchie* and the Moscow courtiers), had become detached from the great majority of nobles. They were now completely isolated from the provincial nobility and performed their service exclusively from the 'Moscow list' (based in the capital), which greatly increased their dependence on the state. This pattern of development of the sovereign's court was to continue under Ivan Groznyi's successors. As a result, the upper echelons of the nobility (the members of the sovereign's court) had their ties with the provinces broken; they lost touch with local interests and became completely dependent on the monarchy. They were essentially turned into state officials, and as such they began to implement in the localities the harsh policies of the autocracy, which ran counter to the corporate interests of various groups of the population, including the provincial nobility.

Similar developments took place during Ivan Groznyi's reign in the evolution of the urban population. As a result of the forcible resettlement of merchants throughout the 1570s and 1580s, the commercial districts of the provincial towns lost their most influential and prosperous élites, and the urban population was turned into a homogeneous tax-paying mass. The merchant élite – the 'guests' and members of the guests' and clothiers' hundreds – were granted considerable privileges, but at the same time they were recruited into state service, and thereby became counterposed to the majority of the urban population.[43]

It is clear from all this that in the last third of the sixteenth century the social estates did not undergo a process of consolidation, but rather they became divided into status groups, split into privileged élites on the one hand, and lower orders without rights on the other. This led not only to a weakening of the estates, but also to a change in their very character, as they lost their ability to promote their corporate political interests vis-à-vis the central authorities.

The *oprichnina* inflicted significant damage on the local institutions of estate self-government. In the years of the *oprichnina* the *guba* institutions were further subordinated to the state. For example, they were obliged to take part in implementing the *oprichnina* policy of land reallocation that had such a ruinous impact on the nobility,[44] and this completely transformed their character as institutions of noble self-government. The *oprichnina* government's policy of large-scale allocation of state lands to noble landowners meant that in the central districts of Russia the peasant *volost'* was virtually destroyed,[45] and this seriously harmed *zemstvo* peasant self-government. As a result of the policy of relocating the most prosperous and influential merchants and artisans, the institutions of estate self-government in the towns were seriously weakened. The policy of enserfment which the government began to implement in the final years of Ivan Groznyi's reign acted as another significant obstacle to the development of a 'third estate'. In practice, this policy affected not only the peasants on private landowners' estates, but also the peasants on state lands and the townspeople who were brought into the tax-paying classes.[46]

The decline of the system of estate self-government in the localities was accompanied by a marked increase in central government control over the provinces. At the end of Ivan Groznyi's reign the new form of local government – by *voevody* – was developed. *Voevody* were now introduced not only in frontier towns but also in the interior and in the north, where traditions of local self-government were particularly deeply entrenched. The local institutions of estate self-government became gradually subordinated to the *voevody*, who were representatives of central government. The increased centralisation of the administration was also reflected in the development of the system of special institutions with territorial jurisdiction, the so-called *Chetverti*: chancelleries which established administrative, juridical and financial control over the population of the districts they supervised.[47]

Thus Ivan Groznyi's tenacious campaign to consolidate 'autocratism' in Russia was not undertaken in vain. In the years of his *oprichnina* and post-*oprichnina* rule the power of the state was able to dominate society and bring it under its strict control. Admittedly, even after Ivan's death the Russian monarchy retained some of its traditional features, such as its hereditary aristocracy and the sovereign's practice of appealing to public opinion. The *zemstvo* continued to play a part in the administration of the state in the seventeenth century, but it never became an estate-representative institution of the western European type,[48] and the activity of the *zemstvo* organs of local self-government was limited to the performance of state service. As a result of his *oprichnina* and post-*oprichnina* policy, Ivan Groznyi achieved his main aim: he ensured the triumph of autocratic principles over the principles of estate representation, and Russian statehood took a definitive step in the direction of autocracy.

Notes

1 Veselovskii, *Issledovaniya*, p.199.

2 *ChOIDR*, 1912, vol.2, section 3, p.29.

3 Gryaznoi appears in somewhat romanticised form as one of the characters in Rimskii-Korsakov's well-known opera, 'A Bride for the Tsar'.

4 D.N. Al'shits, 'Novyi dokument o lyudyakh i prikazakh oprichnogo dvora Ivana Groznogo posle 1572 goda', *Istoricheskii arkhiv*, 1949, vol.4, pp.3–71; A.L. Stanislavskii, 'Kniga razdach denezhnogo zhalovaniya 1573 goda', *Istoriya SSSR*, 1976, no.4, pp.136–40.

5 *Rude and Barbarous*, pp.292–3; *Pskovskie letopisi*, vol.2, Moscow, 1955, p.262.

6 *PSRL*, vol.34, p.192.

7 *Poslaniya Ivana Groznogo*, pp.195–6.

8 Likhachev, Panchenko and Ponyrko, *Smekh v drevnei Rusi*, pp.26–7.

9 P.A. Sadikov, *Ocherki po istorii oprichniny*, Moscow and Leningrad, 1950, pp.43–4; cf. G.V. Vernadskii, 'Ivan Groznyi i Simeon Bekbulatovich', in *To Honor Roman Jakobson*, vol.3, The Hague and Paris: Mouton, 1967, pp.2133–51.

10 *Rude and Barbarous*, pp.166–7 (Giles Fletcher), 275 (Jerome Horsey); V.I. Koretskii, 'Zemskii sobor 1575 g. i postavlenie Simeona Bekbulatovicha "velikim knyazem vsea Rusi"', *Istoricheskii arkhiv*, 1959, vol.2, pp.149–50.

11 *PSRL*, vol.34, p.192.

12 For a genealogical table illustrating Simeon's links with the royal house, see Ostrowski, *Muscovy and the Mongols*, p.194.

13 Pritsak, 'Moscow, the Golden Horde, and the Kazan Khanate', pp.577–8; Ostrowski, *Muscovy and the Mongols*, p.188.

14 Uspenskij, 'Tsar and Pretender', pp.268–72.

15 Klyuchevskii, *Sochineniya*, vol.2, p.178; Platonov, *Ocherki po istorii smuty*, pp.118–19.

16 V.I. Koretskii, 'Zemskii sobor 1575 g. i chastichnoe vozrozhdenie oprichniny'; S.M. Kashtanov, 'O vnutrennei politike Ivana Groznogo v period "velikogo knyazheniya" Simeona Bekbulatovicha', *Trudy Moskovskogo gosudarstvennogo Istoriko-arkhivnogo instituta*, vol.16, 1961, pp.427–62; R.G. Skrynnikov, *Rossiya posle oprichniny*, Leningrad, 1975, pp.5–39; S.P. Mordovina and A.L. Stanislavskii, 'Sostav osobogo dvora Ivan IV v period "velikogo knyazheniya" Simeona Bekbulatovicha', *Arkheograficheskii ezhegodnik za 1976 god*, Moscow, 1977, pp.153–93.

17 Mordovina and Stanislavskii, 'Sostav osobogo dvora', pp.159–60.

18 The conciliar courtiers (*dumnye dvoryane*) comprised a rank in the boyar duma along with the boyars and *okol'nichie* (and later the conciliar secretaries (*dumnye d'yaki*)). This rank was definitively established as a separate category in the *oprichnina* period. Its creation enabled the tsar to draw into the highest spheres of government low-born men who because of their humble origin could not aspire to the higher duma ranks of boyar or *okol'nichii*.

19 Koretskii, 'Zemskii sobor 1575 g. i chastichnoe vozrozhdenie oprichniny', p.43.

20 Pavlov, 'Zemel'nye pereseleniya v gody oprichniny', p.97.

21 Mordovina and Stanislavskii, 'Sostav osobogo dvora', p.156.

22 Platonov, *Ocherki po istorii smuty*, p.119.

23 For fuller details of Russian foreign policy during the first (1572–3) and second (1574–6) interregnums in the Polish-Lithuanian Commonwealth, see B.N. Florya, *Russko-pol'skie otnosheniya i politicheskoe razvitie Vostochnoi Evropy vo vtoroi polovine XVI – nachale XVII v.*, Moscow, 1978, pp.46–120; Florya, *Ivan Groznyi*, pp.296–309, 324–37.

24 V.V. Novodvorskii, *Bor'ba za Livoniyu mezhdu Moskvoi i Rech'yu Pospolitoi (1570–1582 gg.)*, St Petersburg, 1904.

25 Skrynnikov, *Rossiya posle oprichniny*, p.48.

26 B.N. Florya, ed., 'Dokumenty pokhodnogo arkhiva voevody kn. Vasiliya Dmitrievicha Khilkova 1580 g.', *Pamyatniki istorii Vostochnoi Evropy*, vol.3, *Dokumenty Livonskoi voiny*, Moscow and Warsaw, 1998, pp.197–236.

27 Florya, *Ivan Groznyi*, p.355.

28 *Pskovskie letopisi*, vol.2, p.263.

29 R.G. Skrynnikov, *Sibirskaya ekspeditsiya Ermaka*, Novosibirsk, 1982, p.145.

30 Mordovina and Stanislavskii, 'Sostav osobogo dvora', p.159.

31 *Agrarnaya istoriya severo-zapada Rossii XVI veka: Novgorodskie pyatiny*, ed. A.L. Shapiro, Leningrad, 1974, pp.67, 69.

32 *Pistsovye knigi Moskovskogo gosudarstva*, St Petersburg, 1877, part 1, section 2, pp.291–403; Skrynnikov, *Rossiya posle oprichniny*, p.182.

33 S.B. Veselovskii, *Feodal'noe zemlevladenie v Severo-Vostochnoi Rusi*, vol.1, Moscow and Leningrad, 1947, p.96.

34 *Correspondence*, pp.192–3; *Rude and Barbarous*, p.304.

35 Veselovskii, *Issledovaniya*, p.338.

36 N.P. Likhachev, *Delo o priezde v Moskvu Antoniya Possevino*, St Petersburg, 1903, p.58.

37 Florya, *Ivan Groznyi*, p.381.

38 *Zak. akty*, p.60 (no.42).

39 M.M. Gerasimov, 'Dokumental'nyi portret Ivana Groznogo', *Kratkie soobshcheniya o dokladakh i polevykh issledovaniyakh Instituta arkheologii*, vol.100, Moscow, 1965, pp.139–42.

40 *Rude and Barbarous*, pp.304–6.

41 See, for example, V.I. Koretskii, 'Smert' Groznogo tsarya', *Voprosy istorii*, 1979, no.9, pp.93–103.

42 Pavlov, *Gosudarev dvor*, pp.27–50.

43 Florya, 'Privilegirovannoe kupechestvo'.

44 V.A. Kolobkov, 'Oprichnoe samoupravlenie', *Politicheskie instituty i sotsial'nye straty Rossii (XVI–XVIII vv.). Tezisy mezhdunarodnoi konferentsii 2–3 oktyabrya 1998 g.*, Moscow, 1998, pp.56–61.

45 Yu.G. Alekseev, *Agrarnaya i sotsial'naya istoriya Severo-Vostochnoi Rusi XV–XVI vv.: Pereyaslavskii uezd*, Moscow and Leningrad, 1966, pp.168–85.

46 Skrynnikov, *Rossiya posle oprichniny*, pp.189–93.

47 Pavlov, *Gosudarev dvor*, pp.233, 240.

48 Torke, *Die staatsbedingte Gesellschaft*.

Conclusion

The developments leading to the consolidation of autocracy which we outlined at the end of the previous chapter occurred after 1564, and they ran counter to the reforms of the 1550s, which had strengthened the position of the estates. In spite of the dramatic nature of the events which heralded the introduction of the *oprichnina*, the change in policy was not a sudden one. After Ivan's illness in 1553 his relationship with Adashev and Sil'vestr deteriorated. He increasingly mistrusted his formerly close advisers, resenting the way they had obliged him to remove the Zakhar'ins from power. At the beginning of the Livonian War the tsar blamed Adashev, in particular, for the diplomatic blunder which led to military setbacks in 1559. The underlying cause of Ivan's breach with Adashev and Sil'vestr in 1560, however, was the tsar's growing awareness of the discrepancy between the ideology of autocracy on the one hand, and its reality on the other. Metropolitan Makarii and others had instilled into the young tsar the idea that his power was divinely ordained and unlimited by earthly institutions; in practice, Ivan felt himself constrained by the tutelage of his advisers, by the need to consult his boyars, and by the prospect that the reforms would require him to take account of the interests of the emergent estates in future decision-making. The dismissal of Adashev and Sil'vestr did not resolve the problem: instead, it provoked hostility from the princely aristocracy, and the growth of opposition to Ivan's policies was countered by repressions which in turn led to further resistance. Finally the tsar attempted to break out of the vicious circle by introducing the *oprichnina*.

Ivan's posthumous reputation is based mainly on the violence which characterised the *oprichnina* and post-*oprichnina* periods. The scale and nature of the executions and tortures shocked contemporaries as much as they have horrified subsequent generations of historians and their readers. The reign of terror reached its peak in 1570, with the attack on Novgorod and the Moscow executions. Mass repression of this kind was, however, relatively short-lived: like similar dreadful episodes at other times and in other places, it was self-limiting and ended up devouring its initiators. In any case, few regimes maintain themselves in power by coercion alone, and Ivan's Muscovite autocracy was no exception. From the time of his coronation onwards, the tsar's advisers were determined to enact public rituals and ceremonies which conveyed the splendour of the ruler and helped to promote the integration and cohesion of the realm. In a largely illiterate society, visual symbols played a particularly important role: St Basil's Cathedral, at the heart of Moscow, provided a striking reminder of the significance of the conquest of Kazan'. Annual events in the Church calendar, such as Epiphany and Palm Sunday, were marked with public ceremonies in which the tsar participated; and key moments in the ruler's own life-cycle, such as his coronation, his marriages, and the christenings of his children, were lavishly celebrated. The tsar's personal leadership of his armies in the field, and his participation in victory processions, made him a familiar figure to many of his subjects outside the narrow confines of the court and the capital, and his frequent pilgrimages to holy places throughout his realm also served the purpose of showing him to his people.

Perhaps as an extension of the theatricality of everyday royal life, many major political events in Ivan's reign were carefully stage-managed. The most obvious example is of course the introduction of the *oprichnina*, a dramatic scenario which was evidently well planned. Ivan's mock abdication in favour of Simeon Bekbulatovich also contained elements of play-acting, as did the organisation of his court at Aleksandrova Sloboda on the lines of a monastery, with the tsar as abbot and his *oprichniki* as monks. The exact meaning of these performances is not always clear, but they were evidently designed to convey complex messages about the nature and purpose of the tsar's power.

Even the terror sometimes assumed theatrical and ritualistic forms. The 'enthronement and dethronement' of I.P. Fedorov-Chelyadnin involved an enactment of the crime of which the boyar was accused; and the massacre in Novgorod was clearly intended to demonstrate the dreadful fate which awaited traitors, as were the Moscow executions of 1570 and the horrible deaths of I.M. Viskovatyi and N.A. Funikov, in particular. Some aspects of these gruesome killings suggest that Ivan was trying to act out his concept of the tsar as God's representative on earth, with a duty to punish traitors in the ways that sinners were tormented in hell. At other times the tsar was crudely populist, employing the idioms of folk culture in order to mock his victims, as when Archbishop Pimen of Novgorod was publicly attired as a *skomorokh*, and his successor Leonid was sewn into a bearskin and baited with dogs. Such carnivalesque devices may have been adopted as an attempt to bid for popular support for the terror, by presenting it in the guise of public entertainment;

certainly Ivan's bizarre forms of punishment and humiliation made a strong impression on contemporaries, and were frequently recalled with fascinated horror by posterity. From his encounter with the hostile mob after the Moscow fires of 1547, Ivan had drawn the conclusion that crowds could be manipulated. It was a lesson that he took to heart: in future, the people were to be incited by the tsar against the 'traitor-boyars', rather than vice versa. At the time of the introduction of the *oprichnina*, Ivan elicited from the citizens of Moscow a promise that they would personally destroy traitors, and in 1570 he sought their approval for the public executions in the capital. Although the repressions affected all sectors of the population, the tsar seems to have enjoyed some success in communicating to the ordinary people his own concept of the *oprichnina* terror as the deserved punishment of traitor-boyars and corrupt officials: that, at least, is how it was often remembered in folklore.

In spite of the failures and disappointments of the Livonian War, Ivan had demonstrated that Muscovy was a force to be reckoned with in Europe. The state which he bequeathed to his son and successor, Tsar Fedor (1584–98), was much more extensive than the realm which Ivan himself had inherited from Vasilii III. Admittedly, the territorial gains had been made in the east and south-east; and, with the exception of Ermak's Siberian triumphs of the 1580s, most of them had occurred before 1560. Russia's successful growth took place at the expense of the Tatars; this, together with the fact that the eastward expansion began soon after Ivan's coronation in 1547, has suggested to some that the Muscovite authorities saw the tsar as the successor to the khans of the Golden Horde. We have found little evidence to support this view. The conquest of Kazan' and Astrakhan' was legitimised as the repossession of the patrimony of the grand princes of Kiev, and as a religious crusade against the infidel Muslims who had usurped their lands. Similar ideological justifications were offered for the Livonian War: it was a campaign to regain territory which had belonged to the house of Ryurik, but had subsequently fallen under the sway of non-Orthodox rulers. Dynastic and religious concerns provided stronger motivations for Muscovy's expansion than considerations of national or ethnic reunification (concepts which were in any case only embryonic in the sixteenth century): the Baltic peoples of Livonia – like the Turkic and Finnic peoples of the Volga basin – were not, after all, Slavs. Byzantine ideas exerted a powerful influence on Russian religious and political doctrines in the sixteenth century, but in Ivan's reign the concept that the link with Byzantium came through pre-Mongol Kiev (the Monomakh legend) was stronger than the notion of the transfer of imperial status from Constantinople after 1453 ('Moscow – the Third Rome'). Continuity with Kiev was a major theme, which influenced Muscovy's foreign policy as well as its political imagery. As a result of his defeat in the Livonian War, Ivan failed to become tsar of 'all Rus'', but it was an ambition which he passed on to his successors.

Chronology

9th century – Ryurik the Viking supposedly comes to Rus'
988 – Prince Vladimir of Kiev converts Rus' to Christianity
1036–54 – reign of Yaroslav 'the Wise' as grand prince of Kiev
1054 – 'Great Schism' of eastern and western Christianity
1113–25 – reign of Vladimir Monomakh as grand prince of Kiev
1147 – the town of Moscow is first mentioned in a chronicle
1237–40 – Mongol invasion of Rus'
1243 – the Mongols confirm Yaroslav Vsevolodovich as prince of Vladimir
1299 – Metropolitan Maksim moves from Kiev to Vladimir
1328 – Prince Ivan Daniilovich of Moscow (Ivan I Kalita) becomes grand prince of Vladimir
1354 – Moscow becomes the seat of the metropolitan
1380 – battle of Kulikovo: Grand Prince Dmitrii Ivanovich (Donskoi) defeats Mamai
1389–1425 – reign of Grand Prince Vasilii I
1425–62 – reign of Grand Prince Vasilii II
1437 – Council of Florence begins
1448 – Russian bishops name Bishop Iona of Ryazan' as metropolitan
1453 – Constantinople falls to the Ottoman Turks
1462–1505 – reign of Grand Prince Ivan III
1472 – Zoe (Sofiya) Paleologue becomes second wife of Ivan III
1475 – Crimean khan becomes vassal of the Turkish Sultan
1478 – Moscow annexes Novgorod
1480 – the 'stand on the Ugra': Ivan III confronts Akhmat Khan
1485 – Moscow annexes Tver'
1487 – Russians establish Magmet-Amin' as khan of Kazan'
1497 – Law Code issued
1498 – Ivan III crowns his grandson Dmitrii as his co-ruler and heir
1502 – destruction of the Great Horde by the Crimean Tatars
1505–33 – reign of Grand Prince Vasilii III
1510 – Moscow annexes Pskov
1514 – Moscow captures Smolensk
1521 – Moscow annexes Ryazan'

1525 – Safa-Girei becomes khan of Kazan'
1525 – Vasilii III divorces Solomoniya Saburova
1526 – Vasilii III marries Elena Glinskaya
1530 (August) – birth of Elena's son, Ivan Vasil'evich
1532 (October) – birth of Elena's son, Yurii Vasil'evich
1532 – Russian client Enalei becomes khan of Kazan'
1533–84 – reign of Ivan IV
1534–8 – regency of Elena Glinskaya
1535 – Safa-Girei is restored as khan of Kazan'
1536 – death of Prince Yurii of Dmitrov
1537 – death of Prince Andrei of Staritsa
1538 – death of Elena Glinskaya
1538–47 – period of 'boyar rule'
1542 – Makarii becomes metropolitan
1547 (January) – Ivan's coronation as tsar
1547 (February) – Ivan's marriage to Anastasiya Romanovna
1547 (June) – fires and popular uprising against the Glinskiis in Moscow
1547/8 – Ivan heads an expedition against Kazan'
1549 (February) – 'Council of Reconciliation' convenes
1549 (March) – death of Khan Safa-Girei of Kazan'
1549/50 – Ivan heads a second expedition against Kazan'
1550 – new ('Royal') Law Code introduced
1551 (January–February) – 'Council of a Hundred Chapters' convenes
1552 (October) – conquest of Kazan'
1552 (October) – birth of Tsarevich Dmitrii
1553 (March) – Ivan's illness and disputes about the succession
1553 (June) – death of Tsarevich Dmitrii
1553/4 – Richard Chancellor comes to Moscow from England by the White Sea route
1554 (March) – birth of Tsarevich Ivan
1554 – Prince Semen Rostovskii is accused of treason
1555/6 – abolition of 'feeding' (*kormlenie*)
1556 – *zemstvo* reform; 'Code on Service'
1556 – annexation of Astrakhan'
1557 (May) – birth of Tsarevich Fedor
1558–83 – Livonian War
1558 – Russian invasion of Livonia
1559 – Livonia becomes a protectorate of Lithuania
1560 (August) – death of Tsaritsa Anastasiya
1560 – dismissal and 'trial' of Adashev and Sil'vestr
1561 (August) – Ivan's second marriage, to Mariya Temryukovna

1562 – Russia goes to war with Lithuania

1563 (February) – Russians capture Polotsk

1563 (summer) – trial of the Staritskiis

1563 (December) – death of Metropolitan Makarii

1564 (January) – Russians are defeated by Lithuanians on River Ula

1564 (April) – Prince Andrei Kurbskii flees to Lithuania

1564 (July) – Ivan's first letter to Kurbskii

1564 (December) – Ivan's departure from Moscow for Aleksandrova Sloboda

1565–72 – *oprichnina*

1565 (February) – Ivan returns to Moscow, issues decree on *oprichnina*

1565 – exile of princes to Kazan'

1566 (June) – the first 'Assembly of the Land' convenes

1566 (July) – Filipp Kolychev becomes metropolitan

1567/8 – investigation of treason charges against I.P. Fedorov and others

1568 – Metropolitan Filipp is removed from office

1569 – 'Lublin Union' of Poland and Lithuania

1569 (September) – death of Tsaritsa Mariya Temryukovna

1569 (October) – Prince Vladimir Staritskii is executed

1569/70 – Ivan's punitive expedition against Novgorod

1570 – public executions in Moscow

1571 (May) – Moscow is burned by the Crimean Tatars

1571 (October–November) – Ivan's third marriage, to Marfa Sobakina

1572 – Ivan's fourth marriage, to Anna Koltovskaya

1572 (August) – Crimean Tatars are defeated at battle of Molodi

1572 (autumn) – abolition of *oprichnina*

1572–3 – interregnum in Poland-Lithuania after death of Sigismund II

1574–6 – second interregnum in Poland-Lithuania after flight of Henri of Anjou

1575/6 – Simeon Bekbulatovich is given the title of 'Grand Prince of All Rus''

1576 – Stephen Bathory becomes King of Poland-Lithuania

1577 – Ivan heads Russian campaign in Livonia

1577 – Ivan's second letter to Kurbskii

1579 – Poles recapture Polotsk

1580 – Ivan's seventh marriage, to Mariya Nagaya

1581 – introduction of 'forbidden years', restricting peasants' freedom of movement

1581 – successful Russian defence of Pskov against Bathory

1581 (November) – death of Tsarevich Ivan

1581–4 – Ermak's Siberian expedition

1582 – compilation of 'Memorial List' of Ivan's victims

1582 (January) – peace of Yam Zapol'skii between Russia and Poland-
Lithuania

1582 (October) – birth of Tsarevich Dmitrii

1583 – peace of Plyusa between Russia and Sweden

1584 (March) – Ivan's death

1584–98 – reign of Fedor Ivanovich

1591 – death of Tsarevich Dmitrii

1598–1605 – reign of Boris Godunov

c.1603–13 – 'Time of Troubles'

Glossary

appanage (Russian *udel*, pl. *udely*) – A small principality; in the sixteenth century, the semi-autonomous lands granted to the younger brothers of a grand prince.

boyar (Russian *boyarin*, pl. *boyare*) – In the narrow sense, the highest rank of member of the boyar duma (q.v.). More broadly, a member of those aristocratic clans whose senior members were eligible for appointment to boyar status.

boyar duma (Russian *boyarskaya duma*) – The council of advisers of the Muscovite ruler.

chetvertchiki – Servicemen who received their remuneration in the form of money distributed by the *Chetverti* (q.v.).

Chetverti – Chancelleries with administrative jurisdiction over specific geographical areas.

Chingisid – A descendant of the thirteenth-century Tatar warlord Chingis (Genghis) Khan.

'court' (Russian *dvor*) – After 1572, the territory which was under the tsar's direct control; the successor to the *oprichnina*. Sometimes also known as the 'sovereign's appanage'.

deti boyarskie – Literally, 'boyars' sons': petty servicemen, 'gentry'.

duma – Council, especially the boyar duma (q.v.).

estate (Russian *soslovie*, pl. *sosloviya*) – A social group, order or class, e.g. nobility, clergy, townspeople, peasantry.

estate-representative institutions – Elected self-government bodies for the estates (*sosloviya*), e.g. the *guba* and *zemstvo* institutions (q.v.).

'feeding' (Russian *kormlenie*) – The payments in cash or kind which were made to the *namestniki* (q.v.) by the local population under their jurisdiction.

Gediminid – A descendant of the fourteenth-century Lithuanian prince, Gedimin.

groznyi – Dread, formidable; cf. *Groznyi* – [Ivan] 'the Terrible'.

guba – Administrative areas with elected self-government institutions of the nobility.

'guests' (Russian *gosti*) – The wealthiest and most privileged category of merchants.

hetman (Polish) – Army commander-in-chief.

kravchii – Taster; a courtier who was in charge of the tsar's food.

namestnik (pl. *namestniki*) – A provincial governor.

okol'nichii (pl. *okol'nichie*) – The second rank (below boyar) in the boyar duma (q.v.).

oprichnik (pl. *oprichniki*) – In 1565–72, a member of the tsar's bodyguard, holding land in the *oprichnina* (q.v.).

oprichnina – In 1565–72, the division of the realm that was directly under the tsar's control (cf. *zemshchina*). By extension, the *oprichniki* (q.v.) and the reign of terror that they implemented.

pomeshchik (pl. *pomeshchiki*) – Service noble, holder of a *pomest'e* (q.v.).

pomest'e (pl. *pomest'ya*) – Landed estate held on condition of the performance of military service (cf. *votchina*).

prikazchiki – Urban officials with administrative powers.

pyatina (pl. *pyatiny*) – Literally, 'fifth'; one of the five administrative subdivisions of the Novgorod district.

Ryurikid dynasty, Ryurikids – Descendants of Ryurik the Viking, the semi-legendary ninth-century ancestor of the Grand Princes of Kiev, Vladimir and Moscow.

sejm (Polish) – The Polish Diet, parliament.

skomorokh (pl. *skomorokhi*) – A minstrel, popular entertainer.

stol'nik (pl. *stol'niki*) – Literally, table-attendant; a rank of courtier.

strel'tsy – Literally, 'shooters': infantrymen armed with handguns. In the sixteenth century, their arms were harquebuses; in the seventeenth century they were replaced by muskets.

stryapchii (pl. *stryapchie*) – A rank of courtier.

tsar (Russian *tsar'*) – From 1547, the official title of the Russian ruler (previously grand prince). Cf. tsaritsa (tsar's wife); tsarevich (tsar's son).

uezd (pl. *uezdy*) – An administrative area ('district').

voevoda (pl. *voevody*) – A provincial governor, especially in a frontier region.

volost' (pl. *volosti*) – A rural administrative area, a sub-division of an *uezd* (q.v.).

volosteli – Governors of *volosti* (q.v.).

votchina (pl. *votchiny*) – Family lands, a hereditary estate (cf. *pomest'e*).

votchinniki – Owners of *votchiny* (q.v.).

zemshchina – After 1565, the territory which was excluded from the *oprichnina* or the 'court' (q.v.).

zemskii (pl. *zemskie*) – A nobleman who held land in the *zemshchina* (q.v.).

zemstvo – Elected self-government institutions of the peasants and towns-people.

zhilets (pl. *zhil'tsy*) – Literally, 'a resident': a rank of courtier.

Select Bibliography

The following bibliography comprises only works in English. In the case of secondary sources, it takes the form of 'suggestions for further reading' and gives preference to works published in the last twenty years. References to other authorities consulted, including those in Russian and German, can be found in the endnotes to each chapter.

Primary sources

Bond, E.A., ed. *Russia at the Close of the Sixteenth Century*, London: Hakluyt Society, 1856.

The Correspondence between Prince A.M. Kurbsky and Tsar Ivan IV of Russia, ed. and trans. J.L.I. Fennell, Cambridge: Cambridge University Press, 1955.

The Domostroi. Rules for Russian Households in the Time of Ivan the Terrible, ed. and trans. Carolyn Johnston Pouncy, Ithaca: Cornell University Press, 1994.

Hakluyt, Richard, ed. *Voyages* (Everyman's Library Edition [1907]), vols. 1–2, London: Dent, 1967–/3.

Herberstein, Sigismund von. *Notes upon Russia*, trans. and ed. R.H. Major, 2 vols., London: Hakluyt Society, 1851–2.

Morgan, E.D. and C.H. Coote, eds. *Early Voyages and Travels to Russia and Persia by Anthony Jenkinson and Other Englishmen*, 2 vols., London: Hakluyt Society, 1886.

The Moscovia of Antonio Possevino, S.J., trans. and ed. Hugh F. Graham, Pittsburgh: University Center for International Studies, University of Pittsburgh, 1977.

Prince A.M. Kurbsky's History of Ivan IV, ed. and trans. J.L.I. Fennell, Cambridge: Cambridge University Press, 1965.

Rude and Barbarous Kingdom. Russia in the Accounts of Sixteenth-Century English Voyagers, ed. L.E. Berry and R.O. Crummey, Madison, WI: University of Wisconsin Press, 1968.

Schlichting, Albert. 'A Brief Account of the Character and Brutal Rule of Vasil'evich, Tyrant of Muscovy (Albert Schlichting on Ivan Groznyi)', ed. and trans. Hugh F. Graham, *Canadian-American Slavic Studies*, vol.9, 1975, pp.204–72.

Staden, Heinrich von. *The Land and Government of Muscovy: a Sixteenth-Century Account*, trans. and ed. Thomas Esper, Stanford, CA: Stanford University Press, 1967.

Tolstoy, George, ed. *The First Forty Years of Intercourse between England and Russia, 1553–1593*, St Petersburg, 1875.

Secondary sources

Bogatyrev, Sergei. *The Sovereign and his Counsellors. Ritualised Consultations in Muscovite Political Culture, 1350s–1570s*, Helsinki: Academia Scientiarum Fennica, 2000.

Bushkovitch, Paul. 'The Epiphany Ceremony of the Russian Court in the Sixteenth and Seventeenth Centuries', *Russian Review*, vol.49, 1990, pp.1–18.

Bushkovitch, Paul. *Religion and Society in Russia: the Sixteenth and Seventeenth Centuries*, New York: Oxford University Press, 1992.

Crummey, Robert O. *The Formation of Muscovy, 1304–1613*, London: Longman, 1987.

Crummey, Robert O. 'New Wine in Old Bottles? Ivan IV and Novgorod', in Hellie, ed., *Ivan the Terrible*, pp.61–76.

Davies, Brian L. 'The Town Governors in the Reign of Ivan IV', in Hellie, ed., *Ivan the Terrible*, pp.77–143.

Flier, Michael S. 'Breaking the Code: the Image of the Tsar in the Muscovite Palm Sunday Ritual', in Flier and Rowland, eds., *Medieval Russian Culture*, vol.2, pp.213–42.

Flier, Michael S. and Daniel Rowland, eds. *Medieval Russian Culture*, vol.2, Berkeley: University of California Press, 1994.

Grobovsky, A.N. *The 'Chosen Council' of Ivan IV: a Reinterpretation*, New York: Gaus, 1969.

Halperin, Charles J. *Russia and the Golden Horde: the Mongol Impact on Medieval Russian History*, London: Tauris, 1987.

Hellie, Richard. *Enserfment and Military Change in Muscovy*, Chicago: University of Chicago Press, 1971.

Hellie, Richard. *Slavery in Russia, 1450–1725*, Chicago: University of Chicago Press, 1982.

Hellie, Richard, ed. *Ivan the Terrible. A Quarcentenary Celebration of his Death (Russian History/Histoire Russe*, vol.14, 1987).

Hellie, Richard. 'What Happened? How Did He Get Away With It? Ivan Groznyi's Paranoia and the Problem of Institutional Restraints', in Hellie, ed., *Ivan the Terrible*, pp.199–224.

Hunt, Priscilla. 'Ivan IV's Personal Mythology of Kingship', *Slavic Review*, vol.52, 1993, pp.769–809.

Kappeler, Andreas. *The Russian Empire. A Multiethnic History*, trans. Alfred Clayton, Harlow: Longman, 2001.

Khodarkovsky, Michael. 'Four Degrees of Separation: Constructing Non-Christian Identities in Muscovy', in Kleimola and Lenhoff, eds., *Culture and Identity in Muscovy*, pp. 248–66.

Khodarkovsky, Michael. 'Taming the "Wild Steppe": Muscovy's Southern Frontier, 1480–1600', *Russian History/Histoire Russe*, vol.26, 1999, pp.241–97.

Kivelson, Valerie. 'Political Sorcery in Sixteenth-Century Russia', in Kleimola and Lenhoff, eds., *Culture and Identity in Muscovy*, pp.267–83.

Kleimola, A.M. 'Ivan the Terrible and his "Go-Fers": Aspects of State Security in the 1560s', in Hellie, ed., *Ivan the Terrible*, pp.283–92.

Kleimola, A.M. and G.D. Lenhoff, eds. *Culture and Identity in Muscovy, 1359–1584* (UCLA Slavic Studies, New Series, vol.3), Moscow: ITZ-Garant, 1997.

Kollmann, Nancy Shields. 'The Grand Prince in Muscovite Politics: the Problem of Genre in Sources on Ivan's Minority', in Hellie, ed., *Ivan the Terrible*, pp.293–313.

Kollmann, Nancy Shields. *Kinship and Politics: the Making of the Muscovite Political System, 1345–1547*, Stanford, CA: Stanford University Press, 1987.

Kollmann, Nancy Shields. 'Pilgrimage, Procession and Symbolic Space in Sixteenth-Century Russian Politics', in Flier and Rowland, eds., *Medieval Russian Culture*, vol.2, pp.163–81.

Kollmann, Nancy Shields. *By Honor Bound: State and Society in Early Modern Russia*, Ithaca: Cornell University Press, 1999.

Lehtovirta, Jaakko. *Ivan IV as Emperor. The Imperial Theme in the Establishment of Muscovite Tsardom*, Ph.D. Dissertation, University of Turku, 1999.

Lotman, Ju.M. and B.A. Uspenskij. *The Semiotics of Russian Culture*, ed. Ann Shukman, Ann Arbor: Michigan Slavic Contributions, 1984.

Martin, Janet. *Medieval Russia, 980–1584*, Cambridge: Cambridge University Press, 1995.

Miller, David B. 'The Coronation of Ivan IV of Moscow', *Jahrbücher für Geschichte Osteuropas*, vol.15, 1967, pp.559–74.

Miller, David B. 'The Velikie Minei Chetii and the Stepennaia Kniga of Metropolitan Makarii and the Origins of Russian National Consciousness', *Forschungen zur osteuropäischen Geschichte*, vol.26, 1979, pp.263–382.

Miller, David B. 'The Viskovatyi Affair of 1553–54: Official Art, the Emergence of Autocracy and the Disintegration of Medieval Russian Culture', *Russian History/Histoire Russe*, vol.8, 1981, pp.293–332.

Miller, David B. 'Creating Legitimacy: Ritual, Ideology and Power in Sixteenth-Century Russia', *Russian History/Histoire Russe*, vol.21, 1994, pp.289–315.

Nørretranders, Bjarne. *The Shaping of Czardom under Ivan Groznyj*, London: Variorum Reprints, 1971.

Ostrowski, Donald. *Muscovy and the Mongols: Cross-Cultural Influences on the Steppe Frontier, 1304–1589*, Cambridge: Cambridge University Press, 1998.

Pelenski, Jaroslaw. *Russia and Kazan. Conquest and Imperial Ideology (1438–1560s)*, The Hague: Mouton, 1974.

Perrie, Maureen. 'The Popular Image of Ivan the Terrible', *Slavonic and East European Review*, vol.56, 1978, pp.275–86.

Perrie, Maureen. *The Image of Ivan the Terrible in Russian Folklore*, Cambridge: Cambridge University Press, 1987.

Perrie, Maureen. 'Outlawry (*Vorovstvo*) and Redemption through Service: Ermak and the Volga Cossacks', in Kleimola and Lenhoff, eds., *Culture and Identity in Muscovy*, pp.530–42.

Perrie, Maureen. *The Cult of Ivan the Terrible in Stalin's Russia*, Houndmills: Palgrave, 2001.

Platonov, S.F. *Ivan the Terrible*, ed. and trans. J.L. Wieczynski, Gulf Breeze, FL: Academic International Press, 1974.

Poe, Marshall. 'What did Russians Mean When They Called Themselves "Slaves of the Tsar"?', *Slavic Review*, vol.57, 1998, pp.585–608.

Poe, Marshall. *'A People Born to Slavery': Russia in Early Modern European Ethnography*, Ithaca: Cornell University Press, 2000.

Rowland, Daniel. 'Did Muscovite Literary Ideology Place Limits on the Power of the Tsar (1540s–1660s)?', *Russian Review*, vol.49, 1990, pp.125–55.

Rowland, Daniel. 'Biblical Military Imagery in the Political Culture of Early Modern Russia: the Blessed Host of the Heavenly Tsar', in Flier and Rowland, eds., *Medieval Russian Culture*, vol.2, pp.182–212.

Rowland, Daniel. 'Moscow – the Third Rome or the New Israel?', *Russian Review*, vol.55, 1996, pp.591–614.

Shaw, Denis J.B. 'Southern Frontiers of Muscovy, 1550–1700', in J.H. Bater and R.A. French, eds, *Studies in Russian Historical Geography*, vol.1, London: Academic Press, 1983, pp.117–41.

Skrynnikov, R.G. *Ivan the Terrible*, ed. and trans. Hugh F. Graham, Gulf Breeze, FL: Academic International Press, 1981.

Skrynnikov, R.G. 'Ermak's Siberian Expedition', *Russian History/Histoire Russe*, vol.13, 1986, pp.1–39.

Stevens, Carol B. 'Banditry and Provincial Order in Sixteenth-Century Russia', in Kleimola and Lenhoff, eds., *Culture and Identity in Muscovy*, pp.578–99.

Thyrêt, Isolde. *Between God and Tsar: Religious Symbolism and the Royal Women of Muscovite Russia*, DeKalb, IL: Northern Illinois University Press, 2001.

Uspenskij, B.A. 'Tsar and Pretender: Samozvančestvo or Royal Imposture in Russia as a Cultural-Historical Phenomenon', in Lotman and Uspenskij, *The Semiotics of Russian Culture*, pp.259–92.

Willan, T.S. *The Early History of the Russia Company, 1553–1603*, Manchester: Manchester University Press, 1956.

Wortman, Richard S. *Scenarios of Power. Myth and Ceremony in Russian Monarchy*, vol.1, Princeton, NJ: Princeton University Press, 1995.

Index

Note: Page numbers in bold refer to Maps or Figures.